Making a Difference in the Journey:
The Geography of Our Faith

Anabaptist Center for Religion and Society Memoirs

RAY C. GINGERICH, SERIES EDITOR

This series of autobiographical accounts is typically published by Cascadia Publishing House LLC and copublished with the Anabaptist Center for Religion and Society (ACRS), based at Eastern Mennonite University. ACRS/EMU sponsors the series, determines the particular focus of each set of stories, and in consultation with the publisher, volume editors, and authors, is responsible for the content.

Volume 1, 2007, 2009
Making Sense of the Journey: The Geography of Our Faith
   Robert Lee and Nancy V. Lee, Editors

Volume 2, 2009
Continuing the Journey: The Geography of Our Faith
   Nancy V. Lee, Editor

Volume 3, 2016
Re-Envisioning Service: The Geography of Our Faith
   Ray C. Gingerich and Pat Hostetter Martin, Editors

Volume 4, 2017
Making a Difference in the Journey: The Geography of Our Faith
   Nancy V. Lee, Nancy M. Farrar, Audrey A. Metz, and Kathy D. Fisher, Editors

ACRS MEMOIRS, VOLUME 4

Making a Difference in the Journey: The Geography of Our Faith

Brethren and Mennonite Stories Integrating Faith, Life, and the World of Thought

Edited by
Nancy V. Lee, Nancy M. Farrar,
Audrey A. Metz, and Kathy D. Fisher

Foreword by
Lee Snyder

Cascadia
Publishing House
Telford, Pennsylvania

copublished with
**Anabaptist Center for Religion and Society
Eastern Mennonite University
Harrisonburg, Virginia**

Cascadia Publishing House orders, information, reprint permissions:
contact@CascadiaPublishingHouse.com
1-215-723-9125
126 Klingerman Road, Telford PA 18969
www.CascadiaPublishingHouse.com

Making a Difference in the Journey
Copyright © 2017 by Cascadia Publishing House,
a division of Cascadia Publishing House LLC
Telford, PA 18969
All rights reserved.
Library of Congress Catalog Number: 2017040098
ISBN-13: 978-1-68027-007-5; ISBN 10: 1-68027-007-9
Book design by Cascadia Publishing House
Cover design by Dawn Ranck, with engraving of the man born blind by Jan Luyken

The paper used in this publication is recycled and meets the minimum requirements of American National Standard for Information Sciences—Permanence of Paper for Printed Library Materials, ANSI Z39.48-1984.

All Bible quotations are used by permission, all rights reserved and if marked NRSV are from *The New Revised Standard Version of the Bible*, copyright 1989, by the Division of Christian Education of the National Council of the Churches of Christ in the USA; NIV from the Holy Bible, *New International Version*. Copyright © 1973, 1978, 1984 International Bible Society. All rights reserved throughout the world. Used by permission of International Bible Society; NKJV from *The New King James Bible*--New Testament, Copyright © 1979, Thomas Nelson, Inc., Publishers; TEV from *Good News Bible*. Old Testament Copyright © American Bible Society 1976; New Testament Copyright © American Bible Society 1966, 1971, 1976; TLB from *The Living Bible* © 1971 owned by assignment by Illinois Regional Bank N.A. (as trustee). Used by permission of Tyndale House Publishers, Inc., Wheaton, IL 60189. All rights reserved.

Library of Congress Cataloguing-in-Publication Data
Names: Lee, Nancy V., 1931- editor.
Title: Making a difference in the journey : the geography of our faith / edited by Nancy V. Lee, Nancy M. Farrar, Audrey A. Metz, and Kathy D. Fisher ; foreword by Lee Snyder.
Description: Telford, Pennsylvania : Cascadia Publishing House, 2017. | Series: ACRS memoirs ; Volume 4 | Includes bibliographical references.
Identifiers: LCCN 2017040098 | ISBN 9781680270075 (6 x 9" trade pbk. : alk. paper) | ISBN 1680270079 (6 x 9" trade pbk. : alk. paper)
Subjects: LCSH: Eastern Mennonite University--Biography. | Mennonites--Biography. | Brethren (Brethren churches)--Biography. | Service (Theology) | Christian life--Mennonite authors. | Christian life--Brethren authors.
Classification: LCC BX8141 .M35 2017 | DDC 289.7092/273 [B] --dc23
LC record available at https://lccn.loc.gov/2017040098

To
Lois Mary Gunden Clemens,
who, in a French Mediterranean town during World War II,
risked her life to save many Jewish children and Spanish refugees. In
fact, in January 1943 the Germans imprisoned her for more than a year.

On January 27, 2016, the Embassy of Israel in Washington, D.C., with Yad Vashem (the World Holocaust Remembrance Center), named her posthumously as Righteous Among the Nations. She is only the fourth American (of more than 24,800 people) to be thus honored.

After she was back in America,
she wrote the book Women Liberated.

CONTENTS

Foreword by Lee Snyder 11
Series Editor's Preface by Ray C. Gingerich 13
Editor's Preface by Nancy V. Lee 15
Introduction by Richard (Dick) Benner 17

PART I: MAKING A DIFFERENCE THROUGH CHURCH LEADERSHIP

Robert Earl Alley   23
    A Journey in Formation, Re-formation, and Trans-formation

Martin W. Lehman   45
    My Faith Journey: From Youthful Conformist to Senior Nonconformist

Fred W. Swartz   69
    Listening to God's Word in Every Step

PART II: MAKING A DIFFERENCE THROUGH EDUCATIONAL LEADERSHIP

Beryl H. Brubaker   93
    Filling Many Roles in One Special Place

Joseph L. Lapp   119
    Joining the Family Business: By Birthright, by Choice, and by Divine Call

W. Robert McFadden   145
My Journey as a Thinker, Scholar, and Teacher

Lee M. Yoder   169
From Farming to a Life of Educational Leadership

PART III: MAKING A DIFFERENCE THROUGH LEADERSHIP ABROAD

Douglas (Doug) Hostetter   195
My God Was Too Small: God Is Bigger Than We Think

Paul Swarr   213
Laborers Together with God

Richard (Rick) Yoder   237
Redeeming the Assets of the Empire

PART IV: MAKING A DIFFERENCE THROUGH LEADERSHIP IN UNEXPECTED WAYS

Richard (Dick) Benner   259
Moments of Grace

Lawrence H. (Larry) Hoover   283
Mediation and Peacebuilding: Ways to Make a Difference

Allon H. Lefever   303
My Life Journey: Business as a Calling

Peggy B. Shenk   327
From the Home of an Evangelist to a Desk in EMU's Presidential Suite

Shirley H. Showalter   353
Why Writing Memoirs Is Hard . . . and Why You Should Do It Anyway

Appendix: Vernon E. Jantzi   365
The Editors   371

FOREWORD

We make sense of our lives by the stories we tell, writers confess. Telling our stories opens new and different ways of seeing—both for the reader and the writer. As a story lover myself, I was drawn in by the wide variety of these selections. They include all the elements of a good read: suspense, outrageous encounters, and examples of courage and uncommon grace.

This volume, fourth in the series of faith journey accounts, asks "What difference did it make?"

At one of the college commencement ceremonies I recently attended, the president asked the graduates to look ahead. "What difference would it make if you knew the end of the story?" he asked.

Here we have a chance to enter into the lives of leaders reflecting on that question. We are permitted insights into the worlds of international affairs, educational institutions, denominational conflicts, professional and journalism intrigues, and entrepreneurial risk-taking. We have here not simply a record of faith journeys moving from past to present but, more importantly, intimations of the future—how fifteen individuals in a particular time and place made a difference in ways which continue to shape the future.

Fittingly for this *Geography of Our Faith* series, time and place serve effectively as organizing themes. Readers will move from pulpits to board rooms to courtrooms; from lecture halls to get-your-hands-dirty refugee camps. Settings include the familiar Shenandoah Valley and other rural enclaves of Mennonite and Brethren communities. But these stories are global in scope, reflecting experiences in such places as the Middle East, Afghanistan, Africa, and Vietnam.

What moves me about these stories is a sustained sense of awe in life's unfolding surprises. As one writer puts it, "God is always creating something new." There is evidence of deep faith embedded in these accounts. But often that faith must wrestle with personal failure and with life's unsettling ambiguities and paradoxes—an acknowledgement that we have no assurance of order or clarity.

This is wisdom literature, offerings by sages, creative thinkers, professionals in the trenches, individuals called to second and third careers—an inspiring source for any reader who might wonder, "What difference would it make if we knew the end of the story?"

In a world of complexity and unrelieved turmoil, a time when many are infected by despair and desperation, the last word must be given to Martin Lehman, a church bishop who dared to ask questions that were not allowed. He offers hope for the journey, citing 1 John 2:8 as the compass giving direction to his life: "The darkness is passing and the true light is already shining." Martin's assurance is based on his own sense of the ending of the story. These marvelous accounts point to that "true light" for all of us on the journey.

—*Lee Snyder, President Emeritus, Bluffton University; Academic Dean and Vice President, 1984-1996, and Interim President, 2016, Eastern Mennonite University; Author,* At Powerline and Diamond Hill

SERIES EDITOR'S PREFACE

In spring 2010 a small committee of ACRS representatives—including the late Al Keim, a cornerstone among the founders of ACRS—met to plan new directions in our series of Monday Morning Breakfast stories. (See "Appendix, vol. 2, n. 4 in this series for a fuller account of how such a series got started.) The current collection of memoirs represents the second in our "new directions"—the fourth and likely final volume of stories (memoirs) in this series.

In our extended deliberations, we agreed to invite Brethren and Friends (Quakers), in addition to Mennonites (to which the first two volumes were limited), to share their stories. Of equal or greater significance, however, was the decision that "service" was to be the leitmotiv of volumes 3 and 4.

I interviewed the contributors to all four volumes before their presentations at the Monday Morning Breakfast and offered them written guidelines on the thematic nature of the current series. Underlying this set of memoirs was the concern for sharing with the audience and readers the experiences of making a difference through a transformative life of service—whether deliberately chosen, providentially destined, or what might appear as "cultural happenstance."

As a friend to friends, the authors of these stories shared them in a spirit of vulnerability with an awareness that the primary differences made through their service happened not only to others (as may have been the original intent or the agency assignment) but also to themselves in a personal life-giving transformation. Here are stories of service that at times redirected the entire course of the storyteller's life as well as stories of events that slowly and sometimes rapidly shifted the character and direction of entire communities and the religious bodies or denominations of the storytellers.

This final volume of the ACRS Monday Morning Breakfast Stories is being released as part of EMU's centennial celebration. It is therefore a fortuitous coincidence to have Donald Kraybill, the author of EMU's centennial history, astutely observe that "*service,* more than any other phenomenon, provides the unifying thread throughout the entire century of EMU's history." (Kraybill at EMU's Donor Appreciation Banquet, Oct. 14, 2016). My hunch is that this generalization on service and its accompanying metamorphic effects (often under the rubric of discipleship) might apply to the entirety of both the Mennonite and the Church of the Brethren denominations.

—*Ray C. Gingerich*
  ACRS Series Editor

EDITOR'S PREFACE

The popular Anabaptist Center for Religion and Society (ACRS) Monday Morning Breakfasts, managed so capably for many years by Ray Gingerich, continue under the leadership of Margaret Foth, Terry Burkhalter, and Vernon Jantzi. All are welcome at these monthly events at Eastern Mennonite University during the academic year (usually with pastries, coffee, and tea at the early hour of 7:30 a.m.). However, since the nature of the presentations has changed, and barring unexpected developments, this fourth volume is expected to be the final collection of memoirs; it represents those given at breakfasts December 2010-April 2013. Chapters have then been revised and updated up to the point of their 2017 publication.

These authors, like those in the three previous volumes, have all served in responsible positions. Like the previous presenters, they trace the influences that shaped them from early years through adulthood. However, the world they discovered often challenged them to respond in ways that differed from those of their predecessors.

In Part I, Church of the Brethren and Mennonite leaders describe efforts to found new congregations, help those congregations grow, lead successful building programs, and respond with open hearts to protests inspired by the Vietnam conflict and social injustices. Their work made huge differences in their communities.

Among the educational personnel in Part II are a woman who held seven different administrative positions, including that of interim president, and a man who led in building from scratch a K-12 school overseas. Another author describes his own exploration of attitudes toward war and the ways he led students through the same process. Still another tells of guiding a university through a challenging building program during difficult events. Each of these individuals had a significant impact on many colleagues and students.

Two of the memoirs in Part III come from men who provided life-saving and life-giving help to numerous groups of people in dangerous areas abroad. A third writer recalls learning how to listen and then how to to be a Christian pastor in Jerusalem. These leaders made long-lasting contributions, often to people in great peril and need.

In Part IV, contributors reflect on how they changed lives in unexpected ways: one as a courageous journalist and newspaper owner; another as a leader in mediation and peace building; one as a caring businessman; another as assistant to a university president; and yet another as a professor and college president. This group made amazing differences not only in familiar settings but also in distant places.

In fact, all these authors are still influencing the lives of many— and their insightful yet humble narratives continue to stretch and change our minds and hearts.

On the book's cover, the historical engraving in which Jesus Blesses the Man Born Blind (John 9: 1-7) exemplifies the compassionate actions of the authors of these memoirs. This engraving by Jan Luyken (*or* Luiken) was taken from a volume by David Martin (1639-1721): *Historie des Ouden en Nieuwen Testaments bverrykt met meer dan vierhondred printverbeeldingen in koper gesneeden [History of the Old and New Testaments: translated with over 400 engraved copper plates by Jan Luiken]*, published in 1700 by Pieter Mortier, Amsterdam.

Special thanks for their encouragement and advice go to Lee M. Yoder, ACRS Steering Committee chair, and ACRS Publication Committee co-chairs Margaret Foth and Vernon Jantzi (who is also vice-chair and director of the ACRS Steering Committee).

It has again been a pleasure to work with Michael A. King, president and publisher, Cascadia Publishing House LLC, who brings to this task a vision for the publication needs of ACRS-EMU as well as high standards and Christian commitment.

As the lead editor of this volume, I wish to thank co-editors Nancy Farrar, Audrey Metz, and Kathy Fisher for their much appreciated and most valuable assistance.

—*Nancy V. Lee*
  ACRS 4 Managing Editor

INTRODUCTION:
THEIR STORIES ARE OUR STORIES

Personal stories of a people finding their way during a time of unprecedented change in culture and religion are the best indicator of its endurance, its unique character and its determination to stay true to itself.

The following pages will give you, the reader, a good grasp of how several accomplished yet humble folks with a shared spiritual heritage—followers of Jesus in a European-rooted Anabaptist tradition—have found their place in a changing, secular-prone North American culture. Their struggles, their tenacity in face of obstacles, their international experiences open a window into the contours of a minority faith community.

But don't be misled by the word *minority*. These persons, admitting to every human frailty while at the same time demonstrating unusual resourcefulness and intelligence, should not be underestimated. They punch way beyond their weight, to use a cliché. Indeed, most of us, in the Anabaptist tradition sharing our stories, come from a humble beginning; but that is only a common starting point.

We are historically a rural people, many of us learning the important lessons of hard work and endurance on the farm. We lived in small provincial enclaves of like-minded people, some of us treating our other-religious neighbors with regrettable suspicion. But as our world expanded beyond those confines through higher education, international experience, and professional ventures into the wider culture, we began to shed parochialism while clinging to basic values of our spiritual heritage.

The theme of coming of age within restrictive environments runs through all of these stories. They read like a novel, except these characters are real, the plot lines unravelling with actual experiences. The characters are resilient, sometimes dramatic, but never boring or dull. They have developed their life narratives with skill and intrigue.

Stories are powerful because they are so personal. We learn from them because they reveal things about ourselves. Many of these storytellers are my friends. I know whereof they speak. Their descriptions are not exaggerated or pompous. They tell it like it is. Their narratives are authentic. They talk of failures along with successes. These are real persons telling us they share our humanness, our frailties, but in equal measure our hopes and dreams.

Some of us have had difficult conversations with our parents, articulated so well by Doug Hostetter, whose introduction to and enlightenment from a wider world put him in conflict with a high-profile father. But underlying that struggle was an undying love between parent and child that kept the relationship intact. This is a tale of redemption.

On the other hand, there is the exhilarating story of Peggy Shenk whose progressive father, well ahead of his time, gave succor not only to his immediate family but also to many in his church leadership circle and beyond. While it cost him a leadership position in one of our major educational systems, it proved to be a shining light that helped lead us out of some of the darkness of the twentieth century. Hers is a moving love story.

In like manner, there is the honest struggle of Martin Lehman, who fought courageously and valiantly for the acceptance of sexually marginalized persons—a leader who came to change his traditional views and worked zealously to make room for these hurting people in a still-reluctant religious community working through its prejudices and moral principles. His is a story of steadfast courage.

There is the thrilling story of an expanded worldview as told by Rick Yoder as he takes his Anabaptist peace and justice values to the world stage through his work with the United States Agency for International Development (USAID). He was able to take his work and spiritual ethics from a small farm in Elverson, Pennsylvania, to the ends of the earth to provide, in his words "jobs, higher incomes and better quality of life for lots of people." His is an inspirational story of "seeking justice."

Another story of a farm boy honing his skills to become an educational leader at home and abroad is that of Lee Yoder, growing up in one of the more closed enclaves of what is known as Big Valley in central Pennsylvania. Further east in a more urbanized setting, Joseph Lapp broke with family tradition of denominational leadership (his father another high-profile leader) to study law and later use his skills to lead Eastern Mennonite College to university status.

Another pioneer in law is the story of Larry Hoover Jr. of Harrisonburg, Virginia, who directed his work in mediation to world affairs, working with the United States to a more creative approach to conflict in such places as the Philippines—another farm boy taking his values to the world stage and making a difference.

There is the inspiration of a business entrepreneur, Allon Lefever, who brought his Anabaptist values and skills to the management of hundreds of employees in one of the largest Mennonite-owned enterprises, Victor F. Weaver Inc. in New Holland, Pennsylvania. He modeled what it means to be fair in labor relations and to keep the profit motive from being the guiding force in the private sector.

These are only a sampling of the many stories that pulsate through these pages. Apologies to those not noted here. All of them are compelling in their own way. They define for us who we are as a people. The narrative they form comes from a generation of creative persons who, grounded in small congregations with the Bible as their center of religious learning, instructed in the basic lessons of life from parents with many times only an eighth-grade education, took those tools and expanded them into high-value leadership positions and professional skills that have contributed to our culture in important ways.

The stories are told with candor, with a good dose of self-effacement and humility, providing a delightful read and giving hope for the future.

The only critique I would offer is that there are far too few stories from women. At a time when women are gaining their rightful place in our faith communion and in our society, we need to hear more about their struggles and aspirations, the pain and constraints under which they surely have lived over the past half-century. Their nurturing component to our story is still often untold—even as the telling would make us a more perfect communion.

—*Richard (Dick) Benner*
  Editor and Publisher, Canadian Mennonite *magazine*

PART I

Making a Difference
... Through Church Leadership

Robert Earl Alley

Pastor and Denominational Leader

Once intending to be a math teacher, Robert Alley in his memoir traces the influences that shaped him as a pastor. After leading a successful church planting, he accepted the call to a second church and later to the Church of the Brethren in Bridgewater, where he led the construction of the beautiful new church building. After serving in various denominational leadership positions, he was elected Moderator, Church of the Brethren Annual Conference, and participated in the 40th Anniversary of the Church of North India, where a great-uncle had served. Photo by Linda L. Alley

ROBERT EARL ALLEY

A Journey in Formation, Re-formation, and Trans-formation

As a pastor helping families prepare for memorial services, I often asked, "What made your relative who he or she was?" People seldom hesitated very long before they gave meaningful responses. In preparing this memoir, I asked that same question of myself: "What has made me who I am?" Responses have centered in the family, faith community, and community at large. In simple terms, these relationships have been crucial to my journey. As I sought to give order to these reflections, I was drawn to the formula *Formation, Re-formation, Trans-formation*. While such a formula follows a chronological sequence, the seeds planted in one part bear fruit in a subsequent part. The threads weave together in such a manner that the sequence is more than the sum of its parts.

FORMATION

I was formed in the womb of family, born out of the love of two people after a marriage of twelve and a half years as their only son, both their oldest and youngest child. The day I was born, my father returned home to announce to a neighbor couple, "Well, I got that boy!" It was Sunday morning, May 25, 1947, 5:36 a.m. at the old King's Daughters' Hospital in Staunton, Virginia. (The hospital later became a Mary Baldwin College dormitory and eventually was demolished.) It was not just any Sunday. It was Pentecost Sunday, a designation that held no meaning for my parents with their nonliturgical faith. However, that special connection would later hold important meaning for their small son.

My parents were common folk. My father was a house painter who would establish his own painting contracting business when I was four. My mother, a factory garment presser before I was born, had skills in homemaking that far exceeded all else. Although her formal education had ended with high school, she would become my father's assistant, keeping the books for his business, securing the cash payroll each week, and fulfilling all the responsibilities of a secretary and accountant, learning as she went. My father completed only the fifth grade, but his skills in house painting made him popular with many patrons in the Staunton area. His business acumen, acquired through experience and common sense, gave him the ability to manage from six to twenty-two men, depending on the season of the year. My parents' devotion to home and work was instrumental in giving me a similar work ethic. They taught me the value of work, the importance of doing a job right, and the need to stay with a task until it was complete.

The rural setting of our family home also influenced my formation in those early years. We were not farmers, but we did have a garden, a milk cow until I was about four, chickens, beehives for honey, several dogs and cats, two or three hogs, and two beef cattle. I learned responsibility while tending some of the animals and helping with the annual butchering.

One very important event in my family formation occurred when I was ten years old. Interested in securing camp property to use for fishing and hunting, my father purchased a hundred-acre tract of mountain land southeast of Deerfield in Augusta County, Virginia. A year later, with assistance from several persons, we built a simple cabin that served our family for weekend vacations, my parents for fishing, and my father and his friends for hunting. Today it still provides a place for refuge and family getaways. It has become the common ground for all the generations of our family.

Home extended beyond my immediate family to include grandparents, aunts and uncles, and cousins. One particular great-aunt and uncle filled the role of grandparents because my father's parents had died before I was born and my mother's parents were both deceased by the time I was twelve. From this extended family I learned where I belonged in the long procession of generations. This awareness was enhanced for me in the fifth grade. After completing the reading workbook exercise to create a family tree for the family in the story we had read, the teacher asked each of us to create our own family tree. That assignment planted seeds that have borne fruit for me many, many times in over fifty years of doing genealogical research and writing. Genealogy became my "golf," and family reunions, along with the research, deepened my appreciation for the extended family in which I was formed.

While I was being formed in the family, I was also being formed in the faith community. My parents and I seldom missed the weekly church service and Sunday school unless we were ill, out of town, or faced with a snowstorm. We attended Barren Ridge Church of the Brethren, near Staunton, where my father was a member and where his family had belonged and attended for several generations.

My mother had grown up attending a Methodist church in Weyers Cave and remained a member of that congregation all her life. However, she participated in the Church of the Brethren for more than sixty-five years (her entire married life), attending Love Feast, wearing a prayer covering on those occasions, and contributing. (The Love Feast is a Church of the Brethren service centered around the Last Supper of Jesus with his disciples. It includes moments of reflection and confession, the washing of one another's feet, a simple meal, and the bread and cup of communion.)

I attended vacation Bible school each summer, the Loyal Temperance League (the children's division of the Women's Christian Temperance Union), youth fellowship when I became a teenager, junior choir, and yearly revival services. Since we lived a couple of miles from the Church of the Brethren, I also attended programs and services at the nearby Laurel Hill Baptist Church, including Sunbeams (for children kindergarten through third grade) and Royal Ambassadors (for boys age ten and older), vacation Bible school, and revival meetings.

Because my father grew up before his family had an automobile, he had also attended this Baptist church as a child unless the family was visiting relatives near the Church of the Brethren. My grandmother served there as church sexton, and Baptist ministers often assisted Church of the Brethren ministers at family funerals.

At age ten, I made my first public commitment to Christ at this Baptist church at the close of vacation Bible school. During that Friday morning session, the minister simply asked those who wanted to follow Jesus to come forward. I wanted to do that, so I did along with others of my peers. When I was eleven, I went forward at the close of Sunday morning worship at the Church of the Brethren. About ten days later I was baptized along with my peers in Meadow Run, a stream near our church that had long served as a baptismal site. It was August 19, 1958. That date was significant because it was the month marking the 250th anniversary of the baptism that initiated the Brethren movement.

My parents expressed their faith through participation in these two faith communities as well as through practices in our home. For example, my mother attended one of the Baptist women's circles monthly. When I was young, I accompanied her to the Ever Ready Circle, where I often took up the collection and handed out the songbooks. One year the Circle even listed me as a member!

At home, my father offered our family's mealtime blessing until I was able to say this simple child's prayer: "Thank you for the world so sweet; thank you for the food we eat; thank you for the birds that sing; and thank you, God, for everything." When we visited other homes, my father was often the one called on to offer the mealtime prayer. After my mother and I left the hospital where Daddy died, one of the first things I did was to write down his daily prayer: "Kind and gracious Heavenly Father, bless this food; bless it to its intended use and us to Thy service. Amen." It was a cherished link to his spirituality.

In addition to the influences of family and faith communities, the community at large also helped to form me. It included friendships with people in the village of Laurel Hill, east of Verona; music lessons in flute, accordion, piano, and harmony in Staunton, where my music professor taught both African American and white students; my parents' friends (whose children were often several years older than I); and experiences in the schools I attended. In high school, I participated in prose reading for forensics and, during my senior year, served on one of the debate teams and sang in a choral class. I excelled in almost every subject but particularly enjoyed history and math. At the end of high school, I applied to college with the ambition to become a math teacher.

The wombs of family, faith community, and community at large in those first eighteen years of life formed much of my identity. When I graduated from high school, my mother gave me a quilt that she and my great-aunt had made. My great-uncle referred to their work as "love stitches." Clearly, the wombs of my early formation did create many "love stitches" in my life. They prepared me to be re-formed.

RE-FORMATION

Upon graduation from high school, I entered several decades of *re-formation*. This re-formation also began on a Pentecost Sunday: June 6, 1965, in the Barren Ridge Church of the Brethren, when I was licensed to the ministry. However, I did not yet envision ministry to be my full-time profession. I still planned to be a math teacher who would serve the church as a good lay minister. The previous December I had preached my first sermon, about forty-five minutes in length! A couple months later, when we youth were gathering to rehearse a play for our church's centennial, our pastor's wife asked me if I had ever considered being licensed to the ministry. Soon after that, our local ministry commission chair, Ray Coffman (a close family friend), and the church moderator, Guy Stump Sr., visited me and my parents. The commission, they said, wanted to recommend me for licensing. I agreed, the congregation voted, and I was licensed.

As a child, I had emulated our local pastor, Homer Miller, who was a good preacher and pastor. After church on Sundays, while my mother prepared Sunday dinner, I would often move some of the dining room chairs to the living room, pull out an end table, and "hold church." But my childhood interest in preaching had shifted to teaching by the time I was finishing high school. Yet on class night at the time of graduation, I dressed as my great uncle, who was a Brethren missionary in India for thirty years. The class prediction was that I, too, would become a missionary.

My re-formation continued at Bridgewater College, where my studies expanded my world; I majored in math, intending to become a teacher. Yet the church relicensed me year after year. Several times each summer I would be invited to preach at different churches when the pastor was absent. Then in the middle of my junior year, as I listened to a sermon by Dr. Robert Sherfy at the Bridgewater Church of the Brethren, I was challenged to change my career track. Later that year I decided I could no longer follow two paths, so I shifted my major from mathematics to philosophy and religion. Ministry had become my career goal, and I looked forward to entering a seminary after college.

At Bridgewater College, some who fostered my re-formation were philosophy and religion faculty such as David Metzler, Bob McFadden, and William Willoughby. Roger Sappington, who taught Church of the Brethren history, nurtured my history interests. My term paper in his course was titled, "The Life and Mission Work of Howard Lee Alley" (my great-uncle). Apart from college work, I also completed "A History of the Laurel Hill Community" and "A History of the Joseph Alley Family." I continued the study of music with piano taught by Olivia Cool and organ by John Barr, both Bridgewater College faculty members.

Between my junior and senior years, I spent the summer in Maryland as an Earn and Serve Worker in the Westminster Church of the Brethren. The church provided my room and board; I worked daily at Wampler Furniture, helping to deliver furniture and doing other jobs. Evenings and weekends I devoted to church opportunities, which included assisting the pastor, Curtis Dubble, who later became an Annual Conference moderator.

A climactic event in my re-formation occurred during my senior year at Bridgewater College. In response to invitations from friends, I started attending a charismatic prayer group hosted by one of the college professors. As I learned about the Holy Spirit, I began to identify with the Christians at Ephesus (Acts 19), who said they had never even heard there was a Holy Spirit. During one of the prayer meetings, I moved to a room apart from everyone else to avoid group pressure and invited God to be real in me. The Holy Spirit became real in my life that night.

The affirmation of that infilling came when I realized that William Holman Hunt's painting of Christ standing at the door and knocking no longer reflected my experience. I had opened that door, and Christ had entered. So meaningful was this experience that I asked someone to go to my dorm room and remove that picture from the wall. It would be many years before I returned a copy of that painting to my church office and eventually to my study room at home. My re-formation now involved more than education, vocational choice, and distance from home; it had reached my inner being. When I told my parents about the Holy Spirit's infilling, my father responded in a simple manner: "If you don't have the Spirit, you don't have anything."

During this time, I discovered more about the Holy Spirit through *The Cross and the Switchblade*,[1] by David Wilkerson, with John and Elizabeth Sherrill. (The pastor at Laurel Hill Baptist Church had given me this book several years earlier, but I had not yet read it.) Another element of re-formation occurred when I began to use *Good News for Modern Man*,[2] a translation of the New Testament into modern English. Previously I had been totally devoted to the King James Version. Later in my re-formation period, I would come to cherish insights I gained through reading *The Living Bible*,[3] *The New English Bible*,[4] and the *New Revised Standard Version*.[5]

I also became more aware of the implications of the verse that the Laurel Hill Baptist Church pastor, Charles Boyer, had written on the graduation card he sent to me in 1965: "Do your best to win full approval in God's sight, as a worker who is not ashamed of his work, one who correctly teaches the message of God's truth" (2 Tim. 2:15, TEV). Over the years, this and several other verses have become spiritual touchstones: "In everything you do, put God first, and he will direct you and crown your efforts with success" (Proverbs 3:6, TLB); and "I am confident of this, that the one who began a good work among you will bring it to completion by the day of Jesus Christ" (Philippians 1:6, NRSV).

The infilling of the Holy Spirit was only one special element in my re-formation, though a pivotal one. Following college graduation, I traveled to the Ozarks of Missouri to serve as the summer pastor at a small rural church, Peace Valley Church of the Brethren. Then for one year I attended the Church of the Brethren seminary, Bethany Theological, at Oak Brook, Illinois. (In 1994 it relocated to Richmond, Indiana, adjoining the Earlham School of Religion).

I fully intended to graduate from Bethany. While there, I especially appreciated the leadership of President Paul Robinson and professors such as Donald Durnbaugh in Church and Brethren History at Bethany and Reidar B. Bjornard in Old Testament at Northern Baptist Seminary, the neighboring seminary that shared some classes with Bethany. Bjornard wove together a passion for scholarship and spirituality that deepened not only my appreciation for the Old Testament but also my trust in the authority of scripture. Scholarship enhanced trust in biblical authority; it did not diminish it.

After my first year in seminary, I was assigned to be the summer pastor at First Church of the Brethren in Harrisonburg, Virginia, as part of my seminary studies. At that time this was the largest Church of the Brethren congregation in Virginia. Its pastor had left in May, and the new one would not arrive until September. I was the church's only pastor that summer!

During that summer ministry, I learned about Eastern Mennonite Seminary (EMS) in Harrisonburg. I turned to prayer and sought the counsel of a Bethany Seminary professor, a district executive, and the director of church relations at Bridgewater College. As a result, I transferred to EMS, planning to return to Bethany for my senior year.

However, the transfer resulted in further re-formation and in the decision to complete my seminary studies at EMS in May 1972. At EMS this re-formation continued through the preaching instruction of John R. Mumaw, the Hebrew instruction of G. Irvin Lehman, and the evangelistic instruction and inspiration of George R. Brunk II and Myron Augsburger. During my two years at EMS, three important events occurred: I was called to my first pastorate, a new church-planting near Martinsburg, West Virginia; I met my future wife, Linda Lefever; and I had the privilege to tour the Holy Lands and Europe between my middler and senior years with G. Irvin Lehman and about twenty-five others.

Two years after meeting Linda in a supper line at Eastern Mennonite College (EMC), I invited her to become Mrs. Robert Alley. She accepted! By then I was serving in my first pastorate and had purchased a home. Linda, an English major, graduated from EMC the year after my seminary graduation. She had grown up on a dairy farm in Lancaster County, Pennsylvania, where her family were members of the Mennonite church. We were married in October 1974 at East Fairview Church of the Brethren near Manheim, Pennsylvania, by Raymond Charles (her Mennonite bishop) and Paul Munday (a young Brethren minister who later became a denominational staff member in evangelism and then pastor of the largest Church of the Brethren in Frederick, Maryland).

Linda has invested herself in the life of the congregations where I served but never simply as "the pastor's wife" and never expecting accolades as such. She directed vacation Bible schools and accompanied me for several revival meetings. She occasionally served as worship leader, preached on two occasions when I was ill, and participated in women's groups. At our wedding, when Raymond Charles offered the meditation, he commented that he had always thought the greatest vocation was that of being a minister. But in talking with Linda, he said he had learned of a higher vocation. She had told him that she saw herself as "a minister to the minister." That "vocation" has contributed significantly to my re-formation and later trans-formation.

Being re-formed as a husband led to re-formation as a father. We would be blessed with three children—Leanne, Linetta, and Jonathan—all now married adults. Like Linda and me, they and their spouses, would eventually earn degrees from Eastern Mennonite University at the college or seminary level. However, our daughter Linetta and her husband first studied as undergraduates at Bridgewater College, as I did.

RE-FORMATION CONTINUES: SET-APART MINISTRY

Re-formation had now occurred through education and vocational change, through a Holy Spirit infilling, through family life, and through the early stages of a ministerial career. On May 21, 1972, I was ordained to the set-apart ministry in the Church of the Brethren at my home congregation at Barren Ridge. (While the Church of the Brethren believes in the priesthood and thus the calling to ministry of all believers, it calls some persons for licensing and ordination; this is known as the set-apart ministry.) My childhood pastor, Homer Miller, preached the ordination sermon, and one of my college professors, Bob McFadden, officiated on behalf of the district. Again it was Sunday but no ordinary Sunday. It, too, was Pentecost Sunday!

Following graduation from seminary and ordination to the ministry, I accepted the call to become the full-time pastor of the new church planting in Martinsburg, West Virginia, where I had begun pastoring on weekends a year and a half earlier. When I first began pastoring this Church of the Brethren fellowship, they were not yet even recognized by their church district. I asked my father for his counsel about whether or not to accept the ministry there. His answer was that I had nothing to lose.

Moreover, the director of church relations at Bridgewater College, Sam Harley, provided a list of four ingredients that promised growth for a new congregation: "solid church families; fellowship within the church unit; purpose, goals, and objectives; and gainful employment." I found all of them in what would be named Fellowship Church of the Brethren, which I would serve for eleven years and help grow from an attendance of thirty-five or forty to seventy-five or eighty each Sunday. I would also walk with them through a building program and work with them toward being self-supporting.

As a new church planting, the congregation had no traditions except the ones that the members brought with them. Thus, it was a time of formation for the congregation; for me, it was a time of re-formation, of discovering afresh what really shaped congregational life and what fostered both spiritual and evangelistic growth. One of the key ingredients in ministry at Fellowship Church of the Brethren was the ministry of prayer, which continues to be central in the life of that congregation today. It has also become a congregation that ministers to people who come into its life for only brief periods. In September 2010, I had the privilege to preach at its fortieth anniversary.

Ministry at Fellowship Church took my re-formation in ministry beyond the local scene. I served six years on the Mid-Atlantic District Board as a member of the Ministry Commission. For five of those years, I was chair of the commission and hence a member of the board's executive committee. During these years, my learning curve was strengthened by association with District Executive Don Rowe and by the tensions and eventual withdrawal of the Broadfording Church of the Brethren, west of Hagerstown, Maryland. At the end of my years at the Fellowship Church, I was serving as moderator-elect of the district.

After eleven years in ministry at the Fellowship Church (1970-1981), I was ready for further re-formation and accepted a call to the pastorate at Everett Church of the Brethren in Everett, Pennsylvania.

An older congregation of size and influence, this church was a vital presence in its community. With a growing family and increased congregational responsibilities, I resolved no longer to accept elected positions of church leadership beyond the local community. I did agree, though, to chair Middle Pennsylvania District's Goals and Budget Committee and to serve a two-year term as one of the district's delegates to the Annual Conference Standing Committee. I also associated with the Pennsylvania Council of Churches through its annual Pastors' Conference and through its Trucker-Traveler Ministry in Breezewood, Pennsylvania.

All was going well in Everett. Our family was settled, and I appreciated the way the congregation was developing. I intended for the Everett Church to be a long-term pastorate. True, I had sometimes desired to return to the Shenandoah Valley in Virginia and had even prayed that such an opportunity would arise. But not even in my wildest dreams did I ever consider that the future might include the Bridgewater Church of the Brethren!

In the fall of 1988, I first learned of the pastoral vacancy at the Bridgewater church, but I took no special interest in it. When I attended the Spiritual Life Institute at Bridgewater College in March 1989, several persons mentioned the pastoral vacancy to me. I simply brushed their comments aside. Then on Wednesday evening of the Institute, while I was sitting in the worship service in the church sanctuary, an inner voice spoke to me: "You will be in that pulpit." I said, "No, Lord." But the voice persisted. It was clearly not just a personal passion. After I returned to Pennsylvania the following day, I shared the experience with my district executive. At the end of our conversation, we agreed that neither of us should take any initiative in pursuing it.

About two months later at lunch, I heard the home phone ring; the voice on the other end was that of Merlin Shull, district executive for the Shenandoah District where Bridgewater was located. I knew immediately what he wanted—my profile to share with Bridgewater. After receiving the paperwork, Linda and I prayed and considered a possible call to that church. I completed the profile with assistance from my district executive and personally delivered it. The following weekend, I resolved that I did not want to move. On Monday morning I called to have my profile removed from consideration and then took our car to be serviced for the coming trip to Annual Conference in Florida. While waiting, I felt myself to be the most miserable of all people. I realized in my heart that I had to leave my profile in the search or I would never know what was truly God's call. So I called and had the profile re-entered.

What a summer's journey! I had to postpone plans for a sabbatical, though I was able to attend a continuing education experience on family systems at Union Theological Seminary in Richmond, Virginia. At the end of August, I received the call to serve as the pastor of the Bridgewater Church of the Brethren, beginning December 1. Our family prepared to move; Bridgewater awaited us; Everett grieved our leaving. Re-formation continued in listening to the call of God.

The call to the Bridgewater Church put me in the position of speaking every week before professors I had studied under in college. When I mentioned this awkward situation, a member comforted me by saying, "Well, you listened to them for a while; now it's their turn to listen to you!" And they listened most graciously, as did a dozen or more retired ministers and their spouses in the congregation, along with several hundred others who worshiped there regularly. Indeed, pastoring the Bridgewater congregation turned out to be a delight and a challenge. It called forth not only my best preaching, worship planning, and pastoral skills but also my administrative skills. The ministry there put me in leadership of a multiple staff, summoning my skills in recruiting staff as well as in providing organizational expertise for the entire congregation.

During the tumultuous years of decisions related to the construction of a new church building on the hill just beyond Bridgewater College, one dissatisfied member asked, "So what are you going to do?" I replied, "I'm going to preach the gospel, care for the people, and seek to maintain some manner of administrative order." Through the remarkable leadership of numerous lay persons, we processed the building decisions with most of the congregation intact. Approximately twelve years after creating its building fund and five and half years after moving into its new church building, the congregation was worshiping in a five-million-dollar structure that was totally debt free. Today that congregation continues to worship in and serve from a facility that allows it to be who it wants and needs to be in the community.

TRANS-FORMATION

While at Bridgewater Church of the Brethren, I began to recognize not only signs of re-formation but also glimmers of trans-formation. Re-formation emerges through the improvement of what has already been formed. Trans-formation emerges through changes in one's basic identity. The completion of the building program at the Bridgewater Church opened opportunities for me to experience trans-formation.

In my family life, trans-formation ushered me into the older generation with the death of my mother in 2000. (My father had died in 1980, twenty years earlier.) It continued through the marriage of our three children and the birth of four grandchildren. I also became the husband of an ordained minister, my wife Linda, who in 2010 began her own ministry in spiritual formation and direction. No longer would I merely undergo re-formation, improving the person I already was. Now I would be trans-formed, changed into something more than I had been before.

Within the faith community, I cultivated preaching and ministry skills with a new focus called spiritual formation. This focus was cultivated through my sabbatical in 2000, when I visited the Celtic center of Iona, and through my enrollment in the summer Spiritual Formation Institute at Eastern Mennonite Seminary over a three-year period. In these studies and experiences I discovered God as more than a designated being; God became for me the Holy One.

The writings of Morton Kelsey, an Episcopal clergyman, professor, and writer, along with those of Henri Nouwen, a Catholic clergyman, helped inform my trans-formation. I particularly appreciated Kelsey's *Healing and Christianity*[6] (especially his definition of faith on page 301) and Nouwen's *The Living Reminder*.[7] More recently, Marcus Borg and N. T. Wright contributed to this trans-formation. Borg's *The Last Week*,[8] co-authored with John Dominic Crossan, and Wright's *Surprised by Hope*[9] were especially important.

Along with educational and pastoral opportunities, I also found that conversations with a spiritual director provided illuminating insights. Above all, the inner voice accentuated the recurring message, "Trust me." The ventures in this season of trans-formation called forth that trust, which became so crucial when I accepted the call to become moderator for the Church of the Brethren Annual Conference.

Early in this period of trans-formation, my ministry was transformed while I was praying en route to a pastoral visit at the University of Virginia Hospital in Charlottesville. As usual, I prayed for God to be with me in the visit. The inner voice transformed that prayer: "You don't need to ask God to be present in the visit. God is already there with you. You need to pray to be attentive to God's presence." And so I have prayed ever since.

Trans-formation extended into my passion for history. In 2002 I was invited to serve on the board of directors for the newly formed Valley Brethren-Mennonite Heritage Center (VBMHC). A year later, two board members, Nate Yoder and Al Keim, invited me to chair that board. Those calls brought faith and history together in my service with VBMHC. I am amazed as VBMHC continues to develop. Also, in 2010 the Brethren Encyclopedia Board invited me to chair the steering committee to plan the fifth Brethren World Assembly in 2013. Again, this opportunity strengthened my passion for history and incorporated it with my devotion to the faith community.

After I passed my sixtieth birthday, I began to ask questions about how long to continue in pastoral ministry, particularly at the Bridgewater congregation. Prayer, reflection, and the counsel of trusted friends helped me to decide when it was the right time for me to leave that ministry and retire from full-time pastoral service. I had devoted almost half my pastoral career to Bridgewater Church of the Brethren, and I did not want to sacrifice either the congregation or myself by winding down during my sunset years. No inner voice spoke as clearly as it had at other times, but many times over, I have given thanks to God for the decision to retire from full-time pastoral ministry at the end of April 2009.

Trans-formation then shifted me from a pastoral ministry into a broader ministry. Over the years, several people had suggested my serving as moderator for the Church of the Brethren Annual Conference, and I had always dismissed the possibility. In fact, when I moved to Bridgewater in 1989, I resolved to focus only on serving the local church and community until my children finished high school. I honored that resolution. But trans-formation now moved me in another direction.

I confess that I had wondered whether I would like being the Annual Conference moderator at some point, though I never felt enough passion to pursue that role. Then, as I prepared to retire, someone again asked permission to submit my name to the nominating process. In November 2008 I laid the application on my desk. A few weeks later, while I was ringing the Salvation Army bell at the Bridgewater IGA, another person stopped to talk. I hardly recognized him because he was so bundled up for the cold weather. He too inquired about submitting my name to the nominating committee. It was Earle Fike, another veteran Brethren minister, leader, and former moderator.

Linda and I reflected and prayed about the possibility. I remember praying as I lay in bed that night, realizing that once again I had to let my name be considered or I would never know what God's call was. Then I said to God, "I cannot do this by myself." And as it has many times before and since, that inner voice said, "Trust me." The next day, after further consideration and prayer, I called the person who had given me the application and told her that she could submit it. It was Kathy Miller Williar, the daughter of my childhood pastor. Through the election process at the 2009 Annual Conference, the call was extended for me to become moderator.

Being moderator for the Church of the Brethren transformed me in both the faith community and the community at large. The call typically extends over three years: one is first the moderator-elect, then the moderator, and finally the past moderator. As moderator-elect, I chose to participate in numerous Brethren gatherings to broaden my perspective of our denominational life. I attended the National Older Adult Conference (NOAC) for the Church of the Brethren, the Progressive Brethren Gathering, the President's Forum at Bethany Theological Seminary, our Intercultural Conference, and our New Church Planting Conference. I met also with some of the leadership of Brethren Revival Fellowship. Furthermore, in the first two years, I shared a place at the table of our Mission and Ministry Board as well as our Annual Conference officers and our Program and Arrangements Committee. As moderator, I chaired the latter two groups. During all three years, I participated in our Interagency Forum and chaired it in the third year.

Being moderator extended my world into the geographical districts of the denomination and beyond. In two instances, I participated with groups never before visited by the moderator: (1) some of the leadership of the Brethren Mennonite Council for Lesbian, Gay, Bisexual, and Transgender Persons; and (2) the Forum for the Fellowship of Brethren Homes. All of these were transforming my experience of faith community from local congregation and community to the denomination and world.

The highlight of my moderator year came in October 2010, when I joined our Global Missions Partnership Executive Jay Wittmeyer to travel to India to represent the Church of the Brethren at the fortieth anniversary of the Church of North India. Fully received as a ministerial colleague there, I helped to consecrate deacons and ministers in one congregation, dedicated pulpit furniture in another, participated in breaking the ground for a new school, and preached in eight to ten congregations.

Robert Alley, with Archbishop of Canterbury Rowan Williams, releases a pigeon during the procession to the service celebrating the 40th anniversary of the church of North India, October 1970.

The climax of the visit was the Fortieth Anniversary Service itself, with several thousand people in attendance and with Archbishop of Canterbury Rowan Williams as the featured preacher. I assisted with various liturgical duties (including serving Eucharist Communion) with ministers representing other denominations. This visit to India brought to at least partial fulfillment the high school Class Night prediction that I would become a missionary. I actually visited all three of the mission stations where my great-uncle Howard Alley had served for over twenty-nine years and preached in one of them.

To show the continuing support of the Church of the Brethren (COB) at the 40th anniversary for the Church of North India, which the COB helped to create in 1970, Robert Alley joins in the ceremony, "International Delegates Light Candles with the Faithful."

Back home, at the Annual Conference in Grand Rapids, Michigan, in July 2011, I led the gathering of the Brethren as they worshiped and fellowshiped together and as they tackled business items, two of which were controversial because they dealt with matters related to same-sex relationships. Our conference theme, "Gifted With Promise: Extending Jesus' Table," featured the story of Jesus feeding the 5,000 from Mark 6:30-44. My sermon to open the Annual Conference was titled "A Tale of Two Tables."

Retirement Challenges

Upon trans-formation into retirement, I found myself needing a new church home for the first time in my life. While our church membership and primary giving continue at Bridgewater church, our worship participation has been less frequent there out of respect for the new pastor and for my need to attain distance from my former ministry. After visiting some other Brethren, Mennonite, United Methodist, and Presbyterian churches, Linda and I have been worshiping at the Muhlenberg Lutheran Church in Harrisonburg fairly regularly. I feel deeply blessed by the liturgy, the music and arts, the preaching, and the warm fellowship there.

Muhlenberg has given me the opportunity to worship apart from the responsibilities of being moderator and leader in the life of the Brethren. The liturgy and the sermons have spoken to my journey and the challenges of being moderator. The trans-formation in this arena has also helped me to taste grace. When I changed seminaries forty years earlier, my deep concern was that I not diminish or lose connection with the Church of the Brethren. I did not do so then, and I do not plan for that to happen now, even though I deeply appreciate the liturgical life, fellowship, and pastoral care in a Lutheran church,

With retirement from full-time pastoral ministry has come the opportunity to devote energy to the "golf" in my life—genealogy research and writing. My ambition is to write at least four family histories and a history of my home community in the next decade or two. I submitted my resume to become a certified genealogist through the Board for Certification of Genealogists, which is part of the National Genealogical Society. While I did not receive certification, the process allowed me to gain important genealogical writing skills.

Formation, Re-formation, Trans-formation—these three processes have woven the strands from family, faith community, and community-at-large into varying patterns from one season to the next. My early formation occurred in the wombs of family and faith community with connections to the community at large. My ongoing re-formation occurred through education, vocational change, a Holy Spirit infilling, marriage and family, and pastoral ministries. My eventual trans-formation occurred because of spiritual formation, fresh insights into the presence and practice of the Holy One, new callings in ministry, family extensions and grandfathering, and service as Church of the Brethren moderator.

What connects all these stages in my life's journey? While listening to a Sunday morning sermon at Muhlenberg Church, I discovered what seems to me to be the common thread. For the first time, I applied Frederick Buechner's observation to myself: "The place God calls you to is the place where your deep gladness and the world's deep hunger meet."[10] I cannot count the number of people who have told me that they felt I was called to be Church of the Brethren moderator. They identified my pastoral skills and spirit as a good match for the needs of the denomination in the 2011 Annual Conference. And it seems to me that this intersection also existed in the pastoral callings I received, in the educational environments I enjoyed, and in the family who surround me. As I wrote earlier, relationships have been integral parts of my life. Family members, teachers, parishioners, writers, and all those whom God has put in my path have contributed to my formation, re-formation, and trans-formation. The most important relationship of all has been my relationship with the Holy, in Jesus Christ and through the Holy Spirit.

I trust that God, the Holy One, will continue the work of transformation in me, especially as I devote attention to what Apostle Paul defines as *grace* in the book of Romans (see Romans 5:1-5, NRSV). Where that process will lead, I do not know. Sometimes it feels a bit scary, but I must trust the Holy One. In *The Sense of the Call*, Marva Dawn writes,

> To discover our ministries is as never-ending a process as fulfilling them. God is always creating a new thing, widening the Kingdom's work through us. We ought not to worry (though I confess that I do) if after many years of service we still are asking how best we can serve God and fulfill our call; it is worrisome if we have stopped asking.[11]

April 2011
Revised July 2015

NOTES

1. David Wilkerson with John and Elizabeth Sherrill, *The Cross and the Switchblade* (New York, N.Y.: The Berkley Publishing Group, 1962; reissued New York, N.Y.: Jove Books, 1986).

2. *Good News for Modern Man*, trans. Robert Bratcher (New York, N.Y.: American Bible Society, 1966; Grand Rapids, Mich.: Zondervan, 2001). The

complete Bible, known as *The Good News Bible*, appeared in 1976; it is also known as *Today's English Version*.

3. *The Living Bible*, paraphrased by Kenneth Taylor (Wheaton, Ill.: Tyndale House Publishers, 1971).

4. *The New English Bible with the Apocrypha* (Oxford, United Kingdom and Cambridge, United Kingdom: Oxford University Press and Cambridge University Press, 1970).

5. *New Revised Standard Version* (Nashville, Tenn.: Thomas Nelson Publishers,1989).

6. Morton T. Kelsey, *Healing and Christianity* (Minneapolis, Minn.: Augsburg Fortress, 1973). *Psychology, Medicine and Christian Healing: A Revised and Expanded Edition of Healing and Christianity* (San Francisco: Harper & Row, 1968, reprinted 1995).

7. Henri Nouwen, *The Living Reminder: Service and Prayer in Memory of Jesus Christ* (New York, N.Y.: Harper Collins, 1977, 2009).

8. Marcus Borg and John Dominic Crossan, *The Last Week: What the Gospels Really Teach About Jesus's Final Days in Jerusalem* (New York, N.Y.: HarperCollins, 2006).

9. Nicholas Thomas Wright, *Surprised by Hope: Rethinking Heaven, the Resurrection, and the Mission of the Church* (New York, N.Y.: HarperCollins, 2008).

10. Frederick Buechner, *Wishful Thinking*: *A Theological ABC* (New York, N.Y.: Harper & Row Publishers, Inc., 1973), 95.

11. Marva J. Dawn, *The Sense of the Call: A Sabbath Way of Life for Those Who Serve God, the Church, and the World* (Grand Rapids, Mich.: Wm B. Eerdmans, 2006), 30.

Martin W. Lehman

Bishop with an Open Heart

Sent as a missionary superintendent to Florida with his wife Rhoda (Krady), Martin Lehman was later ordained bishop and then became the first General Secretary of the Southeast Mennonite Convention/Conference. In his memoir he shows how his insights moved from loyalty to restrictive conservative beliefs and cultural practices to an openness to God's grace for everyone. He found his voice in articles like "The Day I Went Public with My Faith" and now continues, in his blog, "The Old Fool—Martin Lehman," to advocate for inclusion of all. Photo by Ray C. Gingerich, at Lehman's ACRS Breakfast Presentation

MARTIN W. LEHMAN

My Faith Journey: From Youthful Conformist to Senior Nonconformist

While I was putting the final touches on this manuscript, the preacher in me told me that it needed a Bible text. A little search brought me to the following: "Always be prepared to give an answer to everyone who asks you to give the reason for the hope that you have. But do this with gentleness and respect" (1 Pet. 3:15, NIV). This text reminds me to prepare to be questioned about what I believe, to welcome every opportunity to give a reason for my hope, and to be gentle and respectful always toward all who hear me.

A RURAL, SOMEWHAT PROBLEMATIC, BEGINNING

I feel kindly toward the old gentleman who named me. I was born on March 14, 1926, in a small farmhouse in the slate hills west of the Conocheague Creek in Franklin County, Pennsylvania. My parents intended to name me Martin Weagley Lehman: *Martin* after my mother, Ruth Martin, *Weagley* after the country doctor who came to our house to preside over my birth, and *Lehman* after J. Irvin Lehman, my father. But the good doctor had the final word. On my birth certificate he wrote "Martin W. Lehman."

Our family lived on a thirty-five acre, sustainable farm. As a boy I learned to milk the cow, churn ice cream and butter, and trust honeybees. I slopped the hogs, gathered eggs, split wood, decapitated and plucked chickens, and worked in the garden. I learned to build a compost pile with chicken litter and all our vegetable refuse, which we spread over our garden soil. From this grew all manner of fruits and vegetables to be sold at the farmers' market in Chambersburg and to the customers who sought us out.

One Sunday at church I was playing with some toys in an empty space on the bench beside my mother when I became aware that the man in the pulpit was my father and that he was saying something important. I remember that moment, and it was perhaps then that I received my first call to preach. At age nine I stood to accept Jesus as my Savior; and, baptized at age ten, I became a member of the Marion Mennonite Church, which belonged to the Washington County (Maryland) and Franklin County (Pennsylvania) Mennonite Conference, the smallest Mennonite conference at the time. Sadly, it was a troubled conference whose members disputed among themselves about many things.

My father, the secretary of the conference, often met with the bishops to record their actions. His nervousness related to this work sometimes caused his beard to stop growing in spots. (I know because I watched him shave at the kitchen table with his straight-edged razor.) He regularly had an upset stomach as the annual conference sessions approached. My mother called it his conference stomach. Ever since, I have had a deep distaste for divisions in the church.

Life outside my small circle in Franklin County began at Eastern Mennonite School (EMS). There, from 1940 to 1943, Dorothy Kemrer led me through three years of hard study of Latin. My English vocabulary has grown through knowledge of Latin roots.

Also, in my freshman year of high school I got a brief glimpse of Rhoda Krady, daughter of D. Stoner and Francis Krady, when she visited EMS for one weekend. She returned as a student for her sophomore year and then left for Lancaster Mennonite School for her junior year, but I pursued her by writing a letter to her on her sixteenth birthday. I do not mention Rhoda as often as she deserves in this treatise, but she was almost always by my side, in fact and in thought.

Memorable Civilian Public Service (CPS) Events, North Fork, California

On January 5, 1945, I entered CPS at Grottoes, Virginia, to do Soil Conservation Service; in May that year I was transferred to the forest service camp at North Fork, California. I was selected by lot (from names pulled from an Amish hat) to be one of the several hundred conscientious objectors to go to California because of the danger of fires caused by Japanese fire bombs launched by balloons. We traveled by troop train through the level green wheat fields of Kansas and the cacti growing in the great desert of the Southwest to the San Joaquin Valley of California, where the train stopped at Fresno, and we boarded trucks for North Fork, the headquarters of the Sierra National Forest and the home of CPS Camp No. 35. The journey impressed me with the vastness of our beautiful country.

Camp Grottoes, the first camp for conscientious objectors, had the most homogeneous population of all the camps; the North Fork camp was different. It had a wider range of Mennonites and Amish as well as COs of other persuasions, including Christadelphians, Jehovah's Witnesses, and Russian Molokans (known as Spiritual Christians, with a history dating back to the 1760s when they broke with the Russian Orthodox Church and its practices). Further, although one would expect fire prevention work to seem useful, the morale of the fellows who welcomed us might be measured by the following: On my first morning there I said, "Good morning," to the man brushing his teeth next to me. He asked, "What's so damn good about it?"

The highpoint of my life in California was the four months living alone in a cabin perched on a steel fire tower. Each of these cabins had a cot, a gas stove, a short wave radio, a telephone, and an Osbourne fire finder and was surrounded by a catwalk. I walked the catwalk and looked for smoke every ten minutes of every waking hour. For many years afterward, if there was smoke on the horizon, I saw it.

I took with me the black Mennonite Hymnal published in 1927 and my Bible and read and reread the epistle to the Romans. Sixty years later I am still guided by what I read, which may be summed up thus: All have sinned, and no law, not even a good and perfect law from God, can save me. The law of sin and death operates within me, exploits my weakness, and seeks to seal my fate. Yet there is hope for me, for the law of life in Christ Jesus sets me free.

I spent part of each day singing through the hymnal. Some hymns were prayers, like "O Master, let me walk with Thee" (Frances R. Havergal and Robert A. Schumann) and "Lord, speak to me that I may speak/ In living echoes of thy tone" (Washington Gladden and H. Percy Smith). These prayers, which I sang often, reflected the deep longing of my soul. I will always cherish the memory of those four months alone with God in the mountains.

A Furlough Month

Early December 1945, I was granted a month-long furlough and a bus ticket from Fresno, California, to Gulfport, Mississippi, by way of Greencastle, Pennsylvania. Traveling for six long days on that bus, I wondered if I would ever get out of Texas! On arriving home I borrowed my father's car and went to Lancaster to see Rhoda Krady. East of Chambersburg I expected to go over South Mountain. It was not there. My eagerness to get to Rhoda no doubt helped make the mountain disappear, but my visual perspective had changed so much that the mountains and trees of Appalachia did not look to me as they had less than a year earlier.

Gulfport, Mississippi

The furlough passed quickly, and I was soon on my way by bus to the elite CPS unit at Gulfport, Mississippi, where fellow COs introduced me to the values of the old South, including attitudes toward African Americans. My first assignment was to work with a small team of men who used red squill as a poison to control the rat population along the Gulf Coast—in mansions owned mostly by whites and in the shacks of the descendants of slaves, who lived in slum-like ghettos not far from the scenic Gulf shore. After that project, I joined the staff in the camp kitchen, where I washed dishes, graduated to meal preparation, and ended my civilian public service career as a dietician for the forty-to-fifty person unit.

During my time at Gulfport, I wrote an original piece called "The Antithesis of Job." The main character of my booklet, tested by his wealth (especially in comparison to others), was admonished by liberal, conservative, and ultraconservative brothers. I included the piece in my letters to Rhoda, who returned the drafts to me in her letters with commas put in their places along with other grammatical corrections. *The Sword & Trumpet* (a monthly publication in Harrisonburg, Virginia, edited then by my father, J. Irvin Lehman) published it in 1949, not only in the third issue of volume 17 but also as a booklet in which Associate Editor George R. Brunk II described it as unusually mature thinking for a man so young.

October 10, 1945, was my last day in CPS.

NOVICE MISSIONARIES IN FLORIDA

On April 5, 1946, Rhoda Miller Krady and I were married and began to put down roots in Franklin County. We built a cottage on a beautiful corner of my parents' farm, bought a well-preserved, one-owner 1931 Chevrolet coupe, and soon became the parents of a beautiful daughter we named Rachel Elaine.

All this was interrupted by an invitation to attend Eastern Mennonite Board of Mission's six-week Missionary Training Institute in Philadelphia, which focused on practical methods of evangelism and church planting. Not many months later, we received a letter from Henry Garber, the president of Eastern Mennonite Board of Missions, inviting us to his home to consider a call to serve as a mission superintendent couple in either Brewton, Alabama, or Tampa, Florida. Since we knew some of the people serving in Alabama, we decided on Brewton as our first choice.

However, Tampa turned out to be the only choice. A few hours before our arrival at the Garber home, another couple had accepted the call to Brewton. This now seems providential. The mission superintendents in Alabama were mission-minded but older than Rhoda and me and resistant to change. The younger mission superintendents in Florida, who had worked in cities or in migrant communities, were often willing and eager for change.

We sent Rachel's crib ahead of us with a friend and crammed ourselves and our personal belongings into and on top of the coupe. We began our trip on February 1, 1950, and arrived on February 4. We knew we were venturing into a new phase of life. Over and over we sang a song we had learned at the Pond Bank Summer Bible school the summer before:

I will not be afraid, I will not be afraid;
I will look upward, and travel onward,
And not be afraid.
He says He will be with me, He says he will be with me;
He goes before me, and is beside me,
So I'm not afraid.

(The first two stanzas of a song by Ellis Govan, which in China the persecuted missionaries and Chinese believers sang during China's second war with Japan, 1931-1945; copyright status understood to be public domain.)

Yes, we were naïve, but the lyrics confirmed our simple faith as we journeyed with our two-year-old daughter and our few possessions into the unknown future.

Novice missionary that I was, I had in my mental baggage a belief system based on the Bible's verbal inspiration. The Bible, taken at its word, allowed no divorces and no marriage after divorce, required covering a woman's long hair, permitted no musical instruments in public worship, allowed no wedding rings or other jewelry, and forbade women to wear men's clothing. This is only a partial listing of what I now acknowledge to be the dirty laundry in my mental luggage. (If you dislike my use of the term *dirty laundry*, please recall that when the apostle Paul listed his assets, he called them *dung*.)

Almost a year later, on the day before Christmas, I was ordained for the ministry. As I recall, in my preaching in those early years, Jesus was preeminent. But the closer a convert came to church membership, the more likely I would display the dirty laundry in my luggage. The sad fact was that most candidates for church membership left the Mennonites for a Southern Baptist church. There people could go forward to confess faith in Jesus and that very night or no later than the following Sunday be baptized "the right way," by immersion, and join the traditional religious culture of their ancestors.

A middle-aged woman explained to us that as a teenager she had left the Mennonites for the Baptists because she knew she could not be *that* good. I still see the puzzled face of a sincere young man when I explained that before he could be baptized, he must take the ring off his finger. He explained sadly, "But my mother gave me this ring." The last I heard about him, he was in a tank facing down the Russians at the Berlin gate.

I did not see the dirt in my mental laundry. The items in my luggage were all consistent with what I believed to be the wishes of the bishop under whose direction I worked. More importantly, I was blinded to the dirt by my reliance on biblical proof texts. Like the smoke on the horizon, I found in the Bible what I had been taught to look for, not understanding these words of Jesus: "But if anyone causes one of these little ones who believe in me to sin, it would be better for him to have a large millstone hung around his neck and to be drowned in the depths of the sea" (Matt. 18:6, NIV). Now by God's grace, it is not I, but those pastoral sins, along with all my other sins, that are buried in the sea of God's forgetfulness.

LIFE AS A LANCASTER CONFERENCE BISHOP

As the 1950s ended, the Lancaster Conference Bishop Board decided to divide its large southern region into two districts and ordain bishops from among the pastors who resided in the South. The pastors of the new Georgia and Peninsular Florida district met at the Ida Street Mennonite Church to consider who among them should be their bishop. I was troubled and could not sleep the night before nominations were to be made. It does not seem impertinent to me now to say that God and I were in communication. I knew there was a possibility that I would be named. Finally, I went to sleep after I had promised God that if I became a bishop, I would not interfere wherever I sensed that the Holy Spirit was at work. This may have been the time when I began to open my mind to things new.

In the forenoon of the next day, I was named as the one to be ordained. In the afternoon I was examined and instructed by the two bishops present. They asked about my willingness to wear a frock coat like other bishops. They gently asked Rhoda if she was willing to wear a dress with an apron as did her mother and the wives of other bishops. The final question in the series was significant to me. Bishop David Thomas asked if I would promise to give my insights to the Bishop Board even if I were a minority of one. I was ordained the next day.

The congregation greeted Rhoda and me in two different ways as they filed past us at the end of the service. Mennonites of long standing were often teary-eyed as they solemnly promised to pray for us.

They sensed the difficulty of the task before me: that I would be expected to make difficult judgments and might be misunderstood or even disliked. On the other hand, our non-Mennonite neighbors smiled as they congratulated us. To them, being ordained a bishop was a promotion and an honor.

Ordination made me a member of the Bishop Board of the Lancaster Conference. This board met on the third Thursday of every month, and I was expected to travel to Pennsylvania for at least half of the meetings. Thus, for almost twenty years I took a minimum of six trips to Pennsylvania each year and lived a minimum of twelve days with fellow bishops, who became my family for those days. Most of the other bishops had been chosen by lot from among the pastors of their districts. Most had succeeded in a secular enterprise. Among us were schoolteachers, farmers, entrepreneurs, and at least two millionaires. One of the youngest, I lived on a missionary's stipend, but on the Bishop Board we were equals. I learned what it was like to speak my mind and to be a respected minority. I learned to listen quietly to the convictions of others.

The Bishop Board was also subjected to change. Traditionally, the moderator of the board and conference was the bishop with the most years of service. Not long before I joined the board, a senior bishop who realized his limitations declined the honor. The board then instituted a five-year term of office for the moderator second in seniority. Soon after I became a member, the board elected a new moderator, David Thomas, and a secretary, Paul Landis, both of whom were young in age and in years of service. They guided the board through an era when the Mennonite church and the Lancaster Conference allowed significant changes.

However, there was variation in the conference districts. Individual bishops had different styles of leadership based, I think, on the relative strength of their faith as defined by Paul in Romans 14. From my perspective, to the apostle Paul, anyone who knew little of God's grace was weak in faith. Another person more aware of God's grace he described as being strong in faith. Thus the bishops who were less mindful of God's grace tended to regard a word from the conference as a word from God and used conference rules to bind the people they served. Other bishops who were more conscious of God's grace were more gracious to their people.

Geographically, the districts ranged along the eastern seaboard from New York to Alabama and Florida. Some districts were deeply rooted in the conference's rural roots. Others had a shorter history and tended to be on a cultural edge. However, the conference had the simple rule that a bishop should not meddle in another bishop's district. To my knowledge, this rule was carefully observed by all bishops. On the other hand, a bishop could ask the board to appoint bishops to advise him and mediate when he was in need of help.

Lancaster Mennonite Conference met twice each year for all-day sessions on the third Thursday in March and September. The ordained ministers and deacons and their wives met with the bishops for these two days of conference; the women were quiet. Members of the laity were welcomed but seldom spoke and could not vote. On those special days the Bishop Board reported its work and offered statements that became conference positions if approved by four-fifths of the bishops and ratified by a two-thirds vote of the entire body of ordained men.

A bishop of the conference or a bishop from another conference was asked to preach the conference sermon. Soon after I became a member of the board, I was asked to preach one of these special sermons. It was a simple sermon but must have been appreciated because preachers and deacons in the audience came to greet me afterward and to thank me for it. Embarrassed, I wished I could go away and hide. Seeing my discomfort, one of the senior bishops pulled me aside and said quietly, "Martin, it's all right to feel good when God uses you." I have used these simple words to encourage others.

Once I invited a non-Mennonite college professor trained in social anthropology to go to a conference with me. His first observation to me was, "Your women are not happy." He was likely right, because a bishop's ordination affected the whole family. His wife and children were expected to be models of conference decorum. I know because I married the daughter of a bishop. After his death, her older siblings often lamented in reunions the change from the happy papa they knew as children to their father as a bishop who was burdened with the expectations other bishops laid on him. Her younger siblings never knew that happy papa.

In our home we had one child, a daughter, who wished for a brother as we wished for a son. When we visited a new son in another family, we often jokingly said to the parents, "If you don't want him, give him to us." Once we visited a mother of five who had given birth to a sixth. When she realized the frailty of her health, she told her husband that if she should die, to give the baby son to the Lehmans. One month later, she died suddenly, and the baby's father and grandmother brought the baby boy to our door. I decided God had some things to teach me through a son. We named him Jonathan Conrad, which means "God has given good counsel."

CHOICES AS A BISHOP IN FLORIDA

As a bishop, I was soon clearly under the influence of three groups. The first, of course, was the Lancaster Conference Bishop Board. The second to influence me were the ministers of my district, and I am indebted to them for their part in forming me to be their servant. Soon after my ordination, when I convened the ministers for our first meeting, I asked them what they wanted me to do. They said,

Martin Lehman chatting with Omar Meyer, lay leader in the Bayshore Mennonite Church and conference supporter

"Help us to be better ministers." We decided to sponsor a series of seminars with resource persons coming from outside the district. (After one or two of the seminars, we began to invite the pastors who belonged to other conferences to join us.)

Also at our first meeting, the district ministers endorsed the youth camp program sponsored by the Eastern Mission Board and the Tampa ministry and set in motion a process that resulted in the incorporation of the Southern Mennonite Camp Association and the eventual purchase and development of Lakewood Retreat. (We looked to both Eastern Board of Missions and the Sarasota churches for support of the camp program.) Later, with the help of Chester Wenger, Eastern Board's home mission's secretary, we initiated a lay leadership-training program called Project Timothy.

The third group to influence me was Sarasota Mennonite ministers who met monthly for a prayer breakfast. Soon they invited the ministers of all five conferences in the Southeast to their breakfasts. The group's agenda evolved from prayer to consultation, to coordination of events, and to the sponsorship of a youth minister. We had a common treasury and discussed becoming a southeast conference.

My relationship to these three groups was pivotal. Soon I knew that I would need to choose to follow either the counsels of bishops who lived a thousand miles away or the counsels of the pastors who were my neighbors. Deciding on the latter, as I did, meant leading in the direction of change. However, I found that change can be difficult when people assume that their present beliefs and practices are based on biblical texts.

A seminar sponsored in 1963 or 1964 by the Eastern Mission Board at Black Rock Retreat in Pennsylvania provided new light. Harold Bauman used Paul's words in Romans 15:7 to teach us how to relate to others: "Accept one another, then, as God in Christ accepted you" (NIV). This admonition changed the question. It was no longer, has God accepted *them*, but how has God accepted *us*? I believed that God accepted me as I was, a sinner saved by grace; now as a young churchman I was to learn to accept others in that same godly way. I had no idea where this new perspective would lead me.

MORE NEW INSIGHTS

From a book and a trip

In the 1960s one afternoon, driving alone on a lonely road in south Georgia on a hot day, I felt tired and bored. Glimpsing a used bookstore in the small town I was passing through, I slid to a stop and went inside to browse. For five cents I bought a tattered old book I remember as a systematic theology. (Since the front cover was torn off, it was worth no more than the nickel.) What I had learned about changing perspectives when I traveled from the Sierra Nevada in California to the Appalachian hills of Pennsylvania helped me to accept what I understood the old book to teach. It said to me that truth itself never changes but that our views of truth change as we get closer to it.

This metaphor became clearer to me one day when Rhoda and I were traveling north on I-77. I was dozing while Rhoda drove. As my eyelids drooped, I saw a single mountain range on the distant horizon. As we sped onward, I opened my eyes to see a series of mountain ranges. Still closer, I saw valleys among the mountains. Soon, amid the mountains I spotted streams, flowers, trees, and vistas. The mountain range on the horizon had not changed a bit, but what I saw of it changed the closer we got to it.

The metaphor meant that a new view of truth does not change truth. But a new view of truth might not only permit me to change, it may even *demand* that I change both my belief system and my behaviors. I believe we should honestly tell each other about the mountain of truth that we see in the distance. But it is fruitless for any of us to hold too tightly to our present views. That mountain I see before me will surely look different to me farther down the road.

From a sabbatical at
Eastern Mennonite College and Seminary

Another way of seeing came to me in 1966 when Eastern Mennonite Missions gave me a one-year sabbatical at Eastern Mennonite College (EMC). This was a first for the Lancaster Conference, so who would do the work of a bishop in my absence was a logical question. The Home Missions Council allowed me to inform the pastors that they were assistant bishops and that I trusted them and was delegating my responsibilities in each congregation to them. Thus, the pastors baptized and served communion in my absence. When I returned to the district nine months later, I did not reclaim any of these special privileges unless a pastor specifically asked me to do so.

The special study program for pastors at EMC/U allowed me to select classes from both college and seminary programs. I chose New

Testament Theology, taught by Willard Swartley. When he saw that my lack of formal training would force me to study the Bible in English only, he recommended a booklet titled *The Joy of Discovery in Bible Study* by Oletta Wald (Minneapolis, Minn.: Augsburg Fortress, 1975, 2002, 2005). This booklet and James Strong's *Strong's Exhaustive Concordance of the Bible* (Peabody, Mass.: Hendrickson Publishers, 1988) gave me the tools to do inductive Bible study in the English language, and I still experience the joy of making discoveries. Swartley taught me to ask questions.

Oletta Wald taught me to look for repetition and make careful observations. I was surprised to discover what Paul, the Pharisee most zealous for the law, repeats *four times* in his first letter to the Corinthian church, "All things are lawful for me" (6:12, twice and 10:23, twice, NKJV). Could the apostle Paul lawfully do anything a Corinthian did? Just the thought is amazing, perhaps alarming! Yet Paul emphasizes his freedom by repeating it four times in one letter.

Wald also taught me to pay attention to the small words that connect the parts of a sentence. When Paul claims that all things were lawful for him, he always follows that radical claim with the powerful little word *but*, which connects the first clause to a second contrasting clause that asks for prudent use of such freedom. Twice he says that though all things are lawful, not everything is "helpful" (6:12 and 10:23, NKJV); that is, not everything is practical, "beneficial" (6:12, NIV), or advantageous. The fourth time he explains that though all things are lawful, "not all things edify" (10:23, NKJV); that is, not all lawful things are enlightening, enriching, and helpful. The second *but*, I saw, connects to a bold declaration: Though everything is lawful, he, Paul, "will not to be brought under the power of any" (6:12, NKJV). The law has indeed lost its strength, and death has lost its sting.

But why did Paul repeat this radical claim four times in one letter? Perhaps he feared his words might one day be given the weight of law and women far from Corinth in time and space would be required to cover their beautiful, uncut hair. Perhaps he feared that long after he had written words that were appropriate for Corinthians, they would be used to keep women silent in their churches. Women would be denied the right to exercise their Spirit-given gifts, and the church would be robbed of their benefit.

Though no law in the Bible saves me or anyone else, the book still has a purpose. Paul wrote to Timothy that Scripture was useful and able to make one wise for salvation through faith in Christ Jesus. Certainly, the Bible provides adequate bases for the church to change its confession of faith and its practices from time to time. From my perspective, the Bible should be given more attention and respect.

Near the end of my year at EMC, the college sponsored a two-week Evangelism Institute for more than fifty home and overseas missionaries, and pastors from the Southeast joined me there. A pastor from my district confided to Don Jacobs that he believed that his plain suit was a hindrance to his ministry. He had decided to get a regular suit and necktie. "But," the pastor asked, "how can I tell my bishop?" Don replied, "We'll tell him tomorrow morning." Don invited the other ministers from the district to meet with the pastor and me. I do not remember that meeting or what I said. But the pastor assured me later that I told the group that I had decided that anything that stood in the way of making Jesus known had to go.

Choices amid Major Changes

The shifting terrain of denominational organization in the 1960s freed churches to decide what to wear, how to worship, whom to baptize, and with whom to form new alliances. Some in the denomination who could not endure the changes formed separatist groups. Other churches welcomed the opportunity to form new alliances. The churches of four of the five conferences with churches in the Southeast formed a Southeast Mennonite Convention that fully accepted the notion that the locus of authority was in the congregation. Churches in this new convention were given the option of retaining their conference membership. Over time, the churches of my district chose to discontinue their ties with the Lancaster Conference, and I moved gradually from being a bishop to being given new roles in the convention. I am grateful that in these years the denomination and the conferences did not get in the way of congregational autonomy. I regret that in the following decades, the conferences tended to reclaim their status, power, and authority.

In 1982, I was invited to attend a meeting of conference leaders from Region V in Washington, D.C. The purpose of the meeting was to promote homosexual anonymous-type ministries within caring congregations. Counselors described gays and lesbians as deviant but likeable people who intended no harm. A theologian cautioned us not to judge quickly sexual behavior based on a simple reading of the English Bible because biblical scholars were uncertain how to interpret the metaphors used by ancient writers to describe private behaviors. Two gay men from the Washington community were allowed to be present but to speak for only thirty minutes. Their anger at being excluded while they were being talked about rendered them almost speechless and made a lasting impression on me.

Two members of the Region V Executive Council were asked to summarize the Washington meeting. Their second point suggested that the council provide a framework for discussion with gay persons that would minimize rejection and intimidation. Listening would be important. The council appointed a committee, of which I was a member, to create such a framework. As I recall, the framework was not to include judgment of anyone, attempts to change or convert anyone, or affirmation of anyone's orientation. We were to listen only. When the denomination ended its regional structures, the Board of Congregational Ministries (MBCM) continued the listening committee.

Most of our listening was done at general assemblies of the Mennonite Church, where the planners provided us a room, which we used it for our own listening purposes and set aside times when the gay community could use it. On one occasion the committee was asked what it did with what it heard. To satisfy that legitimate concern, we began to report more directly to MBCM and the General Board, the agencies responsible for our appointment. However, we kept confidential the names of those who came out to us. Most homosexuals told us that they knew they were different from others in early childhood. They had long periods of spiritual depression while they pled with God to change them—but received no answer. Finally they found peace and joy when they accepted God's unconditional love for them. I listened to their confessions of faith with respect, feeling as though, with this attitude, I was being more like Jesus than in any other role in my life.

The leaders of the Southeast Mennonite Convention were aware of my listening activities and trusted me. However, one pastor became suspicious, fearful, and angry. He made a motion on the conference floor that was obviously aimed at me and my listening. The motion failed for want of a second. Another member of conference moved that a group be named to study the homosexual "issue" and report recommenddations to conference. This motion passed. As a result, the convention took a conference-like action: For the first time it chose a position later used to obstruct a congregation's mission.

FINDING MY VOICE

The same year, 1982, that I was introduced to listening, I began to find my voice about justice and social issues. I read *The Company of Strangers: Christians & the Renewal of America's Public Life* by Parker J. Palmer (New York: The Crossroad Publishing Company, 1981) and realized that thus far in my life I had preached primarily to friends. That book and an automobile accident one night while Rhoda and I were traveling toward home emboldened me. The accident, which happened on a bridge, had stopped all traffic, and I went to see if I could help. I held a flashlight while others attempted to free the injured persons by prying open jammed car doors with jack handles. That experience prepared me for what came next.

Martin Lehman at his convention/conference office desk

A few months later I volunteered to speak for Mennonites at a rally promoting a nuclear freeze. I had attended some social justice events and heard people wonder why the Mennonites were not there.

I fasted for a week or ten days before I marched and spoke from the front steps of the First Congregational Church in Sarasota. I tried to explain that so few Mennonites supported the nuclear freeze because the goal of a nuclear freeze was too limited. The prophets of the Old Testament foretold of a time when simple, lethal weapons, such as swords and spears, would be reshaped into productive tools. Mennonites believed that Jesus wanted his followers to lay down all weapons and be people of peace.

I explained why I marched in support of a nuclear freeze when other Mennonites did not. I used the accident on the bridge to explain that some matters were so urgent and the future so dangerous for others that strangers had to work together without introducing themselves, discussing faith perspectives, or considering family connections. It was true that I might have held the flashlight for an atheist that night. The possibility did not even occur to me at the moment. We were too intent on helping the injured women who were trapped in the car. I included my speech in an article for the *Gospel Herald* titled, "The Day I Went Public with My Faith." Editor Daniel Hertzler also printed the article in his *Not by Might: A Gospel Herald Sampler with Profiles of the Editors and Selected Writings from 1908 to 1983* (Scottdale, Pa.: Herald Press, 1983).

DISCOVERIES IN LATER YEARS

A book and DISC

In March 1992, at age sixty-five, I retired from conference work. Before the retirement date I learned of an anniversary reunion of the Gulfport CPS unit, which gave Rhoda and me a reason to take a trip immediately after my retirement. Before we left for Mississippi, a friend loaned us a copy of *Transitions: Making Sense of Life's Changes* by William Bridges (Boston, Mass.: Da Capo Press, 1992, 2004). Rhoda read the book to me as we traveled. As I remember Bridges, no one can fully prepare for bereavement, divorce, loss of job, retirement, or other transitions. After a loss there is usually a period of confusion followed by a serendipitous event that opens to the future.

On our return we spent a few hours with a successful Mennonite entrepreneur in Alabama, who told me about the DISC Personality

Profile System promoted by the Institute for Motivational Living. (This is a kind of diagnostic tool that acquaints people with their primary characteristics and how these influence people's behavior with others. D stands for "dominance," I for "influence," S for "steadiness," and C for "conscientiousness.") He said the system had changed his managerial style and his relationships with his peers and his employees. As an example, he said his bishop had annoyed him by asking many questions. The DISC system taught him to value the questions and the questioner. Instead of being annoyed, he decided to hire his bishop so that he could observe more closely and ask more questions.

Could the DISC system be the serendipitous event described by Bridges? Open to that possibility, I immediately ordered the manual to learn the system and within six weeks was certified to administer the DISC assessment tool. The system taught me about myself. I was a "DSC." My high "D" showed that I could be decisive, dare to attempt to do what others doubted could be done, and often do it by defying rules. When under pressure my "SC" behaviors were more prominent than the usual "D." I used my "S" style to try to establish steady and stable environments. I used my "C" style to set and meet competently high standards for myself and for others.

With this new understanding of myself, I moved confidently into the future. I had told my friends that I would approach retirement as if it were a long hallway with many closed doors. It was my responsibility to try the doors to discover which of them would open to me. The first open door was a six-week consulting ministry in a church outside the Southeast. The second open door was a year as a half-time interim pastor for the Pinecreek Chapel in Arcadia, Florida. During these ministries, I honed my skill in the use of the DISC behavioral system.

A talk about the Mennonites

Don Augsburger, pastor of the Bahia Vista Mennonite Church, presented another door for me. He suggested that I represent the Mennonites at the Suncoast Evangelical Association of Sarasota. Charles Heinlein, founder and chairman of the association, welcomed me. At my first meeting with the association, he asked me to tell about the Mennonites in Sarasota County. At the next meeting he asked me to speak about Mennonites and patriotism. I used a small handmade cross and a small flag to illustrate my point. I told them that the U.S. flag was limited to certain boundaries. I explained that the cross was greater than the flag because it knew no boundaries. I said, "I do not pledge allegiance to the flag or the nation for which it stands; I pledge my allegiance to Jesus and his worldwide reign of peace." *The Mennonite* published the speech under the title of "The Flag and the Cross" in its July 2, 2002, issue (vol. 5, p. 17). For a time it was posted on the web site of The Third Way Café to be available to anyone exploring the faith of the Anabaptists. It was also published in a Mennonite Brethren bulletin as part of a discussion of certain aspects of their historical faith. It may have been the most widely read of my writings.

Somewhere in this account I must include a visit from a respected conference minister. He invited me to lunch, at which he urged me to careful and be sure to retire in honor. I understood him to be cautioning me to be wise, but I chose rather to be a "fool" for Christ's sake. I began to refer to myself as "the old fool."

Without shoes

Also, along the way I read a line from J. D. Graber, veteran Mennonite missionary and Mennonite Board of Missions Overseas Secretary, about how to do mission work. He said that the missionary must take off his shoes before he enters another person's "holy of holies" and attempts to rearrange the furniture. That wisdom remained with me through the years and most significantly in my retirement. Though I still had the boldness of a high "D" behavioral style, it was restrained when I took off my shoes to gain admission to the holy of holies of others.

With shoes off, I accepted the position of first vice president of the Suncoast Evangelical Association (SEA). I listened without passing judgment to the testimonies of faith in Christ as told by extreme right-wing Christians even as they took positions and actions that I could not. On at least one occasion I told members of the SEA board that if I were as judgmental as they were, I could have nothing to do with them. Yet they respected me. I felt then and still do that ultimate unity of the church cannot be achieved if we Christians do not exercise grace among ourselves.

Most of these concluding paragraphs describe one-day experiences in a lifetime of events. The Christian Coalition advertised a workshop that would include a video on what was called "the gay agenda." Several lesbians told me they wished they could know what was said at such meetings. I told them I was a friend of the chair and invited them to go with me. With shoes off, I introduced them to the chair. When he introduced the video he acknowledged graciously that many Christian gays and lesbians who lived in Sarasota County did not support the radical gay agenda portrayed on the film.

I was invited to represent Mennonites to a group of people from different backgrounds in search of world peace through individual inner peace. Because I delayed my reply, I was put last on the list of speakers. I took off my shoes and went. The first speaker was a Baptist preacher who gave an evangelical sermon and left the meeting. I stayed while a Native American smoked a peace pipe. He smoked overtime and refused to be interrupted because he was in his holy of holies. Others testified to finding inner peace after not finding it in a traditional church.

Late in the afternoon, the group decided to form a circle and dance. At the end of the dance someone said, "We haven't heard anything from Mr. Lehman." I confessed that I had never before danced in worship and thanked them for the privilege. I then told them that the longer I lived, the more thankful I was for God's grace. A woman leader rebuked me sharply exclaiming, "Oh no! You Mennonites are so good!" (That, I think, is one of our problems. We have appeared to be so good.) I replied by saying that our church meetings were open to the public and invited them to come and hang around with us. I knew that if they knew us better they would understand our need of God's grace.

I was among the few Gentiles who met in a synagogue with mourning Jews when they observed the fiftieth anniversary of the Holocaust. When the rabbi prayed for God to send the Messiah, I prayed, too, with my shoes off.

With shoes off, I met with gays and lesbians in the Sarasota Metropolitan Church when they mourned the murder of Matthew Shepard. A young woman cried as she sat beside me on the back bench. I asked her why she was crying, and she told me her story. I prayed with her.

I continued to refine my skill in the use of DISC System until I was certified to instruct others to administer it. A lesbian minister attended one of my classes and then invited me to hold a workshop for the leaders and members of the Suncoast Cathedral Metropolitan Community Church of Venice. This church was a collection of refugees from main line, Pentecostal, Anabaptist, and other faith traditions. They longed to return to their roots. I accepted this call and informed my pastor of what I was about to do. With shoes off, I moved through the same kind of workshop I had held in Mennonite churches. I found these gays and lesbians to have the same behavioral patterns and the same problems as members of Mennonite congregations.

After my Sunday morning sermon on the "Four Faces of Jesus," the church's tradition called for a communion service. The elders of the congregation stood in front as the members of the church came forward, many as couples, to talk/weep quietly with an elder and receive the emblems. I remained seated behind the pulpit. An elder brought bread and wine to me, which I accepted with thanksgiving. It was the most memorable communion of my long experience as a member of the body of Christ and a minister of the gospel.

That involvement with the Metropolitan Church was reported in a newspaper of the gay community. Mysteriously, it fell into the hands of a member of the Bahia Vista Mennonite Church. I was told about it, but no one told me who had it or showed it to me. At this time the church leadership secured a consultant to assess the health of the congregation. After meeting with the church members who wished to speak with him, the consultant told me that there were members who should talk with me. He arranged for LeRoy Bechler to convene a group of about a dozen men to meet with me. Bechler opened the meeting by saying that the group members had something to say to me. There was a long, uncomfortable silence.

Finally, I broke the silence. I said that if no one had anything to say to me, I had something to say to them. I told them I had heard of a news item that reported my activities in the Metropolitan Church. Had they seen it? I asked. One by one they admitted that they had. I said that I had not seen it. I reminded them that if someone had shown it to me I could have told them what had happened from my perspective. They agreed that they should have shown it to me instead of allowing it to be used to raise suspicions about me. We all agreed to be more brotherly in the future. I still have not seen the newspaper article, but as far as I know it has never again been used against me.

Sometimes I am asked how I avoided harsher sanctions from the conference or denomination for my position regarding homosexuals and lesbians. Perhaps it was because I had done only what the church had asked of me. Neither before nor after retirement have I used pulpit, pen, or other means to advocate the *practice* of same-sex orientation. I do strongly advocate faith in the God of all grace, grace that brings a salvation that justifies, sanctifies, and glorifies all who believe. It saddens me that the marked difference between advocating a practice and being an ambassador of the God of all grace is not yet acknowledged by all churches everywhere.

Through the years I have been asked, "What does your father think of you now?" This was a good question and was asked sincerely. My father is best known for his early conservative positions. Less well known is his later counseling ministry, in which he developed sensitive listening skills. A mission church in the conference led a divorced and remarried couple to faith in Christ. The pastor and church wished to receive them as members. Uncertain what to do, the bishop sought my father's counsel. My father said simply, "The congregation has spoken."

My faith journey has taught me to believe that the Bible, the written word, should be read from beginning to end as an *unfolding* revelation, not a final revelation. Such reading propels the believer on a trajectory that carries the reader to Jesus, the Living Word. That same Jesus taught his disciples that the Holy Spirit would come to teach them more. The Spirit would be as free as the wind to change course and force. My faith journey teaches me that it is futile for a church, Mennonite or otherwise, to try by dead law to shut out those whom God by grace has already accepted.

Real Retirement

In 2000, we were invited to choose an apartment for independent living in Sarasota's Sunnyside Village, where Mennonites, we found, were in the minority. Our required deposit was paid from a special Sunnyside fund intended to help persons who had devoted a lifelong ministry to the church. Accepting this generosity, we moved into a garden apartment and were soon caught up in the activities. We dined with new friends and shared stories, sang in the choir, put puzzles together, joined the clown troop, and attended prayer meetings. I preached occasionally in the village chapel and off campus and lectured about Mennonites to a class on religion in the University of South Florida. I did research and wrote two volumes on Anabaptist history in the Southeast.

In 2006, due to Rhoda's declining health, we accepted the invitation to move from Florida to Goshen, Indiana, to live with Rachel and her husband, Eldon Stoltzfus. On January 3, 2012, my beloved Rhoda quietly slipped away from us. From attending the Forks Mennonite Church, where Eldon was the minister, we had started to attend the College Mennonite Church at Goshen College. After a memorial service at that church, we placed her cremains in the columbarium at the Bahia Vista Mennonite Church, Sarasota, Florida. Another great change was imposed on me.

In my eighty-ninth year I own a fragment of 1 John 2:8 as the compass that gives direction to my life. It reports that "the darkness is passing and the true light is already shining" (NIV). From my present perspective, I understand that the dark past of this world and the shadow it casts over the church and me is fading away and that the kingdom of God is at hand and its glow is already lighting the horizon. So I turn my back on the dark and travel onward with eyes fixed on the easterly glow. I am at peace and live in joyful anticipation. Or as Rhoda and I sang on our way to Tampa in 1950: "I Will Not Be Afraid," finishing with the last stanza of the song by Ellis Govan, in which he celebrates singing onward and upward "To Him unafraid."

November 2012
Revised August and September 2015

Fred W. Swartz

Pastor, Author, Editor, Church Leader

In the above photo, Fred Swartz is serving as the elected Secretary of the Church of the the Brethren Annual Conference in 2003. He is known as an appreciated pastor of congregations in Virginia and Pennsylvania, one of which he helped to found and all of which grew under his care. Invited to membership in the General Board of the Church of the Brethren, Fred Swartz continued his work as an author and in this position wrote and edited many congregational materials and books for the Brethren Press. He also promoted the deacon ministry and led workshops training deacon groups.

Photo courtesy of Church of the Brethren

FRED W. SWARTZ

Listening to God's Word in Every Step

STRANGE EARLY INFLUENCES

Shortly after the horticulturalists developed hybrid corn and considerably before the auto industry invented the hybrid car, I was born—a hybrid. My father's ancestry was German and Mennonite; my mother's was Scot-Irish and Dunker Brethren. My girlfriend (who later became my wife) was Methodist. I was reared the first six years of my life in a Presbyterian church because there was no Brethren or Mennonite church in Craigsville, Virginia, where my father was principal, furnace attender, athletic coach, and teacher in both the elementary and high schools. My dad was Democrat; my mother was Republican. My mother also taught school during my infant and adolescent days, and in Craigsville a young woman who was also a member of the Presbyterian church cared for me. If Freud was right about his theory of formation, I should be endowed with a good dose of Calvinism.

But then we moved to New Hope, Virginia, and promptly became members of the Middle River Church of the Brethren, where my future path was shaped. That congregation was indeed formative for my lifelong faith. I have regretted their system of inducing young people into baptism, however, and carried out my vow never to coerce those whom I have had the privilege to pastor in such a fashion as Middle River treated me. I vividly recall being in the junior Sunday school class to which the pastor came late one Sunday morning to announce that for the next few weeks he would be teaching our class about church membership and that at the end of that time we would all be baptized.

That fateful Sunday came, and all eight of us were herded into the sanctuary to sit in the same pew, regardless of where the rest of our family members were sitting. When the invitation was given, we were supposed to march up and surrender our lives to Jesus and then go home and prepare for baptism in Christians Creek at three o'clock that afternoon. The invitation came (I do not remember what hymn was sung, probably "Just as I Am,"), and some of the class started out of the pew. One other youngster and I lingered. Although I was clearly not ready for this significant step, the teacher diligently and literally shoved the two of us out, and we joined the rest of the victims at the front.

That afternoon, right after lunch, there arose a thunderstorm worthy of the description "a trash mover and a gully washer." Thus, when we arrived at the church to go to the river, the pastor generously gave us the option of going to the river or staying at the church and being dipped into the crudely made baptistery recessed under the planks of the basement floor. Living on a small farm very near Middle River, I knew what the rivers around there looked like after a hard thunderstorm. I chose the church basement, as did all but two of the others. When those two came back from their experience, all they could talk about was how muddy the river was. It was hardly an experience of holy ecstasy!

But of course the formation of my faith began long before I was ten. I remember little about the Presbyterian church except that I learned the song "Eensy Weensy Spider" in vacation Bible school. I also remember forming one of my first impressions of God, the Maker and Doer of all things, when I was four, going on five. One Sunday morning while we were at worship in that church, a fierce thunderstorm rumbled over the area, so loud that it seemed to echo the pastor's neatly prepared diatribe. When the service was over and my dad led me by the hand out of the church, there shivering behind our automobile was my dog Inky. Thunder terrified her. Now our home was a good mile and a half from the church, and Inky had never come with us to that church. I was sure that God had picked her up and placed her there at our car. That thought has never left me; in fact, it has undergirded my belief in miracles, which is now somewhat more sophisticated than imagining the huge hand of God picking up little dogs, but no less certain of the supernatural power of the Almighty.

UNCOMFORTABLE HEALTH EVENTS

A sickly child between the ages six to eight, I was prone to asthma, congestion, and general respiratory illness. My mother gave me injections of a promising new drug several times a day, even waking me up in the middle of the night for one. That wonder drug was penicillin, now somewhat suspect, but a saving grace in my life. Finally the doctors decided I was a prime candidate for another relatively new procedure to combat respiratory problems: X-ray treatments. My mother, a schoolteacher at my elementary school, would take me out of third grade once a month for a treatment at Dr. Noland Canter's office somewhere between New Hope and Weyers Cave. The worst part of that experience was the massive iron lid that pressed down on my scrawny chest, and the best was the big gumdrop Dr. Canter gave me after each treatment. How I loved those gumdrops then! How I cannot stand to eat a gumdrop now! To be sure, my parents were not Christian Scientists!

Thirty years after those x-ray treatments were administered, the government issued a warning to all of us who had been subjected to that medical technique, stating that we were at risk of cancer from radiation. We were ordered to have our thyroids checked. Guess what method was used to pan for the possibility of cancer. Yes, an x-ray! Fortunately I was cleared; however, blood tests indicate that I now have hypothyroidism, the symptoms of which are fatigue, laziness, hair thinning, and a goiter—none of which seems to trouble me. Nonetheless, I follow the doctors' prescription and take the antidote faithfully every day. What do these episodes of ill health events have to do with the formation of my faith? It is amazing how often my memory of them has provided sustaining grace and hope amid other difficulties, or reinforcements for the comfort and encouragement I have offered others as a pastor.

I had a similar experience about twelve years ago when I was with a church group who had for years staged a weeklong trip to the beach at the Outer Banks of North Carolina. The second day we were there, I began having chest pains, not tightening of the chest or trouble breathing, just dull but menacing pains. Since they did not subside after a couple of hours, we decided that I should visit the only emergency care facility on the Outer Banks.

To shorten the story, the doctor and EMTs there thought I was having a heart attack, so I was rushed some fifty miles to the nearest hospital in Elizabeth City, where my daughter was on the staff as a pediatrician. Alerted that I was coming, she had lined up the best care available, including the top cardiologist. I spent the night in intensive care with what seemed to be every conceivable machine and intravenous device strapped on me. I could lie in only one position—on my back. Because I am a side-sleeper, I spent most of the night thinking about the important things in life and literally surrendering myself to God in prayer. My general mood was one of confidence and resolve.

The next day the cardiologist put me through the paces and declared me fit. Though he said he was not entirely sure, he concluded that I had had an attack of pericarditis, an inflammation of the membrane that envelops the heart. I had to wear a heart monitor for a month afterward, but nothing significant ever showed up.

One amusing thing, though, happened during a morning worship service two weeks after my illness. An initial effect of the attack was a sporadic increase in my pulse rate, which had risen as high as 160 during the ambulance dash to the hospital. Afterwards, on an occasion or two my heart began to race, which we now know was still an ongoing side effect of the infection. On the aforementioned Sunday morning, near the end of the closing congregational hymn, I suddenly felt one of my high pulse rate episodes. When I hesitated after the hymn, my co-pastor whispered to me, "Aren't you having the benediction?" All I could get out was, "No, you are." Of course I explained the situation to him later, and we laughed.

Soon those problems ended, and I have had no more such incidents, but the experience drove home to me the vulnerability of this human life and our dependence upon the grace and goodness of God. It has helped me both identify with and show compassion for those who have similar scary moments or stays in the intensive care unit. I do take a baby aspirin each day, for the cardiologist ordered, "You'll take these the rest of your life."

One other medically related incident happened early in my twenties, and I never forgot its spiritual lesson to me as both a pastor and a human being. Very soon in my pastoral career, I found myself dealing with three failing marriages in the congregation. I thought the message from God was, "Look, Son, you've been trained for this situation. Now get busy and save those marriages." I worked hard, believing the message was clear and loud: I was to save those marriages. I began feeling stress, severe stress; being so young, I did not make the connection between that stress and my efforts as a pastor. I made an appointment with Dr. Herman Brubaker, a Brethren physician whom I knew well and whom I trusted to tell me the truth.

After checking me over, the doctor said, "Well your heart's good. I can't find anything wrong, but I can give you some pills to make you feel better."

"What are they?" I asked.

"They're called Valium," he answered.

I had studied psychology, and I knew what Valium was. I sprang up from my chair. "What a fool I am!" I exclaimed. "I'm supposed to be sharing the true peace of Jesus Christ, and I haven't turned to that resource myself!"

Dr. Brubaker just smiled. I thanked him and left his office without the pills but with more knowledge and insight that shaped my pastoral work than I might have received in countless seminary courses. I was learning the meaning of Paul's statement, "I planted, Apollos watered, but God gave the growth" (1 Cor. 3:6, NKJV). I have kept that incident in my memory to remind me that I am to focus on what I can humanly do, do it faithfully, and not try to do God's work for him!

THE BENEFITS OF HARD FARM WORK

My faith has also evolved in part from my having been reared on a farm. When I was seven, our family bought a small forty-acre farm. On this farm we did it all: made hay, planted and harvested crops; milked five cows by hand twice a day; raised hogs, chickens, and beef; and grew and processed most of our food in three large truck patches. One of those truck patches was devoted to potatoes, which my mother served us three times a day since we stored so many in our smokehouse. The smokehouse was also the depository for several country hams, and a long, deep freezer on our back porch was always full of steaks and hamburger.

Hard work filled our lives. Since my only sibling was a brother five years younger than I, I frequently milked two cows, fed the chickens, and completed other miscellaneous chores before coming in, drying the dishes, and then leaving early for the fourteen-mile car ride to school. For the first two or three years on the farm we had to carry water to the house from a cistern about seventy-five yards away, near the barn. Since we had no plumbing, we had a two-hole outhouse, a popular place for black widow spiders. What a joy it was when we installed a water pipe from the cistern to the house and a pump in the smokehouse to have instant water in a kitchen sink and eventually an indoor bathroom!

However difficult those years were, I will never accept any substitute nor make any apology for their wonderful teaching values. I learned to appreciate the resources we are given to sustain our lives. I learned to respect our earth and the necessity to care for it and conserve it, as the following event illustrates. When I was in the sixth grade, I participated in an essay contest sponsored by the Soil and Water Conservation Unit in our county. The slogan we were to use in our essays was "Stop the Water Where It Falls." Because I had regularly attended Sunday school and worship ever since I was two months old and my mother had read me Bible stories, I knew the Bible well enough to use the parable of the houses built upon sand and rock to illustrate the points in my essay. I received second place along with the judges' comment that had I not sounded so much like a preacher, I would have gotten first!

Of course, at that point in my young life the idea of becoming a minister had not entered my mind. I thought I would be an airplane pilot because I could identify every plane that flew. In fact, my first-grade teacher noticed that every time an airplane roared overhead, I held up my hand for permission to go to the bathroom. She later told my mother that she always asked me what kind of plane it was when I returned to the classroom. She said she figured I would learn more in the few minutes I was out of the classroom than I would have by staying in my seat.

Most of all, my farm background taught me the value of hard work and perseverance, values not necessarily honored by today's world of conveniences and forty-hour workweek mindsets. As a pastor I averaged fifty-five to sixty work hours per week, and even then I did not meet my achievement goals. In my final twenty years of pastoral work, I set standards of performance for each six-month period, partly to satisfy the expectations of the congregation but also to give me some sense of accomplishment. In the pastorate, there is no achievement gauge unless the minister establishes one, simply because there is no end to the amount of work to be done if one is conscientious. I have long contended that there is no such thing as a part-time job in any phase of church work. A person may work part time, but she or he will accomplish only part-time results; a person dedicated to the ministry will never be satisfied with those.

Farm life not only trained me for hard work as a pastor but also taught me the value of helping others. Like the other farmers in the community, we knew that harvesting, thrashing, and butchering were tasks that none of us could accomplish alone. We needed the help of one another. I remember hearing, in my first pastorate, that a couple and their three children were snowed in. Both adults had recently had surgery or illness that had sidelined them for several days. Without hesitation, I drove over to their place and began shoveling out their driveway. The young mother came to the door and called, "You're not supposed to be doing that; you're our pastor!" I knew better than to accept that assumption.

In addition, as I reflect on my rural and agricultural background, I realize that it taught me that cooperation and compromise are absolutely necessary for building lasting relationships, whether they are with nature or with people. It is an illusion to believe there is absolute truth in absolute power or, to put it another way, to believe I am always right and the other person is wrong. Such beliefs are about as futile as thinking one can outrun a train to the railway crossing.

On the farm, people cut down their thistles in a pasture, not just to tidy up their own field but also to prevent those nasty weeds from sending seeds to the neighbors' fields. People learn quickly to participate in the community pool of equipment so no farmer has to go bankrupt trying to own it all. If a neighbor's cows get into my corn, I do not call the law; I help the neighbor corral them and drive them back home. If rain compromises the freshness of my new-mown hay before it can be raked up and stored, I remember that rain grew the hay in the first place, and more hay will grow.

It was also from my parents and a chicken farmer that I learned the value of the stewardship of money. My dad was the church treasurer, but he did not usually get around to that task until Saturday night after serving as a school principal all week and tending to the farm chores morning and evening. Occasionally I would look over his shoulder and see him writing a personal check for his and my mother's contribution to the church. I could not believe my eyes when I saw how much he gave to the church while constantly telling me we did not have the money to buy the bicycle I wanted! And Mother, a schoolteacher, washed our clothes with a ringer washer, kept house, and prepared delicious meals in a kitchen without today's modern appliances. She was also chair of the pastoral committee at church, an active deacon, and more.

Later in my college years I heard a chicken farmer testify in a committee meeting that he and his wife, who were rearing three boys, put ten percent of every dollar they earned through their chicken-and-egg business in a jar on the refrigerator and gave it all to the church. I decided then and there that if they could tithe, so could I—and my practice of tithing or giving more than ten percent has continued throughout my life.

In my pastorates and in my relationships with people from other churches and communities, all that I learned translated into respect and non-judgmental attitudes. I tried to take seriously the story of Jesus, who said to the woman accused of adultery, after all her accusers had admitted that they were also sinners, "Neither do I condemn you," (John 8:11, NRSV). He also said, "Do not judge, so that you may not be judged," (Matt. 7:1, NRSV). Even if someone has done something of which I strongly disapprove, I leave the judgment to God and try to help that person see what is best for him or her. The greater sin is trying to play God.

A Mentoring Church

The church of my youth, the Middle River Church of the Brethren in New Hope, Virginia, shaped much of my growing faith. It was a small but highly active congregation, with high-quality pastors who not only preached solid, uplifting sermons but also modeled good pastoral care. With the exception of that one pastor's teaching the junior Sunday school class for six weeks and then baptizing the group *en masse*, I found the three pastors very supportive. They guided me through the process of earning the Boy Scout God and Country Award, they took an interest in my achievements in school and other endeavors, they encouraged me to pursue higher education, and they endorsed my leaning toward ministry.

In that day it was customary for the church to call out ministers; however, I had already made this commitment in a youth revival meeting at which the world-famous pole-vaulter, Bob Richards, was the guest evangelist. Unfortunately, Bob fell from grace as my idol in later years, but in that meeting he had just the right words from God to inspire me toward the ministry.

Rufus Cline, the teacher of the young people in my home church, was a particular influence. Although he caused trouble by objecting to just about everything proposed at the church business meetings, he clearly cared about us. He was always on the alert for a resource that would help us improve or get through a difficult situation. One Sunday he handed me a book and said, "Fred, you might find this interesting." The book was Charles M. Sheldon's little novel *In His Steps* (Grand Rapids, Mich.: Revell, 1985, 2012). It is the story of how one town decided by consensus to ask, "What would Jesus do?" before every action or decision.

I did find it interesting; in fact, I found it not only intriguing but timely, for I read it just before Halloween that year. Some of my buddies wanted me to go with them and an older guy who could drive us around on Halloween night to knock down mailboxes and do other boyish pranks. The peer pressure was great, but I said, "No, I don't believe I'll go," all the while processing in my mind, "What would Jesus do?" That night, one of their pranks was piling fodder shocks and other debris in front of the schoolhouse door. My dad, the principal, had to remove that entire heap before he could open up the school the next morning. He was as furious as I had ever seen him. Was I ever glad I had not been one of the pranksters!

Deacons in the Middle River Church also influenced my values. One was Joe Humbert, a successful farmer who always went out of his way to speak to us young people. One day Joe asked me, a fourteen-year-old, if I would consider joining the chancel choir. "And I want you to sit right by me," he added. Now Joe was someone whose tenor voice I admired; and to have him ask me was something special, especially since there were no other youth in the choir. I did join the choir and sat next to Joe Humbert. I have never forgotten what his gesture of encouragement meant to me.

Another deacon, Oliver Cline, a John Deere salesman, impressed me with his constant smile and humility, as did John Western, a quiet fellow who was always present whenever the church had a work project. These deacons were true witnesses of Middle River Church; they taught me the meaning of Alexander Mack's definition of *Brethren*, based on Jesus' declaration that "you will know them by their fruits" (Matt. 7:20, NRSV).

OPEN DOORS THROUGH THE BOY SCOUTS

Another chapter from my youth merits mention. Most Brethren people will assume I benefited from going to church camps, which I did from the time I was ten through senior high. Those were good experiences but fell far short of the faith maturity I developed through Boy Scouting. I know that many Brethren and Mennonites associate Scouting with military activity because of the uniform and the option of marksmanship with guns. It is true that occasionally a retired Army sergeant scoutmaster will want to be sure his troop knows how to march. However, I was fortunate to have my dad as my scoutmaster. Since he was exempt as a public school administrator, he did not serve in the military. Working on the farm with my dad, plus enjoying a close relationship with him as my scoutmaster, created perhaps the best filial relationship possible.

Scouting opened many doors to me: I achieved the Eagle rank, went to the national and international Scout Jamborees, represented Virginia at the Young Outdoor Americans Conference in Chicago, taught nature classes one summer in a Scout camp, and had opportunities to develop both my speaking and writing skills. I learned more about the church in working for the God and Country Award than in any course or Sunday school class I had before attending seminary!

During both national and international Jamborees, I was recruited by the Staunton *News Leader* and the Waynesboro *News Virgin-*

ian to write and send them articles every day about our experiences. Of course there was no electronic mail then; I wrote everything by hand and mailed in my stories. They would appear in the newspapers several days later, and I received many expressions of appreciation from the parents of Scouts who were also along on those journeys. At the International Jamboree held in Canada, I made friends with several Scouts from other countries and corresponded with them for a few years afterward. Thus, Scouting opened my eyes to the good in people of all cultures and backgrounds.

NANCY'S ENCOURAGEMENT

Another important person in my life who came from a different background was my wife Nancy. We met in high school before either of us was old enough to drive. My dad took us on our first date, which happened to be for a basketball game at which he was a faculty chaperone. Nancy was from Stuarts Draft, at the opposite end of Augusta County, and she was a Methodist. Both sets of parents told us we were too young to limit our dating to one person, but we persisted; the relationship has lasted sixty years, including a marriage of fifty-three years. It troubled me at first that we were from different denominations, so much so that I argued with parents and pastor and peers that all churches ought to merge into one big body. After all, was that not what Jesus said we should do? Well, my plea fell on deaf ears; Nancy, who was wiser than I, saw that I clearly had a call to ministry and therefore chose to be baptized by immersion into the Church of the Brethren. That baptism meant far more to me than my own when I was ten.

I attended Bridgewater College while Nancy went to James Madison College (now James Madison University), and we faced bridging the eight-mile gap between us. Fortunately, the Bridgewater College night watchman sympathetic to our plight allowed me to sneak around to the back window of his office in the college furnace room, raise the window, and use the phone inside to call Nancy every night. I also managed to borrow a car or two from fellow dorm buddies to make an occasional trip into Harrisonburg. Meanwhile, Nancy was encouraging my quest to answer the call to ministry, and she has continued her unwavering support to this very minute.

On the Path to Ministry

As an English major, I found that my college courses further developed my skills in expressing my thoughts in writing and speaking. Did I make a mistake by not majoring in philosophy and religion? I do not know. I do know that one book in particular that I read in college helped form my concept of God. It was entitled *Man's Knowledge of God* by William J. Wolf (New York: Doubleday, 1955). That book, in which the author made God very personal and attainable, was the practical sort of theology on which I have patterned my own religious practice and philosophy. In my preaching I am certain I was closer to Norman Vincent Peale than to Charles Spurgeon or even Billy Graham, though I hope my sermons were at least a little more theologically based than Peale's *Power of Positive Thinking* (Upper Saddle River, New Jersey: Prentice-Hall, 1952, 1956, 1980; First Fireside Edition, 2003; in all, 83 editions). A preaching idol of mine was Karl Barth, whose sermons were much more down to earth than his eight-volume theological treatise, *Church Dogmatics* (G. W. Bromley, trans. and Bromly and T. F. Torrance, eds. Edinburgh: T & T Clark, 1958), which I read from cover to cover.

My first attempt at a sermon occurred while I was in college. By this time I was a licensed minister, a title that simply meant I was preparing for ministry but had authorization to preach. I delivered my first sermon to the congregation at the Cedar Grove Church of the Brethren north of Harrisonburg, who needed (actually who were desperate for) speakers to fill their pulpit. I developed about a fifteen-minute message on the entire paragraph of Ephesians 6:10-17, and in that brief time I covered "the *whole* armor of God," (6:11, RSV)! Of course there are at least two months of sermons in that passage, but I gave them all I knew at that stage of my preparation. But true to our great body of believers, they offered many gracious expressions of enjoyment and gratitude as I shook hands at the door!

Nevertheless, I was ready for seminary the moment I received my college diploma. Nancy and I were married the weekend after I graduated, and that summer we resided in the parsonage of the Mill Creek Church of the Brethren, where I served as student pastor while Paul H. Bowman, the interim minister, was in Europe directing the denomination's 250th anniversary. I had a great time with the youth that summer. We built an outdoor recreational site with nighttime lighting and had twenty to thirty young people there for events on weekend nights. My sermons were better than my first attempt but still fairly generic. A painful test of my call was responding to the suicide of one of the prominent elders of the congregation. With God's help, we made it through the summer.

Bethany Theological Seminary was exciting. Now my study was focused, and my fellow students and I were all on the same track: We studied together, did work study projects together, and worshiped together in this community of learning and spiritual encouragement. Warren Groff joined the seminary faculty the same fall I entered Bethany. I had taken three of his courses at Bridgewater College; now in seminary, I had him for four. His class and my other courses were tough: in six of them I received a B; in the seventh I earned, or was gifted with, an A. Bethany provided excellent preparation in theology, Bible studies, church history, and language studies. The Christian education area was weak, however; and while the seminary president offered a comprehensive course on church administration, he did not teach us how to run a mimeograph machine or how to organize an office. Those lessons came the hard way—by experience, after the first pastorate began!

Entering my senior year, I was not certain I wanted to begin the pastorate right away, or at all. I began looking toward further graduate study, perhaps with an eye toward teaching in a college or seminary. But that fall, our senior class had a spiritual retreat away from the seminary and invited Perry Rohrer, a dedicated layman, to be our resource person. Perry Rohrer made such an impassioned talk on the value and glamour of the pastoral ministry that practically everyone in our relatively large class of twenty-nine returned to the seminary with a firm resolve to answer the call to a pastorate.

MY FIRST PASTORATE

My call came from the Roanoke office of the First District of Virginia to start a new Church of the Brethren in the northern end of the city of Roanoke. I felt it was a genuine call in that I did not know a single person on the administrative board of that district, and I wondered how they knew enough about me to issue such a call of confidence. Since I had no idea how to start a new church, I asked the seminary for help. The answer was, "We have no curriculum for starting a new church." I responded, "Could I then design my own course and you give me credit for it?" The seminary dean agreed, designated a two-hour credit course, and assigned me a faculty advisor. I then designed a course that took me on visits to new church plantings in the Chicago area, listed all the reading materials I could find, scheduled correspondence with pastors of new Church of the Brethren plantings across the nation, and outlined a Plan of Organization for a new church.

In the fall of 1961, this seminary graduate began applying what he had learned in the quest to start a Church of the Brethren in the Roanoke suburb of the Hollins subdivision called Summerdean. A nearby congregation had helped in the purchase of a three-acre site, and the Roanoke office provided a list of thirty-five Brethren families who had expressed interest in a new church in their neighborhood. After a month of visiting these people, I began with a small group of eight families, including Nancy and me, to hold Sunday evening worship services in an elementary school about a mile and a half from Summerdean. Soon the group expanded to fifteen families, and it was not long before we began talking about building a large parsonage on the church site and using it as a first church building. In the next nine years the Summerdean church grew to 140 members, became self-supporting, and erected both a church building and a parsonage.

Starting a new church is a daunting adventure. It takes faith and perseverance. I was glad I was young and energetic enough to have the stamina to knock on doors and issue an invitation to worship with the new church, as well as to coordinate the new strategies in every aspect of church life. The Summerdean church celebrated its fiftieth anniversary November 6, 2011. I was honored to be asked to deliver the sermon.

A CALL TO A DIFFICULT PLACE AT A DIFFICULT TIME

In my nine years at the task of organizing the new church, I became heavily involved in community groups, ministerial associations, and larger community ministries. Now I felt as though I was spreading myself too thin. Resigning from Summerdean, I accepted a call to the First Church of the Brethren in the inner city of Harrisburg, Pennsylvania. Up to this point I had considered myself a country parson (although Roanoke was expanding toward its northern suburbs). I had said openly that I would never go to a big city church, but the Lord does not always listen to our pronouncements. In the fall of 1970 Nancy and I and our two little girls moved to Harrisburg, on the mighty Susquehanna River.

Inner-city work was indeed different. Located amid city rowhouses and well-worn marble steps, this church had been organized before the twentieth century, and many distinguished pastors had preceded me. The congregation had set traditions, as well as an active inner-city program for youth. What I was not prepared for was a different attitude toward race than what I had previously known. For one thing, north of the Mason-Dixon Line, racial prejudice seemed to be based on *fear*. I had been used to a separate but equal kind of relationship between African-Americans and whites in the community in which I had grown up and in Roanoke. In my southern towns we were not afraid of each other; we just (sadly, as I now realize) understood that during the day, we went to different schools and at the end of the day we went to different areas of town to sleep. In Harrisburg I kept hearing fears that the African-Americans were going to take over the neighborhoods. That kind of prejudice was new to me.

I was also a pastor in Harrisburg during the time of the famous Harrisburg Eight trial, when Father Philip Berrigan and his brother Daniel, Sister Elizabeth McAlister, Father Neal McLaughlin, and four others were charged with conspiracy in a plan to blow up the heating towers that served the Pentagon and to kidnap Secretary of State Henry Kissinger. The Church of the Brethren and the Mennonites, who were supporting the protests against the Vietnam War, actively supported the eight accused, believing the charges to be trumped up.

The call came to the Harrisburg church to provide sanctuary and lodging in the church building for the multitude of persons who were coming to stand in protest outside the Federal Court Building. When I took this request to the church board, another war erupted within that room! Some board members were opposed to opening the church doors, some were convinced the Berrigans were guilty, some did not think it would be good publicity for the church, and a few tried to make a case for our witness for peace. In the end, the board left the decision to me. As it turned out, only a few people stayed in the church during the trial.

Active in supporting the Harrisburg Eight, I was among the few privileged clergymen allowed to meet with the Berrigans and Sister McAlister (and possibly a couple of others) in a private meeting outside their cells. They shared with us their intent to save life, not add to destruction. We had a powerful prayer session with them. I took some raw criticism for being a part of that group; nasty letters came from across the denomination, disapproving any part the Harrisburg Church had in relation to the trial. It was a tense time, but we got through it without damage to the church fellowship or its future and with a degree of satisfaction that the Brethren peace position had been maintained.

Inner-city ministry had not only its challenges but also its hazards. On one occasion when I was sitting in my office, I heard a commotion in the alley beside the church. Going out the side door to see what was happening, I found a man and woman in a fierce quarrel. Stepping between them, while trying to stay out of the way of the eight-inch switchblade that the man was wielding, I inquired about the nature of the conflict. Each spit out accusations against the other. While I am not sure I resolved their bitterness, at least I convinced them to go in separate directions. Now, years later, I look back upon the foolishness of my youthful action and thank the good Lord that I escaped the threat of that shiny blade!

At the Harrisburg church I came to appreciate the help an active group of deacons can be to a pastor. First Church's deacon body was well organized when I became pastor, with a pair of deacons assigned to each member of the congregation. It was their responsibility to provide caring, nurturing, and encouragement to those individuals. What a joy it was to share the pastoral work with those deacons, who became a significant model for me when I later became involved in equipping and training deacons in both Mennonite and Brethren churches.

A Doctoral Degree and My First Publication

At Harrisburg, I also began feeling as though I needed to refresh my academic studies through some specific classroom work. Bethany

Seminary had a doctor of ministry program then, but it consisted mostly of colloquiums that a student might attend in Chicago a few times a year. Thus, I explored the Lancaster Theological Seminary (affiliated with the United Church of Christ) and found its doctoral program quite attractive. I also learned that since two other ministers in town were enrolled in the Lancaster program, we could form a travel pool.

I took two classes weekly at Lancaster, in which I was quickly dubbed "Mr. Brethren" because my responses to the subjects we studied were very parochial. I discovered that God wanted me to be more open to what his messengers outside my own denomination were saying. That was truly a healthy experience. The program also included a research project similar to a PhD dissertation, in which the student had to gather rational proof, such as statistics, to support a hypothesis. In addition, a Doctor of Ministry project also had to relate to an aspect of the student's current ministry assignment. Since I changed my ministry assignment three times before I completed the program, I had to change my research topic three times as well. Seventeen years later, in 1992, I finally received the DMin.

While in Harrisburg, mainly as a result of my studies at Lancaster Seminary, I was asked by the Brethren Press to write a study book on the Church of the Brethren and ecumenicity. The volume I produced was titled *All in God's Family* (Elgin, Ill.: Brethren Press, 1977). This was the first of many publications I would help with over the years.

Two devastating floods occurred in Pennsylvania during my time as pastor at Harrisburg, one at Johnstown and one right in downtown Harrisburg. I, along with groups from our church, helped in the cleanup operations at both sites. The visual images of destruction, along with the sad reality of the loss of life in these disasters, have never left my memory.

SEVEN PRODUCTIVE YEARS ON THE GENERAL BOARD

In winter 1977, I began receiving phone calls from our denominational headquarters in Elgin, Illinois, inquiring if I would consider a position on the national staff. The General Board of our church was looking for someone who could write and edit the denominational materials that were being sent to congregations: newsletters,

Deacon resources for both Brethren and Mennonite churches that Fred Swartz either wrote or edited.

brochures, and a variety of resource items. After I had turned down two such inquiries, our family of four gathered to consider the third such request. The vote was three and a half to one-half, the one-half dissenting vote cast by our high school daughter, who was understandably reluctant to leave friends and organizations in which she was involved.

Thus began my stint of seven years on the staff of the General Board of the Church of the Brethren, and for two of those years I was editor of congregational materials and the Brethren Press book editor. Then my boss called me into his office to say that the Administrative Council thought it best to combine the communications and stewardship staff and wanted me to be the director or coordinator. I protested that in my opinion administration had been the weakest link in my previous pastoral work. That was not a concern, my boss countered. "We want someone with pastoral background to put these two *prima donna* staffs together," he announced. I really had no choice, so I added the responsibility of supervising seventeen persons to my already full load.

For five years I carried that load, doing the editing chore most evenings at home. I edited at least fifty books, including Anna Marie Steckley's *A Song in the Night* (Elgin, Ill.: Brethren Press, 1981); she was then on the Mennonite Media Ministries staff 88
in Harrisonburg. Brethren Press had a close relationship with Choice Books at that time, and we produced several paperbacks that were sold by Choice Books. I worked with the late Paul Schrock, Ron Byler, and Ken Weaver, all great colleagues in our cooperative efforts. I also became involved with the Religious Public Relations Council, serving on its executive committee, editing the Council's newsletters for several years, and editing the first Religious Public Relations Handbook. When I left the Elgin staff, the Council honored me with Life Membership in the Council.

In my last years on the denominational staff, we became involved with Mennonites in reviving the congregational deacon ministry. I edited a joint publication titled *Called to Caregiving: A Resource for Equipping Deacons in the Believers Church* by June A. Gibble (Elgin, Ill.: Brethren Press, 1987), and I was active in visiting both Mennonite and Brethren congregations to interpret that booklet and the new call for deacon ministry. I edited the *Deacon Manual for Caring Ministries* (Elgin, Ill.: Brethren Press, 1998) for our own denomination.

These activities launched me into more than twenty-five years of promoting deacon ministry and training deacon groups throughout our denomination and in several Mennonite congregations in Virginia. I also authored a book titled *Essential Servants: Reflections on the Caring Ministries of Deacons* (Elgin, Ill.: Caring Ministries of the Church of the Brethren, 2010), a set of studies and study questions for deacon groups to use in their meetings and training sessions.

TWENTY BLESSED YEARS IN MANASSAS

I consider my time on the denominational staff a long and enlightening sabbatical. My heart was still in the congregational pastorate, but I learned so much from my denominational work that my last pastorate, twenty years at the Manassas, Virginia, Church of the Brethren, was the crowning achievement of my career. Since I was now stronger in administration and blessed with a sense of personal achievement, I was so much better equipped to focus on ministry to people. At Manassas, we increased the membership by at least ten percent each year, and we completed a $1.5 million building expansion project, doubling the seating capacity of the sanctuary and including a new Fellowship and Christian Education unit. It was a wonderful twenty years, from 1983-2003.

I also served on two denominational committees during those years to develop papers guiding ethics for both ministers and congregations. The Associated Church Press has cited the Brethren as having the only known ethics publication for congregations. That paper, created in 1992, is now in the process of being updated, especially in light of the electronic age, which has exploded since the early Nineties. This ethics in ministry paper, revised twice, includes a process for the church to follow in dealing with ministers who are accused of ministerial misconduct.

A NEW RESPONSIBILITY: ANNUAL CONFERENCE SECRETARY

A year before my retirement from Manassas in 2003, I was elected Secretary of the Church of the Brethren Annual Conference—a position I have since labeled a "full-time volunteer job." Not only is the secretary responsible for keeping the records of the denominational conference, he or she is the resource person and updater for the denomination's polity, the repository for corporate history, a participant in many meetings, a personal servant for the moderator, a member of the denomination's Leadership Team, the corporate secretary for the Church of the Brethren, Inc., and a ready source of opinions regarding congregational organization and procedures. At this writing (January 2012), I am in my tenth and final year of that assignment and am ready to release the charge to someone else. It is an elected office, and I am happy that there are qualified persons on the ballot for our Annual Conference in St. Louis in July 2012.

As Annual Conference secretary I learned how much our small denomination has accomplished in over 300 years and what it is still doing in service and witness to the world. We have a message of peace, both in our corporate and personal lives. We have a lifestyle that speaks to fears of a faltering economy, terrorism, despair, and loneliness. We have a commitment that does not rely on a creed for guidance but rather the life and saving grace of Jesus Christ. I am weary of political pushing and pulling in the church; I am weary of people judging one another with shouts of "sinner" and "traitor"; I am weary of those who think it is their mission from God to defend God and his church! God needs no defense; God *is* our defense. Amen!

January 2012

ADDENDUM, DECEMBER 2015

In 2012 the Annual Conference of the Church of the Brethren elected James M. Beckwith of Annville, Pennsylvania, former pastor of the Montezuma Church of the Brethren, Dayton, Virginia, as Annual Conference Secretary.

Fred Swartz telling a children's story in worship at the Bridgewater Church of the Brethren.

I was able to serve as a conference delegate from the Bridgewater congregation for both the 2013 and 2014 meetings. Since 2014 I have served as Moderator of the Bridgewater congregation and have been involved with the congregation's decision to be an inclusive church. This discussion has heightened my awareness of Jesus' love for all persons and of the revelation of God's truth as an ongoing process through all of one's life.

PART II

Making a Difference ... Through Educational Leadership

Beryl H. Brubaker

At EMU: Bridgebuilding Administrator

As a young woman, Beryl Brubaker dreamed of singing opera. Instead, she followed her sister into a "serving" field, nursing-a profession that led her into teaching and high administration at EMU. Her many leadership roles included, successively, nursing department chair, vice president for enrollment, the first provost, and interim president. A truth-telling writer, Beryl describes challenging events at EMU, her goals and actions as an administrator, and her changing perceptions in her faith journey.

Photo by Beryl H. Brubaker; courtesy of EMU Marketing and Communications

BERYL H. BRUBAKER

Filling Many Roles in One Special Place

My story differs from many in this series—those told by persons moving to countries far from their birthplace, others recounted by individuals living in multiple landscapes during a lifetime. My story, unlike those, mostly happened in just two places not far apart on the east coast of the United States. Both were traditional Mennonite communities, though excursions beyond that fold for schooling would be life changing. The Belleville, Pennsylvania, version of the Mennonite world, known as Big Valley, shaped my early life. Later, the much larger Shenandoah Valley would become my second long-term landscape. Thus, no African tales or frequent moves to jobs in new settings will enliven my account, although changes in my position at EMC (Eastern Mennonite College) and later EMU (Eastern Mennonite University) are a vital part of my story.

In writing my memoir, I searched for a theme: "Mennonite Girl: Conformist or Feminist?" or maybe "Mennonite Girl: Compliant or Risk-Taking?" Once I envisioned titling my memoir "A Mennonite Woman's Love/Hate Relationship with Leadership." Another possibility I derived from a popular Mennonite cookbook: "Mennonite Girl Can Cook and Chair a National Board." Or how about "Survivor of 1950s Revivalism"? Yet another choice was "Moments of Truth" since I discovered some of those as I wrote my story.

Finally, ambivalence shaped some of the tales I will share because my strong drive to achieve contended with a sense of inadequacy and anxiety about public appearances. When I was young, we labeled this trait an "inferiority complex." Today, people might call me an introvert even though as a teenager I went door-to-door selling Wallace Brown cards! Reliance on Philippians 4:13 (KJV), "I can do all things through Christ who strengtheneth me," enabled me to lead a life that defied my fears and anxieties.

THE LITTLE GIRL WHO FELT DIFFERENT

Third daughter among five girls, I was a middle child. Is it true that middle children lack self-esteem because they get little parental attention? With my older sisters only one and two years old when I was born and daughters four and five arriving just three and six years later, none of us remained the center of attention very long. Apparently, this middle child became Miss Responsibility and early on took the role of caretaker and fixer, probably manager, too. I would become the daughter that Mother called on for help in her later years.

What early memories could provide hints about me or the person I would become? One of my earliest memories is waking up when Dad got in the car to go to the Barrville (Pa.) Mission for afternoon Sunday school. I had fallen asleep in the car after a spanking at church in the morning, as I remember, and was left sleeping in the car while the family ate Sunday dinner at home.

What was it about me that made me remember this event when I must have been only a couple of years old? Was it church or the spanking for misbehavior that made this memory stick in a child who would try hard to be good and for whom church was a communal binding force? Actually, the fact that my father, following church in the morning and Sunday dinner, was going to a local mission for an afternoon service had much to do with what I would become.

And why do I remember as a four-year-old walking down a sunlit road after Grandpa Kauffman's funeral in New Wilmington, Pennsylvania, or earlier watching Grandpa Kauffman kill a hog in the pen next to the barn on butchering day? Traumatic memories? There are more memories of *trauma*—crying while Mom combed my curly hair, difficulty breathing when I had pneumonia at Christmas time at age six, and at age twelve lying on the couch with a painful abdomen while Hurricane Hazel pounded the windows and Dad, the only driver in the family, was in Goshen, Indiana, doing church business, as usual. When the rain stopped the next morning, Mom found a driver, and I made it to the operating room before my appendix burst. One day, I too would be off doing church business while crises arrived at home.

What was it like growing up in Big Valley, Pennsylvania? I was not a typical Big Valley girl. I did not live on a farm as did most of my classmates, for my father was a painting contractor. I was a town girl—though Mother closely restricted contact with persons who were not Mennonite. My surname was not Peachey, Yoder, or Zook—names common to the Mennonites in Big Valley. My Hartzler aunts and uncles were educated with master's and doctor's degrees, and most were no longer in the Mennonite church. My aunts were not afraid to voice their opinions in the sometimes heated discussions that took place over holiday dinners. I remember one such dispute over chiropractors, roundly denounced by one aunt.

Two of my educated aunts and uncles would serve many years in higher education—Dr. H. Harold Hartzler, or H-Cube as he was known, at Goshen College, and Dr. Eva Hartzler at Juniata College. Uncle Johnny Hartzler took a different route by graduating from the U.S. Merchant Marine Academy and serving as a Merchant Marine ship captain during World War 2. He was later divorced from the smartly dressed wife he first brought to our house. When Uncle Johnny took me for a ride in his convertible, I felt like I was doing something "English," our label for the world outside of Mennonites.

Apparently, my grandfather John M. Hartzler, whom I never knew because he died of a fall long before I was born, was sent off to college because he was not very strong physically. Thus Grandfather Hartzler left this Amish-Mennonite valley to graduate from Juniata College and even teach at Elkhart Institute, the forerunner of Goshen College. He was a teacher and preacher in churches at various locations around the country, including Fort Wayne, Indiana, where he and my grandmother managed the mission work for a short time.

Since Grandma had to make her own way after her husband's untimely death, she both operated a store that attracted the local Amish population and also raised many foster children. She, too, had no trouble speaking her mind.

Connections between my Hartzler grandparents and the eastern Mennonite college came early. Grandma Hartzler's grade school teacher in Logan County, Ohio, was none other than that college's first president, J. B. Smith. And a 1918 catalog in the Historical Library at EMU verifies that an early Eastern Mennonite School trustee was John M. Hartzler, my grandfather. Some forty years later, his son, my father C. Clayton, would serve in that same role at this institution that would become my home.

I was different from many of my peers in at least one other way: I loved school. Belleville Mennonite School (BMS) suited me well. A Christian school that my dad helped to found provided a nurturing environment, fostered my love of choral music, and offered numerous opportunities to hone leadership skills—basketball skills in skirts, also. My home was full of school talk because Dad was president of the board.

My drive to achieve meant that I strived for A's on tests and homework, an effort that did not make me popular with my mostly male classmates. Girls were not supposed to be smart. My habit of arguing with the teacher about which multiple-choice answer on a test was correct only increased their irritation. The guys loved it when our fifth-grade teacher reported that I had picked the wrong multiple-choice answer to define *pasteurized*—the one that said it meant putting the cows out to pasture. What did I know? I didn't live on a farm! Of course, I was convinced that I knew better but had simply made a mistake in marking my answer; nevertheless, the guys teased me about that error endlessly. Because I was "skinny," they called me "Toothpick." Apparently, their teasing did not damage my self-concept too badly because my senior yearbook characterized me as "a strong supporter of women's superiority." Bob Hostetter, a teacher in my senior year, labeled me a feminist.

CHOICES AND DISCOVERIES

It is strange that we can entertain such diverse conceptions of our future. I always knew that I would go to college at EMC, yet I also dreamed of marrying a farmer and becoming a preacher's wife, the highest calling in my world. The big question in my senior year was whether I would major in music in college or follow my sister into nursing. Growing up, I loved singing high soprano and dreamed of singing at the New York Metropolitan Opera House.

Yet how could a Mennonite girl sing on the operatic stage? My religious upbringing had emphasized service. In those days I could not conceptualize that a musical career would fulfill my obligation to serve the world. Besides, I had aspired to be a nurse ever since playing nurse as a child. Now senior year teacher Ron David at BMS was encouraging me to follow my real passion—music. But in the end my religious upbringing, plus my predisposition to do what I thought I should and avoid moving too far out of my secure Mennonite world, won the battle. Or maybe the idea of performing on the stage was just too frightening. While I did spend my first semester at EMC in 1960 majoring in music, I switched to nursing by the second semester. I stayed at EMC a second year before going to Riverside Hospital in Newport News, Virginia, to complete a nursing diploma as part of the EMC-Riverside partnership.

EMC was memorable because it was there as a first-year student that I met my future husband J. Mark Brubaker, a senior about to graduate. Another Mennonite committed to service, he left to teach biology in Tanganyika (now Tanzania), Africa, that fall. Consequently, we carried on a three-year correspondence in pre-Internet days during my sophomore year at EMC and my next two years at Riverside. It turns out that our ancestors, eight generations earlier, had arrived in America on the same ship. Later I would discover that as a young reader of the church paper *Words of Cheer* I had cut out a picture of Mark's family that accompanied his letter to the paper seeking pen pals. That picture of eight boys and one girl likely caught my attention because I had grown up in a family of girls only.

At Riverside I discovered my vocation of teaching. In my senior year I was part of a group of students who traveled around the state sharing a new problem-solving approach to nursing. I remember the moment—a moment of truth—in one of those presentations when I knew I wanted to become a teacher. Maybe I could find a passion in the nursing world after all.

Upon graduation I decided not to return to EMC for the Riverside-EMC baccalaureate degree. Since EMC did not provide an upper-level nursing major, I would have needed to make up certain courses before I could pursue a master's degree. Instead, after practicing nursing for a year, I went to Case Western Reserve University in Cleveland, a decision that would be life-changing in several ways.

I credit Case Western with dramatically changing my study habits. I was used to multiple-choice tests. Memorizing information the night before the test was usually sufficient preparation. At Case Western, I took chemistry my first semester and was taken aback by the first exam. Open-ended questions required me to explain various chemical reactions. I did not do well on that exam. Not surprisingly, I was unhappy about my score and realized I had to change the way I studied for exams.

I would soon discover that thinking through how chemical reactions work was a lot more fun than memorizing formulas. That was also the place where I discovered the caring essence of nursing as I watched my teacher one day while a doctor performed a painful procedure on a patient. I learned what it meant to "be with" the patient rather than to focus on the doctor's needs during that procedure. Later in this essay I will share the shock to my religious upbringing that happened in this setting. Thus, there were several moments of truth at Case Western.

After graduating from Case Western and doing additional hospital nursing, I went on to the University of Pennsylvania for my master's degree in fall 1967. Once again, I held conflicting dreams about my future. I dreamed of raising a big family like that of my husband Mark, a family whom I admired. But I was obviously headed toward a career as well. I dreamed of going to a large university, a place where I could teach, do research, and make my mark on the profession of nursing.

A few days before I graduated with my master's degree in spring 1969, the dean of the nursing school asked if I would join the faculty to teach research in the master's program. In those days nurses with doctoral degrees were scarce. My immediate thought was "No"; after all, I had just completed the program in which she was asking me to teach! But husband Mark said, "Of course you are going to do it." And so I did, but not for long.

EMC/EMU AND NURSING

That fall EMC President Myron Augsburger invited Mark and me to join the faculty there the following fall. A new nursing program had been launched two years earlier, and more faculty were needed for the growing program. Here was an opportunity to give back to the church we both held dear. In May 1970 we left for EMC with the intention of serving for a few years and then moving on. However, the future held a different story for us.

I loved teaching, and I loved teaching at EMC. I remember saying that I was never going to retire. Indeed, I often felt as though I were walking on sacred territory as I read nursing journals and conversed with nursing students who were trying to grow up while also learning to be with sick and dying patients. Professor Vida Huber, chair of the Nursing Department, invited me to assume new roles such as curriculum coordinator and assistant chair. An innovator, she fostered my own creativity as we led the faculty in developing a distinctive nursing curriculum that was mastery-based, eventually self-paced, and one that relied on new teaching strategies. Instead of lectures, we created study guides that required students to find their own information and critically analyze relationships with particular physiological states.

Further, I had been schooled at the University of Pennsylvania in John Dewey's and Jerome Bruner's learning theories. They believed that students must be actively involved in their own learning, and I was now trying to apply their ideas to students in the classroom.

Because I loved physiology, particularly cardiac physiology, I helped my students relate the symptoms of cardiac failure to what they had learned earlier about the heart in their Anatomy and Physiology course. Also, I became very involved in teaching nutrition and other ways to prevent heart attacks. I taught wellness on campus and in the community with the American Heart Association. I worked with the Heart Association to open a free blood pressure clinic downtown. Later an interest in aging and confusion in the elderly in nursing home settings would motivate research I did on a second sabbatical.

Many activities outside nursing added to the excitement at EMC. Mark and I were part of the early days of Earthkeepers, a group who collected newspapers around Harrisonburg and trucked them to Richmond for recycling; this group later became an established club on campus. A feminist group on campus kept my passions stirring. Early on I was involved with Analytical Studies Groups, which met in the summer to do strategic planning and make programmatic recommendations for the institution. I chaired that group long before I felt confident about leading a strategic planning process.

In 1980 I directed the re-accreditation self-study for the Southern Association of Colleges and Schools (SACS) and soon after that chaired a committee to develop philosophy and procedures for salaries and benefits that would express our Anabaptist sense of justice while also allowing us to attract excellent candidates. Still later I was part of a task force to prioritize the building needs on campus. Finally, in 2011, a quarter of a century later, with the completion of the campus theater, every building project we recommended in our final report after many hours of debate had been completed.

I found lots of opportunities in the world beyond EMC, too, as I served on local boards such as the Pleasant View Home for the Handicapped (later called Pleasant View Homes), the Virginia Mennonite Retirement Community, and the Free Health Clinic, as well as a few national boards.

The most interesting board I served on was MMA or Mennonite Mutual Aid (later renamed Everence); I served for twelve years and chaired for the final two years. That board was also the most challenging in terms of its scope of influence. I remember well the meeting at which we decided to stay in health care even though many in the church were abandoning MMA for insurance companies that offered lower rates; however, those companies controlled costs by measures such as refusing to insure persons with serious health concerns. Serving on the search committee to choose the next president of MMA seemed like a huge responsibility in the pivotal days of the early nineties. Our choice, Howard Brenneman, would bring big changes to MMA as it developed a more diverse portfolio and a more sustainable financial strategy.

The year 1979-80 was perhaps the most memorable of my twenty-four years in the Nursing Department. It turned out that we had a faculty member who exhibited behaviors of psychopathy. I could not understand why my relationships with students were strained that year; however, it was a student who finally cued me into what was happening: A faculty member was undermining other faculty. Soon we learned that this faculty member had plagiarized one of my curriculum modules to complete her master's degree requirements at a midwestern university, taken medicines to change her electrolytes, falsified medical records at the local hospital to feign a diagnosis of cancer, and stolen medicines from another hospital. She had convinced the EMC dean of her own superior spirituality and a lack of spirituality in the Nursing Department leadership. You can find the dean's resulting review of the department in the EMU archives. It is not pretty. In the end, my resulting depression sent me to counseling, which became an opportunity to explore the joys and hazards of growing up as a middle child in an imperfect family in Big Valley.

Another moment of truth happened in those days at EMC, a truth that would serve me well as an administrator in later years. Self-pacing and mastery learning had its complications. My job included managing the scheduling of students for clinical experiences in various health care settings. Since students paced themselves through the various study guides and on-campus laboratories that were prerequisite to clinical experience, they signed themselves up in advance for clinical experiences. Many times students signed up for a day in the clinical area and then could not go because they had not yet mastered all the prerequisite learning experiences.

I had to manage the constant changes. During one unpleasant interaction with a student, I suddenly realized that I was making the schedule more important than the student. That was a lesson I often remembered later as an administrator when the piles of paper begged for attention on days filled with one-to-one meetings with staff and faculty. I would remind myself that people were not an interruption to my work—they *were* my work.

THE DOCTORATE AND BEYOND

In the early days at EMC, I intended to use my first sabbatical to complete a doctorate in physiology. But as the sabbatical neared ten years later, my interests were changing because of my involvement in curriculum development. Furthermore, I had become a mother. Heather was born three years after we came to EMC, and that same year we adopted nine-year-old Patty, one of the 100 children that husband Mark's parents had nurtured as foster parents. Managing parenthood and a full-time career was challenging. Furthermore, my dream of ever going to a large university was dimming. Thus, by the late 1970s, I was no longer sure I wanted to get a doctorate.

It was Dean Al Keim who changed my mind when he told me I needed to prepare for an unknown future. Fortunately, I took his advice. I used the sabbatical year plus a one-year leave of absence at the University of Alabama at Birmingham to complete the course work for a doctorate with an emphasis on teaching and clinical research. Weight control was the subject of my dissertation.

I also spent time evaluating the teaching strategies we had put together at EMC. While I had surprised myself by enjoying my role as acting chair during Vida Huber's sabbatical in the late 1970s and had also included a course on administration in my doctoral program, I had planned simply to teach and do research on wellness following graduation. Interestingly, a review of my transcripts confirms that I took a course on administration not only during my doctoral studies but also in my baccalaureate and master's programs, the latter with business students at the well-known Wharton School of Business at the University of Pennsylvania. Those administration courses, unbeknown to me, would be useful to my future.

When I returned to EMC in 1982, I considered whether it was time to move elsewhere, particularly to a university where I could pursue my increasing interest in wellness research and have more time to write. In the end, however, I stayed, and as it turned out, my role was about to change. Dean Al Keim was losing patience with the Nursing Department because of the stream of unhappy nursing students visiting his office. Students in the self-paced nursing program were taking five, six, or more years to graduate; many were so stressed, they contacted the dean.

Eventually, I realized that self-pacing, designed for students who needed more time, was effective for self-motivated students but often disastrous for those for whom it was created. They needed structure. At any rate, the dean felt a change in leadership was needed. In 1984 I reluctantly accepted the position of Nursing Department chair.

Again I surprised myself by enjoying administration. The problems of self-pacing were less challenging than I had feared. In one year's time we revised the curriculum by retaining most of our innovations but reintroducing structure so students could succeed in a timely manner.

For my last several years as chair, some of my load included writing grants for the institution. But in 1994 President Joe Lapp decided to hire a full-time grant writer. My full-time position at EMU felt in jeopardy. At the same time, after ten years as chair, I was at another turning point, restless and needing a change. An invitation to consider a position as dean of nursing at an institution I knew through my accreditation work with the Southern Association of Colleges and Schools looked inviting. That was when Joe Lapp asked me to consider replacing the vice president for enrollment, who had resigned.

My initial response again was "No." I did not think I had the right experience to provide leadership for admissions and financial aid. Several weeks later, though, I changed my mind and applied, partly because my husband had no interest in relocating elsewhere. I still remember how scared I felt when the president took me downstairs to introduce me to the admissions and financial aid staff as their new leader. Because this new appointment did not fit the reluctant-leadership, risk-avoidance side of my self-identity, I needed to do something daring. Accordingly, I went to the Valley Mall and got my ears pierced! Obviously, I was a late adopter of such practices.

Once again I discovered the new position to be enjoyable. Furthermore, at the same time we learned that the federal Title III grant I had written the year before had been approved; I could now lead the campus in becoming computer-networked, along with helping to create this new entity called a university. Incidentally, I also served as chair of the Music Department for two years while I was vice president for enrollment. I did it because Dean Lee Snyder asked me to, and it finally took me into the music world—well, sort of.

In the early nineties I was aware that many folks found President Lapp's talk about EMC's becoming a university to be a bit comical. They felt that the institution was too small and too focused on undergraduate education to pretend to be a university. I remember clearly the Strategic Planning Council meeting when it dawned on me that Joe Lapp's vision for a university was much more than a way to deal with an unwieldy name (Eastern Mennonite College and Seminary), to clarify our identity for schools overseas, or to signal the addition of a few graduate programs.

Lapp envisioned an institution that would play a much bigger role in the Mennonite world and beyond by producing leaders, specifically through the cultivation of graduate programs that could stand alongside the secular programs through which Mennonites currently obtained their graduate degrees. Yet did even Joe Lapp envision the impact EMU would soon have on hundreds of peacemakers from every religion who would join EMU's graduate program in Conflict Transformation before returning to the world's hottest trouble spots?

EMU's First Provost and Interim President

From this transition to a university status would come my most profound role at EMU. In the process of becoming a university, EMU had become a much more complex place, and dissatisfaction was increasing with the administrative structure. Graduate programs reported to two different deans, and the work of the deans was not always well coordinated. A committee advised creation of a new, unified academic structure headed by a provost.

Five years earlier, I had been turned down for the position of undergraduate dean in favor of an outsider. President Lapp had encouraged me to apply for this position, and I thought God might be calling me to do so because God's calls had almost always come through people. So I applied. Before my interview with the search committee, at Park View Mennonite Church on a Sunday morning we sang a song based on Isaiah 6:8 (KJV) where the Lord says to Isaiah, "Whom shall I send, and who will go for us?" Was I to ready to answer like Isaiah, "Here am I; send me"? I cried throughout that song because I felt ambivalent about becoming the dean. The interview with the search committee cast additional doubt because the conversation began rather abruptly with the question, "Why do you want this job?"

Well, I was not sure I did and was taken aback by that stark question. It soon became apparent that God or at least EMU was not calling me to that position. That December became another time to wonder if it was not surely time to leave EMU; once more, I stayed.

Suddenly, in June 2000 I was being asked by the president on behalf of the provost search committee to take the position of EMU's first provost. This surprise call came when the previously selected candidate informed the president two weeks before he was to start that he could not come because of a medical problem.

Given my experience in applying for the dean's position, I had said "No" to the search committee's invitation to apply. But now, with a mixture of fear and excitement, I said "Yes" to the president with the understanding that an evaluation would be conducted within three years to decide if I would continue and if the new position itself was viable. That evaluation would be delayed until after a new president arrived in January 2004 and also until I had served as interim president for some seven months while the newly chosen president prepared for his new role. In the end, I served eight years as provost.

What does one do after being appointed provost at an institution that has never had such a position? And how does the person appointed absorb this new identity in the absence of a long process of application and interviewing to prepare for it? Since none of us knew exactly what a provost was, in July 2000 I took a trip westward to talk to a number of provosts at Christian colleges. Later that fall I attended a meeting of deans and provosts of independent colleges and universities and again listened to others' versions of the provost role. Sometime later I attended a two-week Harvard leadership institute, where I spent many hours talking with other participants about academic leadership roles. Ultimately, we carved out our own understanding of the provost role at EMU—one that is far less authoritarian than that of many provosts, who give the final say on issues of tenure and promotion.

The first decade of the new century was not an easy time to come to leadership at EMU. The 1990s under President Joe Lapp had been a growing time for the university, with increasing diversity of programs and personnel. The faculty had taken on a more adversarial role during a difficult period. A call for more involvement in decision-making by faculty and staff had surfaced in the recent re-accreditation self-study.

A half dozen more years would pass before the campus would come to terms with the need for a Faculty Senate. Whatever unhappiness existed on campus in the year 2000 intensified in November 2002 when the board, in the process of hiring a new president, became alarmed by the activism of some faculty and staff concerning homosexuality. At that point the board issued a statement that some perceived as a threat to academic freedom. It would take years to heal from that event. And homosexuality would continue to be an issue at EMU throughout my tenure as provost. In the meantime, finances needed to be stabilized, and EMU embarked on a prioritization process with inevitable pain as some programs were discontinued or altered.

As I see it, much of the dissatisfaction experienced during the first decade of the new century existed among the undergraduate faculty, who perceived themselves as having lost out in the growth of the university. Energy resided in the growing graduate programs at the same time that undergraduate departments were discouraged from creating new majors due to efforts to raise the comparatively low student-faculty ratio. The biggest revenue producer remained the undergraduate program. Yet many maintained that the graduate and seminary programs were taking dollars from the undergraduate program while the graduate faculty benefited from smaller class sizes and more liberal scholarship options. Furthermore, some undergraduate faculty felt they had lost power because their dean no longer reported to the president.

Intensifying this discontent was the fact that I, the provost, doubled as graduate dean and was thus necessarily perceived to have a conflict of interest that favored the graduate programs. Some faculty, perhaps, were unhappy that I remained eight years as provost when I had not gone through the usual review process for appointment. As I look back, it is my perception that the Faculty Senate has gone a long way toward creating a happier faculty. In addition, the structure was improved when a graduate dean was appointed with the arrival of a new provost after I retired from that position.

EVALUATION AND APPRECIATION

There were many good times during the eight years I spent as provost, and much was accomplished. Undoubtedly, the most important thing any administrator does is to hire the right people. I had close to twenty directors reporting to me; if I was successful as provost, it was mostly because the people I hired or inherited for those positions were so good at what they did. At the same time the deans were hiring a new, younger faculty. In the year 2000 and following, we developed new structures for decision making and proposed many new and revised policies, including a more generous sabbatical policy, a new scholarship/practice policy for graduate faculty, and new standards for promotion.

Nor did we stop creating new educational programs. A writing program came into existence, and we worked with folks at Lancaster Mennonite Conference in Pennsylvania to create STEP, a program to provide training for pastors who lacked formal seminary education. Other new programs off-campus included a nursing degree in Lancaster and a master's degree for teachers at Sarasota Christian School in Florida. The undergraduate departments created new programs, including Digital Media, Photography, Philosophy, and Pre-Law. We continued to find ways to manage costs, such as negotiating an agreement with the local national public radio station to manage the WEMC radio station.

These creative initiatives came from many different people on campus. As I came to know myself as an administrator, I realized that I frequently served as a facilitator for the creative ideas of others. Looking back, I also realize that I enjoyed coaching the persons who reported to me and solving problems together. People are often disdainful of administration; they sometimes call administrators "paper pushers." But administration is much more about working with people. I occasionally wondered whether nursing had been the right path for me. However, nursing had taught me a lot about working with people, and that is not bad preparation for administration. Sometimes the pace of the job was overwhelming. But actually I discovered I enjoyed juggling multiple balls in the air at once and being where the action was.

Even serving as interim president turned out to be a mostly positive experience. I learned that fundraising was less intimidating than I had anticipated because I got to talk to people who loved EMU and wanted to support it. I discovered that people respect the one who carries the title of president. I also discovered that being at the top of the academic pyramid allows one actually to make a few decisions. "The buck stops here" can be enabling rather than burdensome. In addition, I found that presidents had better choose their words with care because they will be repeated! Finally, I learned that needing to make many public presentations had its good points in that it provided opportunities to restate the vision. Sharing the vision is the president's job.

I like to believe that the efforts made in the years I was provost enhanced a sense of ownership, improved communication and transparency, and contributed to a happier faculty. Did the series of conversations we sponsored on homosexuality in 2005-06 help the campus learn to talk in love about this topic? Did Common Grounds Coffeehouse, created with the help of a major Lilly grant, meet our goal of creating a space for difficult conversations? At the commencement speech I made in 2008, I called on students to become bridge builders. Earlier, on a Sunday morning at Park View Mennonite Church, as I had listened to several persons describe how they served within their chosen disciplines, I experienced another moment of truth. I realized that what I aspired to was bridge building. With the increasing diversity on Mennonite college campuses, that skill seems a necessary ingredient of administration.

TRANSITION INTO RETIREMENT

In 2008 I made a transition as I retired at age sixty-six. Well, more accurately, I semi-retired, for once more I said "Yes" when the presi-

Bidding farewell to Beryl Brubaker at her first retirement event—when she left the provost's office in 2008.

dent asked me to write the document for re-accreditation by the Southern Association of Colleges and Schools, and a year later Interim Provost Lee Snyder asked me to direct the library half time. I spent six years in the latter role. Working with a seasoned staff in a less stressful setting provided a good transition into retirement and other unpaid roles with family and community organizations. The Valley Brethren-Mennonite Heritage Center would take up some of my time post-retirement. Its mission, to celebrate the story of Jesus Christ by sharing the values of Valley Brethren and Mennonites, seemed in keeping with my life's work at EMU.

MORE ON MY SPIRITUAL JOURNEY

I wonder who I would be if I had made a career in music or if I had spent a lifetime at a large university. Living and working in Anabaptist Mennonite settings has made a difference. Growing up in Big Valley, I was a believer early on. Church was a big part of our lives—we went at least twice on Sunday and attended Wednesday evening prayer meeting, summer Bible school, and revival meetings at our small church in both fall and spring. I remember at one of those revival meetings inviting a woman who was not a Christian to respond to the invitation by the evangelist. The duty to save the lost hung heavily on me.

We were well versed in the Bible, or so we thought. I remember the summer Bible school I attended when I was in middle school and first heard about pre-and post-millennialism. I had never heard these words before, and now I was learning for the first time that there was a major debate over how the world would end. I felt betrayed by this lack of instruction because the end times were such an important part of our worldview. My upbringing had created a lot of fear about whether we were ready for the second coming of Christ. How could we risk doing anything wrong when Jesus could return at any moment and any unforgiven sin could send us to hell forever?

My sisters and I had a nightly ritual that went like this: "Will you forgive me if I was ugly to you today?" I tried to be good and was shocked when others were not, such as when my sister stole candy from Grandma's store. Later, when she accepted a ride one night with a boy from nearby Lewistown and was raped, I, too, was devastated. I was failing in my role as preventer and fixer.

How many times did I go forward to commit and recommit my life to Jesus in response to preachers George R. Brunk II, Howard

Hammer, Andrew Jantzi, and Myron Augsburger? I was only nine when I made my first commitment. Dad had taken the family to the Brunk tent revivals in Johnstown, Pennsylvania; it was my first exposure to what would become an annual summer ritual in Big Valley. It seemed no one was responding to the preacher's invitation. With guilt a familiar feeling to this nine-year old who tried always to be good and with hell-fire preaching a strong motivator, I literally started down the sawdust trail. I will forever remember that George Brunk called me a little lamb and blessed me because apparently others then followed my lead.

That night I felt all the burdens roll away, and I felt clean and new. Upon baptism, I would finally get to wear the head covering that would mark my entry into the religious community I had learned to love. Later that same covering would symbolize my struggle to move beyond Big Valley religious orthodoxy.

Not until I got to Case Western Reserve University did traditional beliefs start falling apart for me. Certainly I had argued with Dad about the role of women on visits home while I was attending EMC and probably in high school as well. Some church teachings did not make sense to my rational, scientific mind, but I tried to rationalize these conflicts to make sense out of them. After all, in addition to my religious upbringing, I, along with other modern students, was already thoroughly indoctrinated by a scientific worldview so different from the world of the Bible.

It was a course on cultural anthropology that introduced the idea that religion might be a human construct to explain the unknown, an illusion to ease suffering and create hope for the future. That fall I did not take communion at Lee Heights Community Church because I was not sure of my salvation anymore, and I was no longer so sure of what I believed. That course marked my entrance into the world of the doubter as I gained a greater awareness of the tension between the two worldviews in which I lived.

At the same time that I was absorbing these shocking new ideas, I remember explaining to a non-Christian friend that God required a sacrifice to forgive our sins. This explanation of Jesus' death is one that I would find increasingly unsatisfying, especially in light of my scientific worldview. Later, during a counseling session, I was asked to listen to what God was telling me. What came into my mind were these words: "That's why I died for you, so you wouldn't have to be perfect." When I shared these words with the counselor, I protested, "But I don't believe that!" Yet, could it be true? Life and God—both full of mystery.

My inward struggles did not interfere with my decision to serve in a Mennonite college. Apparently, whatever I said in my questionnaire and interview with the Religious Welfare Committee, when I joined EMC a few years after my Case Western Reserve experience, did not raise any significant concerns. I nonetheless arrived with many questions. In those days I could not sing "Just As I Am" without feeling a real distaste. But then the revivalist era ended, and our churches stopped singing "Just As I Am."

Fortunately, EMC provided a setting in which I could continue my spiritual and theological search to reexamine my heritage and make my faith claims. Big Valley Mennonites generally adhered to a fairly literal understanding of Scripture. Now I was asking hard questions: How should we read the Bible and apply it to our times? How could we believe without arrogantly assuming that our truth claims were *the* truth?

EMC/EMU provided many opportunities to feed our thinking. In faculty/staff conferences that marked the beginning of each school year, we read provocative works such as Stanley Hauerwas and William H. Willimon's *Resident Aliens: Life in the Christian Colony* (Nashville, Tenn.: Abingdon Press, 2008.) There were all-school seminars like the one in the '70s called "Christianity and the Future," where we wrestled with questions about how to be faithful followers of Jesus in a modern age. We heard guest speakers such as Francis Collins, head of the National Institute of Health and director of the genome project, who told of his conversion.

Early on at EMC a big issue for me was the head covering. I had been taught to wear it at all times, and I still did for some years after I arrived at EMU. Because I took the Bible seriously, I would not take it off just because others were dropping it. I had to deal with 1 Corinthians 11. A weekend event with Willard Swartley in the 1970s finally put the issue to rest for me. I moved from thinking that I needed to wear the covering because Scripture required it to believing that it was wrong to wear it because it symbolized female subjection, which I no longer saw as biblical. I understood that what was necessary in

Corinth in Bible times was no longer needed in today's context. I came to accept that the principle Paul taught (be aware of how your actions are interpreted by those around you). was more important than any single practice.

In 1979 I also finally cut off my long hair. Long hair, too, had seemed a requirement, according to the writer of 1 Corinthians. I had agreed to let my six-year-old daughter get her hair cut; as I sat in the hair salon that day, I acted on impulse and got mine cut, too. When my mother saw me, she said she had hoped never to me with short hair. The daughter who had always tried to please her parents must have finally grown up. Then at age ninety-nine, Mom had her hair cut short, too, when taking care of long hair became too difficult for her.

Issues related to the role of women in the church and society were always important to me. There was a time when I made up my own pronouns as I sang hymns at church. Maybe my views on this issue are the reason I so often accepted invitations to lead and do things in public despite my ambiguous feelings about public roles. I started saying yes early on. As a young girl at Barrville church, I taught Sunday school, led congregational singing, and presented Sunday evening "topics." Later I became Valley Mennonite Youth Fellowship co-president and a student government leader at Belleville Mennonite School. Many more instances of saying yes followed my arrival at EMC. My desire to achieve, my sense of responsibility, and my feminist values all contributed to my tendency to make a positive response to invitations to leadership.

Besides the seminars, conferences, and speakers that EMU provided, many books became available on campus, volumes such as Willard M. Swartley's Conrad Grebel Lectures, *Slavery, Sabbath, War, and Women: Case Issues in Biblical Interpretation*[1] and Calvin E. Shenk's *Who Do You Say That I Am?: Christians Encounter Other Religions.*[2] Co-teacher Gerald Shenk and I rooted our Faith and Issues courses in Donald B. Kraybill's *The Upside Down Kingdom.*[3] One time that felt like a conversion occurred while I was reading Ted Grimsrud's *God's Healing Strategy.*[4] His emphasis—that the Bible has an overarching story and that this story is God's overwhelming love for us—was for me emotionally moving.

More recent books like Brian D. McLaren's *A Generous Orthodoxy*[5] and Stuart A. P. Murray's *The Naked Anabaptist: The Bare Essentials of a*

Radical Faith[6] have joined the conversation about who I am and who we are. Messiah Professor Sharon L. Baker's *Razing Hell: Rethinking Everything You've Been Taught about God's Wrath and Judgment*[7] and Owen Gingerich's *God's Planet*[8] have provided new thoughts about hell and an affirmation of both science *and* theology.

Over the years I have discovered a God who is less a God of punishment and more a God of love and grace. A painful time at EMU was the year campus pastor Darrell Brubaker took his own life. I remember being astonished when President Myron Augsburger prayed and pleaded for God to have mercy on Darrell's soul. "Could mercy be possible for someone who took his own life?" I wondered. Today, I am less doubtful of that possibility.

As I have indicated, I entered into every leadership role with more than a little trepidation. Was it because I am a female or just a person afraid of failure and self-exposure? I have appreciated Deborah Tannen's books about gender. She suggests that many women do not enjoy engaging in public discourse for fear it will become oppositional. Our female tendency to like pleasing others and to dislike antagonizing people makes us wary of public exposure of our ideas. Imagine what that means for a stereotypical woman leader in a typical faculty meeting in an academic setting.

Despite the gender biases prevalent in our society, I have rarely felt that these biases have been an obstacle to me. Nor have I worried about whether I was just a token female. A few times, however, I felt my leadership was questioned simply because I was female. One such occasion occurred when I was chair of the MMA board. When we were meeting with the executive board of the Mennonite church, one of the executives asked me over breakfast if I had ever chaired a board before. Was this an innocent question? It surely felt condescending. I doubt he would have asked that of a male chair.

On another occasion, conflict related to gender may have threatened my job. At the 1988 annual joint meeting of the Mennonite Medical Association and Mennonite Nurses Association, physician Sam Showalter and I were asked to talk about nurse-physician conflict. Apparently, what I said upset some of the physicians so badly that they considered asking the EMC president to fire me as chair of the Nursing Department. What did I say that was so inflammatory? My introductory comment that I rejected the headship of males, an example of my propensity for directness that occasionally got me into trouble but usually engendered trust, may have been the trigger. Fortunately, Ron Kraybill, a well-known mediator, was present to lead a session that tempered the emotions my speech aroused. I am not aware that the physicians ever contacted the EMC president.

My husband Mark was part of the reason I said yes to invitations to leadership. He always encouraged me to accept leadership positions. After our daughter Heather was born, he was the one who worked part time to provide childcare. I was fortunate to marry a man who does not feel threatened by female leadership or by a wife with a higher salary than his. Actually, in stark contrast to my male high school classmates, Mark would never have noticed me at all if he had not seen my name on the honor roll in the old Administration Building at EMC. Of course, I am not nearly as smart as I thought I was in earlier days. I have worked with too many highly intelligent people over the years not to feel appropriately humbled.

My father, C. Clayton Hartzler, was another important influence on my life. He was an institution builder highly committed to the Mennonite church and a man open to learning. He never had the opportunity to attend college. His father's untimely death when Dad was sixteen meant someone had to stay home and help his mother make a living. This responsibility did not prevent him from becoming very involved in numerous leadership roles, such as founder and chair of the board of Belleville Mennonite School. Until his death in 1972 he encouraged me in whatever I did. Unlike some parents in conservative Mennonite communities, Mom and Dad never discouraged me from pursuing a career or taking leadership positions.

Finally, I give credit to my two daughters, my sisters, many teachers, EMU colleagues, and friends who encouraged me. And I am grateful for my mom, who faithfully worried about me.

So Why Did I Stay at EMU?

At the beginning of my memoir, I explained that my story would center on just two places—Belleville, Pennsylvania, and Harrisonburg, Virginia. I did venture beyond these locations on some special occasions. However, my travels to Africa, Europe, and Central America were mostly to visit family doing service—or to sightsee as my

Four living EMU presidents, from left to right, Myron Augsburger, Joseph Lapp, Beryl Brubaker (interim president), and Loren Swartzendruber.

husband and I did during a three-month honeymoon along the U.S. coastline, down into Mexico, and back across Canada. A 1971 student seminar would take my husband and me to Kentucky for a summer. Our VW camper, bought in Germany on a two-month trip across Europe in 1970, was good for sleeping as we traveled to visit our scattered students in Kentucky. I also spent a few years in several cities—Newport News, Virginia; Cleveland; Philadelphia; and Birmingham—as I earned my educational credentials. However, despite the pleasures I found in these places, I kept returning to Harrisonburg to fill a wide range of roles at EMC/EMU. Why did I stay for forty-five years in this one place at the same institution?

EMU encouraged whatever creativity I was capable of; it provided opportunities for leadership that gave outlets for my desire to achieve; it created space for working on my spiritual journey; and through serving students, faculty, and staff, it enabled me to serve this whole world where our students go to minister. Further, in a 2007 speech I talked about the EMU difference. I suggested that most schools can rightly extol the virtues of their faculty and curricula. They can also show that their graduates prepare people well for their chosen professions and create good citizens. No doubt the faculty at many schools, just like our EMU faculty, care for their students beyond the classroom. But I declared that this is the only school I know that has a vision based upon Micah 6:8. "Do justice, love mercy, and walk humbly with God." That is a compelling vision, one that draws people to EMU.

But are we at EMU really different? Growing up, I did indeed feel different. Actually, in my growing up years, I probably thought Mennonites were the only folks going to heaven. At least I did not expect to see Catholics there! Neighbors across the street and downtown where we shopped were labeled *English* and *worldly*. Yet while I was happy to get to wear the head covering as a nine-year-old, feeling different from the surrounding culture and even my no-longer-Mennonite aunts and uncles was not always comfortable. I could not wear white shoes, and my braids had to be wound tightly to my head. I might want to be attractive, but the Mennonite dress codes in the '50s would make that difficult. Besides, my parents did not even have enough money to get my overbite fixed until late in high school; all their money went to send five girls to the Mennonite school.

That sense of being different would persist through many settings where I went to school. Perhaps the comfort of not being different at EMC/EMU was part of what kept me there. I remember my teenage daughter telling me that Mark and I were different not only from her public school friends' parents but also from her and the person she wanted to be. That criticism hurt at the time, but in afterthought it seemed not so bad. Different is what Jesus calls us to be and what we say we are at EMU, maybe no longer in dress but in some other more important ways. Incidentally, a few years later when her friends were supporting the Gulf War, this daughter discovered that she too was different. She found herself in opposition to the war and decided she was ready to be baptized into the Mennonite church.

Colleagues have frequently commented that I have served many roles at EMU. Apparently, some have said, "If you need someone to do it, ask Beryl." Am I to take that as a compliment? Or should I feel like the last resort? Or maybe they are implying that I was not smart enough to say "No"! In 2015 at age seventy-three, forty-five years after beginning my career at EMU, I fully retired with gratitude that EMU had provided many opportunities for me to play roles I enjoyed, roles that stretched me to my limits. I hope that I made some positive differences. Other paths—professional musicianship, a lifetime of research scholarship—may have been fulfilling, too. Still, I am grateful for the story that unfolded at EMU, a story with surprises I could not have anticipated upon entry in 1970 when Mark and I accepted the call to our alma mater. For that call, we both give thanks.

September 2011
Revised June 2015

Notes

1. Willard M. Swartley, *Slavery, Sabbath, War, and Women: Case Issues in Biblical Interpretation*, Conrad Grebel Lectures (Scottdale, Pa.: Herald Press, 1983).

2. Calvin E. Shenk, *Who Do You Say That I Am?: Christians Encounter Other Religions* (Eugene, Ore.: Wipf and Stock, 2006).

3. Donald B. Kraybill, *The Upside Down Kingdom* (Harrisonburg, Va.: Herald Press, 1978. Revised editions 1990, 2003, 2011).

4. Ted Grimsrud, *God's Healing Strategy: An Introduction to the Bible's Main Themes* (Telford, Pa.: Pandora Press U.S., co-published Herald Press and in association with Eastern Mennonite University, 2000); *God's Healing Strategy: An Introduction to the Bible's Main Themes*, rev. ed. (Telford, Pa.: Cascadia Publishing House, formerly Pandora Press U.S., 2011).

5. Brian D. McLaren, *A Generous Orthodoxy* (El Cajon, Calif.: Youth Specialties Books, 2004).

6. Stuart A. P. Murray, *The Naked Anabaptist: The Bare Essentials of a Radical Faith* (Scottdale, Pa.: Herald Press, 2010; pub. by agreement with Paternoster: Milton Keynes, U.K.).

7. Sharon L. Baker, *Razing Hell: Rethinking Everything You've Been Taught about God's Wrath and Judgment* (Louisville, Ky.: Westminster John Knox Press, 2010).

8. Owen Gingerich, *God's Planet* (Cambridge, Mass.: Harvard University Press, 2014).

Joseph L. Lapp

EMU's First Attorney/College President

Seen above in the Presidents' Library at EMU in 2002, Joseph Lapp, one of the nine children of a Pennsylvania Mennonite bishop, became an attorney, chair of Eastern Mennonite College's board of trustees and then president of the college. He tells a compelling story of a time of change and growth. Among the positive initiatives that he led was the transformation of the college into a university with new graduate programs, a widespread campus renovation program, and major building initiatives that included the EMU Commons.

JOSEPH L. LAPP

Joining the Family Business: By Birthright, by Choice, and by Divine Call

In a roundabout way I learned that someone had referred to me as "being in the family business." I do not know if this was intended to be a negative or a positive remark. Pondering this comment, though, I decided to claim it as part of my story and make it my title.

Using the metaphor of *business* is recognition that from the very beginning, the church, the Mennonite church, was the center of life for my parents and my family. In many ways I grew up in a Mennonite cocoon. Our lives revolved around Mennonite people, organizations, and culture. As my stories show, to us, persons outside the Mennonite world were suspect. Life in the community looked quite secure with opportunities to grow and learn within established parameters. Still, for me there came a time to explore beyond the customary boundaries. Here, my overall focus will be on the social, cultural, and religious influences that shaped the person I became.

LIFE WITH A PACIFIST BISHOP FATHER IN WW II

Those who have read the life story of John A. Lapp, my oldest brother (in *ACRS Memoirs* vol. 2, pp. 51-71), will recognize that he, being ten years older, had different experiences from mine with our same parents and siblings. He would agree, however, with my perception that our family members have enjoyed good relationships.

My father and mother had discovered each other through the Mennonite church activities of the day and were married September 15, 1926. She then gave birth to eight of us plus two still-born babies as home births: John Allen, Mary Louise (Swartley), James Merrill, Daniel Wilbur, Samuel Jay, myself, Sara Jane (Kolb), and Ruth Marie (Guengerich). The ninth, our youngest sibling Rhoda Mae (Lapp), at the doctor's suggestion, was born in the hospital because of my mother's age. The fifth of five boys, I was born on December 22, 1942, a few days more than a year after Pearl Harbor had been bombed by Japan. Early on, I learned that my birthday was "three days before Christmas."

Before my arrival the family had moved a few miles from Lansdale to several acres on Allentown Road for an opportunity to garden and raise chickens and turkeys. In 1930 my father started Lapp's Grocery and Deli in Lansdale. Dad's life-changing event, however, occurred on June 22, 1933. From a group of six men, Dad was chosen by lot at the age of twenty-seven to be the minister at the Plains Mennonite Church. He was the youngest, the only one not fluent in German, and the only non-farmer. Family stories relate that Dad had shared with Mother some sense that he might be called to the ministry. On June 1, 1937, at the age of thirty-one, Dad was again chosen by lot, this time to be a bishop in Franconia Conference. At that time my brother John was four years old, Mary two and one-half, and Jim about to be born on July 20, 1937. None of us children really knows what life would have been like apart from our father's church ministry.

The large story of the time, especially in the early 1940s, was the Mennonites' concern about maintaining a nonresistant faith as war preparations were escalating. By 1941 Dad had become part of the denominational "Old" Mennonite Church's Peace Problems Committee. As war fever increased, Dad became involved with the infancy of the Civilian Public Service (CPS) program. During the war years, he traveled extensively by train and car to attend church meetings and to visit CPS men around the country. To me as a young boy, the names of the various CPS camps became common parlance: Sideling Hill, Pennsylvania; Grottoes, Virginia; and many more. We children accompanied Dad on some of his trips. I recall traveling to Indiana in a train berth and staying in the home of some folks.

As World War II ended and the I-W program developed, my early memories are of Mennonite men coming to our home for assistance with the completion of their Selective Service questionnaires. It was interesting to observe how difficult this task was for these men, some high school graduates but many who had not completed high school. They struggled with such questions as "Why do you oppose war?" and "When did you first develop these beliefs?" Dad assumed that these men knew what the belief in nonresistance was but had difficulty expressing it. As a youth, it seemed to me that he frequently put words into their mouths.

OTHER EARLY FORMATIVE EVENTS

In the early 1950s, Dad came home from the semi-annual Franconia Conference assembly and said soberly, "I was sheriffed today." What Dad meant was that the sheriff had come to the conference session and asked to see him. Dad turned over his moderating duties to the assistant moderator, Elmer Kolb, and stepped out. The sheriff then served him papers for a lawsuit filed by several sons of a minister of the Franconia congregation, alleging that the bishops of the central district and the ministers, deacons, and trustees of the Franconia Congregation had violated the Schleitheim and Dortrecht Confessions of Faith by allowing certain property changes. This event became the subject of many MA and PhD dissertations. Of course, it impacted the church and weighed heavily on Dad, Mother, and the family.

Another tragic event occurred in the mid-1950s when the father of one of my teenaged Sunday school classmates (from a family of seven children) was killed by a drunk driver. Since there seemed to be clear liability, Dad consulted with Mennonite Attorney Elvin Souder as to what could be done without beginning a lawsuit. Along with the funeral director, Paul Hunsicker, Dad negotiated with the insurance company for a financial settlement in the amount of about $100,000.

In summer 1951, the Brunk Brothers Revival Campaign came to the Franconia Conference area. For three weeks our family attended the revivals almost every night. The first day, however, George Brunk II was almost electrocuted and had to spend that night in the hospital. It turned out to be our dad who preached the sermon for the opening session. This is my first recollection of hearing evangelistic preaching in such a dramatic style. At my young age the Brunk family had an exciting life. Yet the meetings created in me fear of hell while also igniting an awareness of the need of salvation, causing me to accept Christ several months short of the age of nine. Following the meetings, a large group of young people received instruction for baptism. As I recall, the late J. C. Clemens was not very satisfied with my progress as the youngest student in this class, but I was baptized at the Plains Mennonite Church with the others.

Many more faith commitment events followed. During the summer of 1962, Myron Augsburger held evangelistic tent meetings at the Christopher Dock Mennonite High School. I found these meetings to be a breath of fresh air, equally dramatic but with a call to discipleship that appealed to my older teenage mind. Besides, this was the occasion when I had my first date with Hannah Mack—though she turned me down the first time because another fellow was ahead of me. That was the beginning of our courtship.

I have frequently thought of the many influential persons who visited in our home: H. S. Bender, Orie Miller, J. C. Wenger, Lancaster conference bishops, Franconia conference bishops, Paul Peachey, J. Lawrence Burkholder, Cal Redekop, John R. Mumaw, C. K. Lehman, George R. Brunk II, Truman Brunk Sr., many of the EMC and seminary faculty, and Goshen College faculty. Many participated with Dad on committees such as the Mennonite Publication Board, MCC, the Peace Problems Committee (later the Peace and Social Concerns Committee), and General Conference committees.

My older siblings attended summer camp at the Laurelville Mennonite Church Center, and I enjoyed going once for a summer boys' camp and once for a junior high coed camp. Henry Swartley, the camp pastor one summer, left a strong impression on me.

FRANCONIA MENNONITE SCHOOL: DISQUIETING MEMORIES

During the war years, Franconia Mennonite leaders, who felt a need for a Christian day school to strengthen Mennonite faith and practices such as nonresistance, founded Franconia Mennonite School (FMS), now Penn View Christian School. My older siblings had been attending the Kulpsville Public School, but Mary, Jim, and

Dan transferred to FMS when it started. Sam and I were the first in the family to begin first grade there. I started first grade at the age of five (probably so my mother would have another child out of the house for part of the day), and my three younger sisters followed as they reached school age. Since FMS had only ten grades, John, Mary, and Jim attended Eastern Mennonite High School in Virginia for their last two years. The principal of FMS was a young minister, Richard Detweiler, and my first-grade teacher was kind Betty Detweiler (sister of Richard Detweiler and later Betty Detweiler King).

Actually, I have less than fond memories of my elementary school experiences. Most of the teachers had had little teacher training. After I finished third grade, the principal, whom my father highly respected, suggested to Dad that I repeat the grade. The resulting changes to my peer groups in Sunday school and grade school classes were painful. However, it was in the first grade that I met Hannah Mack.

CHRISTOPHER DOCK MENNONITE HIGH SCHOOL: BETTER MEMORIES

Christopher Dock Mennonite High School, founded in 1955, offered a better educational experience for me than the Franconia school had. The abusive discipline was gone, and the college educated teachers set high standards. Although some of my learning difficulties continued, Pearl Schrack, Janet Martin, Daniel Reinford, and others have become lifelong friends. Hiram Hershey, our music director, created an appreciation for excellent choral and classical music. Extracurricular activities, socials, and other youth events acceptable to Mennonites became an important part of life. Since I was one of the oldest in my class, I got a driver's license before others; and, though not at the top of my class, I stayed in the general academic track.

MEMORABLE EVENTS IN MY COLLEGE YEARS

In my parental home it was clear that Eastern Mennonite College (EMC) was the most acceptable school for higher education. Though Dad had many contacts at Goshen College, he clearly had more of an affinity for persons at EMC except for the eschatology of some. Thus, late in August 1962, I arrived at EMC in my 1958 Ford Fairlane two-door hardtop with Hannah Mack and Rachael Alderfer (now Hinz) as passengers and all our luggage. Since Emmanuel Martin, the director of admissions, had some concern about my ability to do college work, EMC had accepted my enrollment conditionally.

There I came under the tutelage of administrators and faculty whom EMC historians will recognize: President John R. Mumaw; Dean Ira Miller; Dean of Students Laban Peachey; and faculty members James R. Bomberger, Herman Reitz, Norman Yutzy, Carl Keener, John A. Lapp, Samuel Horst, Al Keim, Catherine Mumaw, Paul Kurtz, Eugene Hostetter, and others.

I recall that in my first year Professor Bomberger assigned a research paper to defend a thesis. My subject was Alger Hiss, one of the many persons caught in the communist hysteria of the McCarthy era. My thesis was that Alger Hiss was framed by Whitaker Chambers, the chief witness against him. This was probably an example of my rebellious streak.

Like many other college students, I did not let the academic work interfere too much with my extracurricular activities. During my first year, Jim Mullenex had gained some notoriety for his WEMC Campus News radio program. After he asked me to take over this program, I had some fun being a muckraker-newsman. Also, in 1962 EMC still had the organized literary societies that provided many social activities, and I followed my family tradition of joining the Smithsonian Literary Society. In my first year, I began attending the Deerfield Mennonite Church, about an hour's drive southwest of the college. Deerfield was a small "Y" church that offered students opportunities to be involved in the worship and Sunday school planning along with visitation in the community.

During this academic year, Hannah Mack and I continued to date. After her first year, Hannah accepted an administrative assistant position at the Mennonite Publishing House (MPH), Scottdale, Pennsylvania, working with Nelson Waybill, the personnel manager.

Continuing in college, I declared a Bible and history major but found my first three years of Bible courses less stimulating than my history courses. With due respect to my friends who were Bible faculty, the 1962-1965 Bible courses left a lot to be desired. Willard Swartley, a new Bible faculty member in 1965, saved the day for me. His senior-level Bible course introduced new resources and a different approach to biblical studies.

Since Hannah was not on campus my second year of college, I needed to fill my spare time with new activities. I kept hearing about the administrative censorship of the college's newspaper, *The Weather Vane* (WV). Although I was not a writer for the WV, I adopted the issue as a broader campus crusade. Ken Reed, Dwayne Martin, and I with the assistance of others decided to produce an alternative campus newspaper. I figured we could make mimeograph copies (two-sided and stapled together with a colored construction strip as a binding) and sell them for ten cents a copy. In addition, we would get some advertisements to defray expenses.

We chose the name *Piranha*. Ken Reed was the editor; Dwayne Martin and I took care of the promotion and business side; and many of the WV writers submitted creative pieces. The idea of the content was to bypass censorship and publish articles/essays/poetry that might contain unacceptable words but were worthy of print. In addition, we advertised the local movies. We published six to ten issues on the alternate weeks when the WV was not published and hawked the copies outside the dining room on Friday evenings, selling about 100 copies per issue.

Tragic off-campus history entered our lives in November 1963 when Henry Rosenberger dashed into our dorm room and announced that President John F. Kennedy had just been shot in Dallas, Texas. After about an hour of conversation, attempting to get news on the radio (no TVs were on the EMC campus in 1963), we jumped into my car and drove to Washington. There we walked around D. C., feeling the national grief everywhere. We stood in line to go through the Capitol Rotunda, where the president lay in state. We spent hours along Pennsylvania Avenue, lined with members of the various branches of the military standing at attention about every twenty-five feet on both sides of the street, waiting for the horse-drawn caisson.

A much happier event during my sophomore year was the realization that Hannah was the one for me, and I made several trips to Scottdale to visit her. Sometime in the fall of 1963 Hannah agreed to my proposal. Our plan, then, was that during summer 1964, I would work at Zeiglers' Apple Cider, and Hannah would terminate at Scottdale to plan the wedding details.

Our wedding was a traditional 1960s Mennonite wedding with vocal music from a small group. It included no ring ceremony, though we bought cheap rings at the Montgomeryville Mart (a flea-market-type place), which we would secretly wear from time to time. Unfortunately during our wedding trip to Cape Cod, I got sick. (Hannah says it was because I had worked eighty hours a week right up to our wedding day.) We then left for Harrisonburg, where a South College Avenue, second-floor apartment owned by Richard Weaver, just north of the recording studio, became our first home.

In my third year of college, I settled into a better study routine and began enjoying my history, church history, and political science courses. Allen Grant Stoltzfus became a philosophizing buddy, introducing me to intriguing books and ideas beyond my knowledge base. In the 1964-65 school year, I was elected to the Faculty Student Senate and then chair. No doubt the purpose of the organization was to connect students and faculty. As a campus leader I was invited to join the national student campaign for Lyndon Baines Johnson for president. Then Dean of Students Laban Peachey invited me to be the editor of *The Weather Vane* for the 1965-66 year. I was not known as a writer, nor had I served on the WV staff. I think Peachey's intention was to rein me in a bit.

It was during this year that we learned that Myron Augsburger would become the college president in 1965. Myron's appointment created anticipation for great change at EMC.

My senior year was busy with the WV editorship with Stuart Showalter as assistant editor, plus the usual struggle with what one will do after graduating from college. During my final semester at EMC, I began gathering information from various seminaries but was not sure that seminary was for me. The war in Vietnam was going strong. Since I had a draft lottery number that indicated a good chance of my being drafted, Hannah and I explored some Voluntary Service (VS) opportunities in the U.S. During the summer of 1966, we were accepted as program directors at Spruce Lake Retreat in Canadensis, Pennsylvania, in the Pocono Mountains. After the summer we became the VS unit leaders at Mennonite Community Chapel, 1113 West Eighteenth Street in Chicago.

CHICAGO: JOINING THE COMPETITION

Our VS unit, supervised by Ken Seitz for the Mennonite Board of Missions (MBM), now Mennonite Mission Network (MMN), was made up of mostly young men performing alternate service. However, it included Esther Allebach (now Kauffman), and we also benefited from the counsel of Sadie Oswald, a long-time Chicago missionary from Shickley, Nebraska, who probably knew more about urban ministry than most ordained men. Also, we were soon joined by Vernice Begley and his family from the Associated (now Anabaptist) Mennonite Biblical Seminary (AMBS). The unit members lived above the Mennonite Community Chapel and worked at the Chicago Rehabilitation Center, providing support for the unit.

As a recent idealistic college graduate, I felt ready to solve all the world's problems. Moving around this old European, African-American, and Hispanic area, I looked for community project ideas. As we played with the children, we learned that many of them were hungry, and so we informally provided them with snacks. In the evenings some of us played pool at one of the local billiard halls. The Hispanics, however, suspected that we were Immigration and Naturalization Service (INS) agents.

During the 1960s, Lawrence Horst was pastoring the Evanston Mennonite Church, which had been started, I believe, to minister to the large number of 1-W men working at the Evanston Hospital. Since I had been a Bible major, Lawrence invited me to preach at Evanston several times when he needed to be absent. I give credit to Lawrence Horst and Sadie Oswald for tutoring me in urban ministry.

During this year, I fondly recall an event with Professor Ed Stoltzfus, who brought a group of students from Goshen Biblical Seminary (GBS) to learn about urban ministry. Vernice Begley and I met with Ed and the students to describe Mennonite Community Chapel's work in the local environment. My recollection is of Ed's quizzing us about urban ministry as only Ed can quiz.

Perhaps it was the quizzing and numerous other events during the year that led me to realize that I had no idea what I was doing. The unit dynamics, however, caused Hannah and me to resign—with regret since the unit had struggled with leadership before we came and we had hoped to bring the needed correctives. Selective Service then approved my employment at Evanston Hospital as a surgical technician, and Hannah accepted a sequence of positions until she became the administrative assistant to an executive of CF Industries, Central Farmers Fertilizer Company. Hannah's excellent employment in Chicago until my graduation from law school in January 1972 was a great gift.

In 1967 several of us participated in a civil rights peace march from State and Wacker Streets south on State to the Chicago Coliseum, where Martin Luther King Jr. and others spoke. I had created a simple poster board sign with the slogan, "Mennonites Support Peace." As I reflect on this event, I recognize the arrogance of saying "Mennonites Support Peace" when I had no authority to speak for Mennonites. However, we shared the desire to support King's civil rights and peace and justice stance.

During 1968, I supported the Eugene McCarthy campaign for President. In the area of Chicago north of the Loop, I became a precinct worker for the campaign, going door to door with literature and registration material. A regret or a blessing, depending on one's vantage point, was not being present for the 1968 Democratic Convention. Since Hannah and I had planned a vacation in Pennsylvania in August, we thus missed the convention and the ensuing protests of that week. During the next several years, I was a spectator in the courtroom trials of the Chicago 8 on the charges stemming from their Democratic Convention demonstrations.

Sometime during our sojourn in Chicago, I began searching for what to do after my service was completed in September 1968. My brother John had once suggested, "Why don't you take the LSAT and try law school?" Being somewhat of a contrarian and needing to be distinct professionally from anyone else in the Lapp family, I took the LSAT. Chicago had several schools with day and night programs with almost open enrollment policies. I ended up at the Chicago-Kent College of Law in January 1969. (Chicago-Kent soon thereafter became associated with the Illinois Institute of Technology.) Since the company where Hannah worked was near that law school, we could commute together.

Those who recall the old movie *Paper Chase* will understand how I experienced law school. The Socratic method with professors intimidating students was the pedagogy of the day for this school. (By the end of the first semester, about half of my classmates, who were from diverse backgrounds, had dropped out.) Classes were in the morning, so after lunch I would go to the County Law Library, on the twentieth floor of the Civic Center, to study. I was able to develop a good routine of study, which usually did not require late nights. I studied the subjects at hand, whether they were contracts, torts, or criminal, property, or constitutional law. I did not make any attempt to introduce theology into the equation since my goal was to become a full-fledged lawyer somewhere.

For several years Hannah and I took an unplanned sabbatical from church. Once, I distinctly recall walking in the Chicago Loop past some Amish folks and saying to the Jewish classmates with me, "Those are my people." Though not Amish, I could openly acknowledge a connection to our common heritage. I knew the Mennonite attitude toward the use of law from observing Dad work through the Benner case without the use of a lawsuit and also the Derstine lawsuit brought against the Franconia Conference, bishops, ministers, and trustees. At this time, my young adult life philosophy was still an unwritten book—the pages were in many ways still blank waiting for my pen.

Getting close to the end of law school meant asking again, "Now what do I do?" During my several years of law school, I had interviewed with attorneys I knew in the Mennonite world, among whom was R. Wayne Clemens, a Franconia Conference Mennonite attorney and friend of several of my brothers. He opened the door to my joining his practice in Souderton; as time drew nearer, I decided to accept his invitation.

REJOINING THE FAMILY BUSINESS

Hannah and I moved into a duplex in Souderton, and I immediately began a cram course for the Pennsylvania bar exam. I had already missed about ten days of the course, which went from 6:00 to 10:00 five nights a week for eight weeks. I began commuting to Philadelphia, leaving about 6:30 a.m. from the Souderton station. In the morning I listened to tapes of the programs I had missed; in the afternoon I crammed for the evening sessions. After a quick light dinner I attended the evening lectures and took the last train back home. The bar exam was scheduled in Philadelphia for the two days before

Good Friday in March 1972. I recall taking the exam, coming home to pack a few items, attending Maundy Thursday communion, and then joining Hannah to start driving to Florida—to "crash."

Re-acculturating into the home community offered some challenges, especially to us as a part of the Lapp family. In Chicago we had established an independence and identity separate from family. However, we now returned to attending the Plains Mennonite Church, the congregation where I was raised.

One Monday morning Dad came to me and advised, "Hannah should wear a covering to church."

I replied that she did not have one.

Dad said, "She knows where to get one (implying the Souder Store, which carried such items).

I recall answering, "I don't think it is necessary."

Nothing more was said, but during the next several years, the wearing of the covering became an issue for discussion at the Plains church. The congregation studied and discussed it but never came to an agreement. Eventually the choice became optional, and that conversation ended.

The Practice of Law

Fortunately I passed the bar exam the first time, and I will never forget the relief from that burden. Working now with Wayne Clemens and Jerry Nulty and developing my own clientele, I learned that people were interested in a Christian attorney and that the Mennonite community liked the idea of another Mennonite attorney in town. Being a young Menno attorney in 1972 meant I was sort of adopted immediately as if my degree and license had suddenly made me an authority with power to do many things. The (Old) Mennonite Church in 1972 had fewer than about ten attorneys who were active in the church. (The General Conference Mennonites had more attorneys. Within the next several years dozens of young Mennos graduated from law school.) I think it was my degree that provided the opportunity for me to be appointed to the EMU trustees in 1973. In many ways that appointment as a trustee was the formative training for my future service at EMU—for thirty years, thirteen years as trustee, one year as president-elect, and sixteen years as president.

After a few years of working with others, back in Souderton I found office space as a sole practitioner. Then Elvin Souder, when we met in the Montgomery County Orphans Courtroom, asked if I would be interested in merging my firm with his. The Souder firm had a good reputation and was considered the Mennonite firm; Elvin was a General Conference Mennonite. With the merger, the firm became Souder, Rosenberger, Lapp, and Bricker and remained my legal practice home until I was called to EMU in 1987.

During our fifteen years in eastern Pennsylvania, we became reconnected to family, church, church organizations, and the local community—and thus again to "the family business." Our circle of friends included those associated with the Mennonite world, those that developed through legal circles, and those that just developed. In the Plains Mennonite Church we became part of a small group, and I was elected to the church council.

Church organizations soon invited me, as a young adult in the legal profession, to participate on boards and committees. The Mennonite Board of Missions (MBM) invited me to be on their Health and Welfare Committee, which worked with hospitals and other social service organizations around the country. Franconia Conference invited me to be on the Conference Ministerial Aid Committee. Bishop Luke Stoltzfus in Philadelphia asked me to serve on the Bethany Child Care Center Board in Philadelphia. Several other organizations I worked with were the Clayton Kratz Fellowship, Spruce Lake Retreat, the local Mennonite Disaster Service (MDS) chapter, and the Legal Aid Committee of the Montgomery County Bar Association. In 1973 I was elected as the Mennonite Church Region Five representative to the Eastern Mennonite College Board of Trustees.

Then Don Hedrick, Vernon Jantzi, Art Defehr, Paul Polak, and John Howard Yoder started International Development Enterprises (IDE) as a non-governmental organization to take on projects using USAID funds, which MEDA had at the time declined using. I became the IDE incorporating attorney. At the same time a Canadian counterpart was formed, making the organization binational.

Professionally I soon discerned that legal litigation was not my forte. Most of my legal practice involved matters pertaining to real estate, estate planning and administration, small business legal work, and some domestic relations-family law. I spent a small portion of time as a public defender at preliminary hearings in district courts in Souderton and Schwenksville. However, while I enjoyed being able to work at resolving individual client issues, I did not enjoy domestic-relations work except for one case. The pastors of Branch Fellowship, an independent non-denominational church that was started by several former Mennonites, brought a woman to me with a unique story. After having had a profound Christian experience at Branch, this woman wanted to settle some legal issues: She was in her fourth marriage but had not dissolved any of her previous marriages. Over several months we annulled the second and third marriages (these marriages were void *ab initio* because of the legal first marriage) and then filed a divorce for the first marriage, finally making the fourth marriage automatically legal. I was grateful to have done a worthwhile legal service for someone wanting to start a new life.

The Adoption of Johanna: Our Becoming a Family of Three

With my professional career established, Hannah and I now began to think about adding to our family. Since nature had not provided us with any children and having chosen not to explore the reasons scientifically, we considered an international adoption at Pearl Buck's nearby Welcome House. Several families in the area had also used the Holt Adoption Agency, a Christian organization with offices in Oregon. In 1977 we began the process with Holt and in the fall received a picture of a girl who was about seven and a half and a note reading, "After much prayer and consideration we would like to place Jung Hai Kyung with you." We had asked for a younger child, but how does one say no to such a letter and picture!

Soon after we received the letter, we shared with the congregation that we were expecting a child from Korea. The quiet people of Plains Mennonite erupted in joyous applause for us. February 4, 1978, Johanna Lynn Lapp arrived at the JFK Airport in New York in the wee hours of the morning. The escorts who brought Johanna from the plane checked our papers, placed her in my arms, and left. A new journey of three Lapps thus began. As it happened, on February 5, 1978, a major snowstorm closed the whole region of eastern Pennsylvania. This gave the three of us a few days to begin the family bonding process of introducing Johanna to us and her new life as part of the Lapp family and our Mennonite world and culture.

EMC&S—EMU

In the fall of 1973 I attended my first meeting of the EMC Board of Trustees, consisting of thirty other men plus one woman, A. Grace Wenger—formerly a popular high school English teacher and then dean of college women at EMC. (Her story appears in the second volume of ACRS Memoirs, *Continuing the Journey: The Geography of Our Faith*, pp. 112-134). Several years later, the board elected me chair of the academics committee. As a committee chair I became a member of the executive committee, which consisted of the board chair plus the committee chairs.

During the 1970s, the executive committee and the board worked with Myron Augsburger, a visionary president with the strong goals of growing the college, seminary, and high school. From 1973 to 1986, however, the board of trustees wrestled with a variety of issues. One involved Dan Yutzy, the academic dean, who was part of a new movement among Mennonites—teaching, preaching, and encouraging the gifts of the Holy Spirit as normal, typical expressions of the Christian life. Yutzy, a sociologist by education, was also a powerful preacher in great demand for his sermons on the empowerment of the Holy Spirit. It soon became an issue as to whether Yutzy was a dean or an itinerant preacher. Could EMC afford having two gifted speakers/preachers spending significant time off campus with events not necessarily directly benefiting EMC? After a review of Dean Yutzy's tenure, it was mutually agreed that he would not continue at EMC.

After he left EMC, the search for a new dean began. To buy some time, three highly respected faculty—Daniel Suter, Jesse Byler, and Willard Swartley—were commissioned as an academic triumvirate. This unusual academic team was in place for one year, following which Al Keim was persuaded to assume the deanship. During Al's tenure, he worked at faculty recruitment, faculty compensation increases, and a revision of the faculty contract system.

During the 1970s, a financial event educated all of us. President Augsburger brought to the trustees a vision for upgrading the chapel, and the board authorized the relatively low estimated price. After the chapel renovation had started, reports came of additional renovation needed; the price tag escalated significantly. Since the funds raised were lower than anticipated, corporate reserve funds were used to cover the project. Later in the decade, the bank declined the application for an addition to the college's line of credit: There would be no more extensions without a larger plan by the board to deal with EMC's financial exigencies. In response, the new financial plan allocated a mandatory budgeted 1.5 percent line item in the total annual budget as a reserve. This plan satisfied the concerns of the bank, which restored the line of credit.

It was after this project that President Augsburger introduced architect Leroy Troyer to the trustees. One of the first projects Leroy began for EMC was a rather comprehensive campus master plan. One of its components was an energy audit that resulted in an energy savings plan that continues to this day.

RICHARD C. DETWEILER, A RELUCTANT PRESIDENT

When Myron Augsburger's term was concluding, the board of trustees appointed a presidential search committee in 1979. The board felt that EMC needed a churchman to maintain a close relationship with the church and focused on Richard Detweiler fairly quickly. Since Richard, a pastor and bishop, as well as the former principal of both Franconia Mennonite School and Christopher Dock High School, had been on the EMC campus serving as dean for a year, he was quite well known here.

I understand that Richard turned down the committee twice before finally accepting the call. If he was not a reluctant president, he at least thought of himself as an interim president and thus served only from 1980 to 1987. One of the reasons for his short term was the illness of his wife, Mary Jane, who developed transverse mylitus, which made it difficult for her to walk and sometimes sent her to the University of Virginia Hospital. She persisted, however, in doing her best to entertain the many guests expected in the home of a college president, and Richard was there to help her.

Toward the end of his term, Richard would tick off the various losses—the termination of faculty, an enrollment decline, and in January 1984 a major fire in the administrative building undergoing renovation. Fortunately important records were not lost since the administrative offices had already been relocated. However, the extended period of inadequate facilities during the new campus center construction contributed to the low morale in the college community. With construction occurring in the heart of the campus, student recruitment also had its challenges. Yet throughout the whole time, Richard exhibited and modeled the presidency as a pastoral role.

While I was chair of the board, Richard began to communicate his interest in terminating as president. When his decision was clear, the trustees and the Mennonite Board of Education (MBE) began again the presidential search process, appointing a committee in fall 1985.

Significant Changes at EMC

During the 1970s, Albert Meyer, executive secretary for MBE, had met regularly with the board of trustees, working to have EMC develop a relationship with MBE. After lengthy discussions at many different levels throughout the church, the trustees agreed to have a "Covenant Relationship" with MBE. This meant that while EMC would participate with MBE, it kept a fallback position in the event that a future board would decide again to go alone organizationally. The "Covenant Relationship" simply meant there would be more formal reporting to MBE by EMC.

Al Meyer wanted all the schools to be Mennonite. This meant that the board members needed to be Mennonites, the chief administrators needed to be Mennonites, the faculty needed to be strongly rooted in the Mennonite faith, and the student body should also be largely from Mennonite churches and homes. Al did not waver much from these items as requisites for being Mennonite schools. He spent a lot of time trying to persuade me, as a younger person on the trustees and vice chair, that EMC should become a full participant with MBE.

Several years into his presidency, Richard Detweiler spoke with me about having the trustees fully join MBE as a sister school with Hesston, Goshen, and AMBS. To accomplish this, we realized major organizational change would be required. When it appeared that there would be support for this change, it also seemed this would be an appropriate time for EMHS to become a separate corporate entity. Since no other high schools were part of the MBE structure, this would allow EMHS to be a true Virginia Mennonite Conference school. The reorganization occurred about 1982. I had the responsibility of asking all thirty-two trustees to resign, with MBE agreeing to appoint twelve of the thirty-two as the new board of trustees. If I recall correctly, only one trustee felt hurt not to be chosen to the new board. I was reappointed and re-elected as chair.

In the early 1980s and until the fall of 1987, EMC experienced annual declines in enrollment. Administrators advised that the decline in the demographic number of Mennonite college-age students meant our enrollment projections needed to be adjusted down. I was not very happy with these reports. This was the same period that Messiah College was growing by leaps and bounds with many Mennonite students.

Other factors contributed to unease. Competition and conflict occurred after Richard appointed two vice presidents, one for administration, one for academics. Faculty felt they were suffering all the budget cuts from declining enrollment. Administrators felt they needed more funds to raise contribution dollars to improve student recruitment marketing. Richard agonized over the divided house.

Then in time for the 1983 Mennonite Church Assembly in Bethlehem, Pennsylvania, George R Brunk II wrote a pamphlet titled *Crises in Mennonite Higher Education*. This widely circulated pamphlet caused great consternation in Mennonite higher education, especially at EMC&S. As a former dean of the seminary, George had influence with a significant constituency in the Mennonite church. During the 1983 Assembly, several sessions were held for George's voice and others to be heard. Richard now had another significant burden: dealing with the "crises in higher education."

THE SEARCH FOR A NEW PRESIDENT

The trustees appointed a presidential search committee in fall 1985. Owen Burkholder, pastor of Park View Mennonite Church (PVMC) at the time, agreed to chair the committee, and recently retired science professor Daniel Suter agreed to serve as staff for the committee. The committee included trustees, alumni, faculty, and

MBE and church representatives. As chair of the board, I was involved in the formation of the committee and in the establishment of some of the selection criteria. However, once some of the initial decisions were made, I was no longer involved with the work of the search committee.

In the early part of 1986 I had expressed to Hannah some boredom with the practice of law. When an opportunity arose to participate in a Witness for Peace team to Nicaragua in the early spring of 1986, I decided to apply for membership on this team. I began reading about the Contra War and the U.S. involvement. In addition, I tried to learn about MCC and Eastern Mennonite Mission's participation in the region. My brother Sam, who had spent some time in Honduras, encouraged me to participate in this peace action.

Almost exactly one week before my scheduled two-week trip to Nicaragua, I received a letter from Daniel Suter, asking me to allow my name to be advanced as a presidential candidate for EMC. I cannot say emphatically enough that this was one of the biggest surprises of my life. My family of highly educated people would not have even thought of a lawyer as EMC's college president. Hannah's response was, "You are restless in your profession. Why not at least go through the process? Furthermore, you have never had to go through rigorous employment screening as I have, so this would be good experience." This was wise counsel.

My first call was to Virginia Schlabach, a fellow trustee and a member of the search committee. My purpose was to explain that the committee's invitation was far from my mind; I was leaving for Nicaragua in a few days. She did not give me any information except to say I should try to answer some of the questions, even if briefly. My second call was to Gerald Studer, my pastor at Plains Mennonite. I indicated to Gerald that my biggest fear was that I would lose some friends. Gerald seemed speechless, clearly not sure that I, a lawyer, was presidential material. I did not feel comfortable discussing the invitation with any of my family, not even Dad.

Hannah agreed that if I would write some brief responses to the questions posed, she would type a letter for me. With Hannah's assistance I put a letter together and again immersed myself in the world of Nicaragua and Witness for Peace orientation. Shortly after I returned from Nicaragua, another letter arrived from Daniel Suter, asking for more information. Then a request came for an interview with the committee. During this time of processing, I was still chair of the trustees. It was not clear yet as to the committee's decision. I continued to feel as if another candidate would surface. Since I considered myself the darkest of dark horses, I said nothing to my law practice partners. Each step along the way I asked the search committee for assurance that they were not playing with me.

Finally, in summer 1986, the trustees and the constituent conferences committee (CCC) called Hannah and me to a special meeting. At this meeting I submitted my resignation as chair and as a member of the board of trustees. The members of each group then individually and jointly approved my nomination as a recommendation to the Mennonite Board of Education, which sent approval several weeks later. In August 1986 I was presented to the EMC&S community as the president-elect.

An important part of the presidential search process was to provide a new president with a period of preparation. Since my appointment was made in August 1986, the plan gave me six months to transition from my professional law practice. I left my practice as of December 31, 1986. In January 1987 I began six months of studies, many of which dealt with issues of higher education. I spent three weeks at AMBS for a seminary course, one week at The Fuller School of Theology for a course, several weeks on the EMC campus living in the dorm for student orientation, and three weeks at Carnegie Mellon University for its program in Higher Education Administration. I gleaned and adopted as my own two principles from that period of preparation: a strategic plan should fit on the back of an envelope; landscaping is academically relevant.

I felt warmly received by the college and seminary community. Through my experience on the board of trustees, I knew that there were good administrators to work with. However, it did not take me long to indicate that I would prefer a different administrative model. I appointed a cabinet of the following: Lee Snyder, vice president and academic dean; George Brunk III, vice president and dean of the seminary; Ron Piper, vice president for finance; David F. Miller, vice president of advancement; Peggy Landis, vice president for student life; Peggy Shenk, assistant to the president; and a new vice president for enrollment management.

President Lapp with his spouse Hannah receives an original Fraktur created by his father, John E. Lapp, commemorating his son's inauguration September 19, 1987.

Later Bob Bontrager, Marie Morris, Bill Hawk, Beryl Brubaker, Daryl Peifer, and Richard Gunden were part of the cabinet for a time. These persons were very supportive and capable in their assignments, and they worked hard to move EMC&S forward. I soon acknowledged Lee as the person in charge when I was away. George was second lieutenant. However, the whole team was generally part of the decision-making process.

It was clear to me that major effort would be required to reverse the enrollment decline. This meant having staff to work hard to counter the Mennonite demographics that showed declining numbers of college age young adults available to recruit.

Although the weather for the weekend of the inauguration in fall 1987 was rainy, the event was a celebration. During the planning, some students had protested about the expense of the event. Dr. Lamar Kopp, a trustee and faculty member at Penn State University, gave a wonderful address, reminding the audience that by the beginning of the twenty-first century, EMC needed to be prepared to educate the children beginning kindergarten that fall of 1987. My father, though his health was fragile, offered a moving prayer of benediction. He prayed to the God of Abraham and Sarah, Isaac and Rebecca, and our Lord Jesus Christ, with many wonderful words of blessing. His prayer hovered over me then and continued to be a source of energy for a long time. Many persons remember nothing other than Dad's prayer from this weekend. A wonderful concert led by Ken J. Nafziger for the guests and campus community climaxed the weekend.

THE HIGH AND LOW POINTS OF MY TENURE AS PRESIDENT

My ongoing goals were the challenges to recruit more students, raise the number of contributed dollars, raise faculty salaries, improve facilities, maintain good constituent relations, maintain an excellent academic program, and recruit faculty and staff with excellent credentials and commitment to the mission of EMU. Changing the community's inferiority complex—the sense that Goshen and Messiah were always better—was also a goal. This did change, not as a named strategic initiative but something I identified as part of the institutional psyche that needed to change.

I looked for potential sources of new revenue consistent with the mission of EMU: the Adult Degree Completion Program; summer use of facilities for conferences; and graduate programs in counseling, conflict transformation, business, education, and clinical pastoral education. I also promoted the development of the Shenandoah Bach Festival as a means of enhancing community relations.

However, several tragedies occurred in the first six months of the 1991. First, the death of the campus pastor, who suddenly took his life because of severe depression, rocked the college and seminary. Two weeks later a Sunday night call came from Leon Stauffer in Lancaster, about the murders of Dr. Clair and Anna Mae Weaver and their daughter, allegedly by their son. Leon asked me to tell the Weavers' son Steve, studying at EMC, about this tragedy.

On my way to the newly constructed apartment building on Mt. Clinton Pike, I was praying about what to say. I found Steve Godshall, Steve Byler, and several others and asked for their help. With these fellows present, I informed Steve and them as much as I knew, leaving us all in a state of shock. Several weeks after that, another student died

President Lapp receives a blanket from Marilyn Hudson as a gift in recognition of EMU's returning Native American artifacts. Mandan elder Edwin Benson watches next to Joseph Lapp.

while at home, seemingly without any explanation. Then about the middle of that semester, a faculty member breached professional conduct standards and was given a leave of absence. Later in June a local businessman and friend, Perry Brunk, died in a plane crash. Needless to say, this was a very difficult six months.

More positively, the beginning of the decade of the 1990s saw discussion regarding the administration of the planned MA in Counseling. With the advent of graduate programs, I began to think EMC could become a university. The first time I mentioned this casually to the trustees, one laughed. Later Hannah gave me a miniature pewter train with an engine pulling three cars with the letters "EMU." Several days after a regular board meeting, Don Kraybill, the board chair, called. "I think we should do this: become a university," he said. Then I knew the change could happen, which it did in 1994. Now it appears this was a good decision.

Architect Leroy Troyer was of major assistance at EMU in continuing to refine the campus master plan and design new facilities. The construction projects included these: outdoor athletics with the turf field; seminary apartments; Park Woods Apartments—replacing the trailer park; the seminary building; Hillside Apartments; an addition to the Physical Plant building; excavation-renovation under the Planetarium for psychology; the North Lawn Residence renovation; the purchase of properties between Mt. Clinton Pike and Dogwood Drive; repurchase of several properties south of Mt. Clinton Pike for the Center of Justice and Peacebuilding (CJP); construction of the University Commons; and the purchase of properties north to Parkway Drive and between College Avenue and Park Road. Attempts to complete a theater building, however, seemed continually out of reach.

MY THIRD CAREER: FINANCIAL SERVICES

In my last several years at EMU, Howard Brenneman, then president of Mennonite Mutual Aid (MMA), indicated that whenever I wanted to make a change to let him know since MMA was interested in having staff with law degrees. Anticipating my submission of resignation at EMU, I asked Howard about a possible position in the Harrisonburg region in 2003.

Thus in summer 2003 I began employment with Everence (formerly MMA) as a Trust and Foundation Representative. I completed licensure to be a financial advisor with the assignment of servicing and developing investment accounts and charitable services. Originally I traveled from Virginia to Florida. Currently, I serve as the managing director for the Everence Harrisonburg core market. This new profession combines my law training and my community and church relationships. With its mission of being a unique faith-based financial organization that assists persons to integrate their faith values with their financial decisions, Everence is an excellent way for me to continue in the family business.

In the last several years I have also served on several church boards: MennoMedia; Eastern Mennonite School; Harrisonburg District Council of Virginia Mennonite Church; Virginia Mennonite Conference Constitution and Bylaws Committee; and the Park View Mennonite Church Council.

When I was first considering a title for this memoir, I thought it would be "By Birthright or by Choice or by Divine Call" until my brother-in-law Willard Swartley said ,"It is not *or* but *and*." I knew immediately that he was correct. I have had what one could say is the opportunity of a lifetime: by birthright, by choice *and* by divine call.

Is it, however, appropriate to identify service with the church and church institutions as *business* or even as *family business*? When I first heard comments about my being in the family business, I took offense at the idea but then realized it made sense and embraced it. My family of origin has given me many opportunities. My parents and all my siblings have been great mentors and encouragers.

Yet along the way, as my story shows, I had choices to make. Many persons hope for one opportunity. I have had the privilege to contribute significantly in three distinct professional roles: law practice; education administration; and financial services. Each profession has been connected indirectly; in each I have seen the role for practicing Christian discipleship in unique ways. I think of my life as a long journey of working with the community of faith to continue the building of God's kingdom for this time and place. At the same time, I recognize that future generations will revise, recreate, and make additions to what all of us do individually in our allotted time.

It is only by the grace and mercy of God that I have been able to make a small contribution. It is all done because this is God's kingdom. It is all done through God's power, and it is all done for God's glory!

April 2013
Revised November 2015

W. Robert McFadden

War and Peace Researcher and Professor

W. Robert McFadden, whose father was a Church of the Brethren minister and pacifist in World War II, focused his research on attitudes toward war. At Manchester College he majored in peace studies. At Boston University his dissertation topic was nuclear pacifism. During his years of heading the Philosophy and Religion Department at Bridgewater College and planning the convocations, he continued this exploration. He participated in many seminars and after retirement taught in JMU's Lifelong Learning Institute.

W. ROBERT MCFADDEN

My Journey as a Thinker, Scholar, and Teacher

DETERMINING MY PEACE POSITION

My father was ordained as a minister at the Paradise Church of the Brethren in Ohio in 1926 at age twenty-two. He was a pacifist during World War II, and my brothers and I learned that perspective and adopted it as our own. I was the only boy in my high school sophomore class who did not buy war stamps or help collect scrap iron. Instead, I bought Brethren Service Committee certificates to help support the Civilian Public Service (CPS) camps and the conscientious objectors housed there. However, I played first trumpet in the high school band; on more than one occasion, I was called out of an afternoon class to play taps when the body of a soldier was brought home for burial in the local cemetery. I also remember that Dad took the family to the large town square to see the celebration when Japan surrendered in August 1945.

Most of the young men in the Church of the Brethren went into the armed forces in World War II. Lowell Miller, former treasurer of Bridgewater College, indicated in an article in the fall 2011 *Bridgewater College Magazine* that he had first registered as a conscientious objector.[1] Six months later, when he was drafted, he decided that, "If no one was willing to fight, we couldn't prevent them from attacking us." Thereupon, he changed his classification and entered the army as a combat engineer. He fought in Italy and later was sent to the Pacific to prepare for the invasion of Japan. His home congregation was the Greenmount Church of the Brethren congregation north of Harrisonburg.

Miller was one of the eighty percent of Brethren young men who joined the armed forces during World War II. Ten percent went into medical service and ten percent entered CPS camps or went to prison as conscientious objectors. After the war, all were accepted back into the church with no disciplinary action. Pastors like my father had maintained contact with members of their congregations, whether in the armed forces or in conscientious objector camps.

During my senior year at Manchester College in Indiana, I heard Andrew Cordier, Assistant to the Secretary General of the United Nations and an ordained minister in the Church of the Brethren, speak at the college on October 27, 1950. He described the role he had played in bringing nations together to respond to the North Korean invasion of South Korea. He said that one had to use social, political, and economic means as well as military means to respond to North Korea.

The first article that I published was a response to that address by Cordier.[2] In it I said that the Church of the Brethren presented a confusing picture to its youth because several different theological stances formed the basis of the so-called "peace position." I identified three such positions.

First, there was *nonresistance*. The Annual Conference in 1785 had said that "the higher powers bear the sword of justice, punishing the evil and protecting the good. . . . But the sword [belongs] to the kingdom of the world. . . ."[3] Yet Christ told his disciples that he had chosen them from the world.[4] The doctrine of nonresistance, I wrote, presupposes that we take literally the teachings of the Sermon on the Mount, that in no way are Christ's disciples to use the sword. Even so, we recognize the government's God-given right to use the sword while we bear witness to a way of perfect love.

Second, there was the position of *nonviolence*. This, I explained, was quite different from *nonresistance*. According to this view, coercion in nonviolent forms is needed to fight evil and to achieve desired political and social goals. It offers a basic change in attitude toward the state. The Social Gospel movement of the 1920s and 1930s maintained that the church should combat evil in society, the state, and the culture. The Brethren were emerging from their sectarian cocoon to do just that. Mahatma Gandhi and Martin Luther King Jr. advocated nonviolence as the way to bring about social change. Gordon Shull, in his article "The Pilgrimage of an Ex-Pacifist," asked if we were refugees from history.[5] This position asserted that we were not.

A third position that developed among the Brethren was *vocational pacifism*. About this position, Reinhold Niebuhr observed that while the church must choose between totalitarianism and war, he also saw the value of a minority witness to the ideals of Jesus in the Sermon on the Mount. He called it a *perfectionistic ethic*. Some, he said, are called to take a pacifist position even though all cannot do so.[6]

The statements of the Annual Conference in 1957 and later conferences implied that we must respect conscience regardless of stance. The Brethren Volunteer Service (BVS) provided a pacifist program of service for those who chose to follow their consciences by rejecting any kind of killing in warfare; it was designed for those who felt called of God to take an uncompromising stand against the sinfulness of war.

By the time I went to graduate school at Boston University, I was still writing and thinking a great deal about war and peace. In the summer of 1959 I took classes at Garrett Theological Seminary in Evanston, Illinois. A class on the life and teachings of Soren Kierkegaard was taught by Gordon Michalson, the brother of Carl Michalson, a well-known theologian at Drew University. The paper I wrote for that class was titled "On Kierkegaard and the Nuclear Dilemma."[7] Dr. L. Harold DeWolf had already made clear his position as a nuclear pacifist.

In my essay, I argued that DeWolf's nuclear pacifism represented a new stage in thinking about war. An all-out nuclear war could never achieve the goals of just war theory. The human race could never again go through a cataclysm such as World War II and survive. Thus, we must learn to handle conflict without using all the destructive tools at our disposal. Like the rattlesnake, we must engage in conflict without biting one another. After all, if rattlesnakes bit one another in fighting, they would exterminate their own species. Nuclear pacifists said that it was wrong not only to use weapons of mass destruction but also to possess them for deterrent purposes. In contrast, the nuclear realists said that they could be possessed but not used. However, possession implied willingness to use them, as those who flew the B-52s and manned the ICBM missile silos could tell you! Thus, there existed both a paradox and a dilemma.

I connected the nuclear dilemma with the views Soren Kierkegaard expressed in *Fear and Trembling*. There Kierkegaard tried to come to grips with God's command to Abraham to sacrifice his son Isaac. He wrote that such a command represented the "teleological suspension of the ethical."[8] In other words, the call to Abraham represented a suspension of the universal ethical command to protect one's children, not kill them. Abraham's action could be understood only as a suspension of God's universal ethical commands. But, I argued, when the incident is seen in the light of historical study, it represents a move from human sacrifice to animal sacrifice. The story is etiological in nature; it is not a story describing a moral hero. The significance of the story is that Abraham went to Mount Moriah a believer in human sacrifice but came down from Mount Moriah no longer believing in human sacrifice. The story explains why the Hebrews believed in a sacrificial system of worship in the temple but opposed the human sacrifice that occurred in surrounding societies.

Similarly, I concluded, while nuclear pacifists had once embraced the principles of just war theory, now they could no longer do so. They had to respond to the need for a new spiritual discipline, a new view of human conflict, and a new perspective on ethics in the human story. The new ethic superseded an older ethic. Unlike the rattlesnake, which acts on instinct, the human race had to act on a new, learned instinct not to destroy itself. We had to learn not to destroy ourselves and human civilization. An all-out war was no longer an option for nations.

Benefiting from Early Experiences

Aside from the continuing challenge of determining my stance on participation in the military, I was early on the recipient of many positive experiences in both town and country and from both Brethren and Mennonite sources. My Burkholder grandparents lived in Smithville and later in Orville, Ohio. My McFadden grandparents had a forty-acre farm between Wooster and Smithville. My father and his parents attended the Paradise Church of the Brethren. The woman who became my mother went with her parents to the Oak Grove Mennonite Church. Both congregations were and still are located just east of Smithville. In 1928, two years after his ordination, my father married my mother. She never forgot the fact that she had to be rebaptized by immersion. Thus, in 1957, when the denomination finally agreed to admit members of other denominations by letter, my father was at the head of those who voted to make the change!

One of three sons, I was born in Smithville, Ohio, in my Burkholder grandparents' home. Smithville had a diner that was famous for its chicken dinners. My Burkholder grandfather was for a time a banker at the only bank in Smithville. One of my Burkholder uncles was the superintendent of the local schools. Nearby Orrville was the home of Smucker's Jellies and Jams. Another uncle on my mother's side was for many years the head cook at Smucker's but none of our relatives was in line to inherit money, and no one in the family thought to buy stock in the company!

My father began as a teacher at Madison High School on the edge of Mansfield, Ohio, having graduated from Manchester College in Indiana. He taught history and penmanship. For training in the latter area, he went to the Zanerian College of Penmanship in Columbus, Ohio, for six weeks in summer 1923 after his first year at Manchester College. He was also a part-time minister. When I finished fourth grade, Dad decided to go to seminary and then enter full-time ministry in the Church of the Brethren. That was in 1939. It was a courageous decision since the country was still in the Depression. His father opposed the move because Dad was on track to become the high school's principal.

I spent my first four years of school in a four-room schoolhouse in Lincoln Heights, Ohio, just outside Mansfield, Ohio. However, when Dad decided to enroll in a seminary, we moved to Michigan City, Indiana, from which he commuted to Chicago on the South Shore Line. The first newspaper headline I remember reading appeared on September 1, 1939: "Germany Invades Poland." At that point I was entering the fifth grade in a school new to me.

After Dad finished seminary, he became pastor of the Troy Church of the Brethren in Ohio, and our family moved to a parsonage just outside the city of Troy, situated about twenty-five miles north of

Dayton, in Miami County. I finished the eighth grade in the county and then attended the high school in Troy, graduating in 1947.

Continuing My Intellectual Journey

Several events stand out as I remember my education at Manchester College, Indiana. First, in my senior year (1950-51) I completed a major in Peace Studies, a program established by Dr. Gladdys Muir in 1948.[9] I was the first major in the program, and two other students, Graydon Snyder and Richard Miller completed a minor. The program included courses such as The Philosophy of Civilization, The Basic Philosophy of Peace, The Techniques and Procedures of Peacemaking, The United Nations, and a reading course. I found it to be a brilliant program and Gladdys Muir an exceptional teacher and mentor.

The second memorable event that happened at Manchester in my intellectual journey was a class taught by Robert H. Miller, who used as our text William Temple's *Nature, Man and God*.[10] For me, it served as a course in basic Christian theology, which was crucial in forming my worldview and laying the groundwork for my continuing growth in Christian theology. Elton Trueblood, the great Quaker philosopher and theologian, had used that book in Earlham College seminars, one of which my father had taken in the late 1940s when he was the pastor at Troy, Ohio. He also thought it was excellent.

The third event that had a lasting influence on me was Andrew Cordier's chapel address, which I mentioned earlier. He was the greatest international civil servant to come out of the denomination.

Inthe fall of 1951, when the Korean War was underway, I entered Bethany Theological Seminary, then in Chicago, Illinois. I had initially registered as a conscientious objector, but my classification was changed to ministerial when I was ordained into the Church of the Brethren ministry that same fall. My draft board in Troy, Ohio, was respectful of my request to go to Europe in summer 1953 and then to extend stay through the fall of that year, thus delaying my last year in seminary. I received my seminary degree in the spring of 1955. I felt that seminary education had given me an excellent background in the history of the Christian church as well as theology.

BEGINNING MY TEACHING CAREER

The spring of 1955 found me serving as interim pastor in the Church of the Brethren in Pampa, Texas. The Ministry Commission of the denomination had arranged for me to be there from April 17 to July 1. I was living in the parsonage and earning $200 a month. I was also becoming accustomed to the windswept plains, sand everywhere, and men who wore cowboy boots to church!

I had been in Texas for about four weeks when I received a letter dated May 12, 1955. The writer, President Calvert Ellis of Juniata College in Huntingdon, Pennsylvania, began, "I was glad to talk with you this morning and to know that you would come to see us on June 9th." The president went on to write that the college could offer me "a salary of $3,600, a room, and meals in the college dining room." In the autumn semester I would be expected to teach four courses: Christian Faith: The Six Basic Doctrines; Church History; The History of Religion, (i.e., World Religions); and Introduction to Philosophy. In the spring semester, I would teach Biblical History, "which is required of all our freshmen."

The president of my Bethany seminary, Paul Robinson, had recommended me for the position. I was to graduate from Bethany at the end of May. However, I would not be present for graduation because I had finished my course work at the end of November 1954 and moved to Pampa, Texas! As I look back on this invitation, the thought of teaching five courses in which I had had minimal training now seems mind-boggling. However, at that time President Ellis thought that a seminary education was sufficient preparation for a person to teach introductory courses at the college level.

That letter changed the course of my life. I taught at Juniata College for three years before going on to graduate school for my doctoral degree, and those three years determined for me my vocation: college teaching. Juniata provided a number of unique experiences. First, I taught Biblical History to 200 freshmen in the spring semester of 1956; every week I delivered two lectures and led ten small discussion groups, each containing twenty students. Thinking I should give some kind of written final exam, I asked the students to define fifty terms in the two-hour exam period. It took me a week to grade those papers. I never again used that test format!

In the second year at Juniata, I proposed to the faculty and then taught a course titled A Theology of Peace. I asked several of my former professors for help. Gladdys Muir, my major professor in peace studies at Manchester College, suggested that I would not learn much from the theologians! She was right. I explored Reinhold Niebuhr's *Christianity and Power Politics*[11] and Umphrey Lee's *The Historic Church and Modern Pacifism*.[12] Both were helpful resources that made an impression on me in my journey toward just war theory.

In my third year at Juniata, I offered the course Philosophy of Religion, in which I used William Temple's *Nature, Man and God*, plus the questions on each chapter provided by Robert H. Miller, my professor at Manchester College. Dean Morley Mays said he had always wanted to read Temple's book and asked to sit in on the class. I felt intimidated, but what could I say? I had three very bright students in the class, and with the help of Dr. Mays, they carried on all the discussions!

WORKING AT ELGIN STATE MENTAL HOSPITAL

Between my time at Pampas, Texas, and my first year of teaching at Juniata College, I spent a month as a student intern at the state mental hospital in Elgin, Illinois. During the summer of 1955, I was one of forty interns in a program for seminary students sponsored by Anton Boisen, the chaplain. We interviewed incoming patients about their religious preferences and conducted worship services in the many wards of the hospital. We were also permitted to attend some of the meetings in which staff discussed releasing patients back into their home environments. I remember conducting a brief committal service for a burial in the state cemetery for a patient who had no family.

Chaplain Boisen led seminar discussions based on his book, *The Exploration of the Inner World*, on the relationships between mental illness and religious experiences. In the introduction, he wrote this significant passage:

> Religious experience as well as mental disorder may involve severe emotional upheaval, and mental disorder as well as religious experience may represent the operation of the healing forces of nature. The conclusion follows that certain types of mental disorder and certain types of religious experience are

alike attempts at reorganization. The difference lies in the outcome.[13]

That seminar formed the lens through which I came to view the religious experience I had undergone a year earlier. On July 14, 1954, I was on the campus of Manchester College in northern Indiana for a committee meeting to plan the upcoming first National Youth Conference at Anderson, Indiana. The previous two years I had felt intense emotional stress, traumatic mental agitation, and uncertainty about my future. My religious life had involved much prayer and soul-searching. During a break in the meetings, I took a walk on a railroad track, which at that time ran through the northern edge of the campus. Out along the tracks, Christ appeared to me at the other end of a field that was adjacent to the tracks. It seemed to me an objective appearance. Recently someone asked me what Christ had said. I answered, "Nothing." But I had a strong feeling that everything would be okay. It was a healing experience. Whether it was a hallucination or

Robert McFadden visits the Gladdys Muir Peace Garden at Manchester University, Indiana, where, as a senior, he was the first to graduate with a major in Peace Studies in 1951. Dr. Muir had established that program in 1948.

reality makes no difference in the perspective of history. For me, it was a landmark that changed the landscape of my spiritual world.

WRITING MY DISSERTATION

When I enrolled in the Boston University School of Theology in 1958, my major professor was L. Harold DeWolf, Professor of Systematic Theology, who was recognized as a just war theologian. Two of the most outstanding pacifists in the country, Walter Muelder and Paul Deats, also taught in the School of Theology. Muelder was dean of the school and Deats was a professor of social ethics. That summer DeWolf preached the sermon "Blind Samson or Christ," in which he argued that under no circumstances could a nuclear war meet the requirements of a just war. In a nuclear war, it is inevitable that "the innocent as well as the guilty are deliberately killed; the resulting evil would far outweigh any good that one could hope to accomplish; and in a nuclear war there is no reasonable hope of victory." He was arguing for unilateral nuclear disarmament, describing a position that became known as *nuclear pacifism* (unpublished manuscript).

When it came time for me to choose a dissertation topic, DeWolf allowed me to write about nuclear pacifism. I turned in the first draft of the dissertation before I left Boston to come to Bridgewater College to teach in 1961. Two months later I received a letter from DeWolf informing me that the dissertation did not fit the university's required format and that the arguments needed more analysis. I had concluded the first draft of the dissertation by quoting German theologians who said that today some Christians must say *yes* to possessing nuclear weapons and that some Christians must say *no* to their possession. To meet the requirements, I had to establish criteria to evaluate the arguments that I had made and reach a conclusion about the validity of those arguments for the nuclear pacifist position. That meant I had to do a different kind of analysis, which took me five years! In the end, I had written a completely new dissertation.

DeWolf had dropped out as first reader when he went on sabbatical leave, so S. Paul Schilling and Nils Ehrenstrom came on as first and second readers. My adopted criteria came from the World Council Study Commission on Faith and Order, on which Dean Muelder was a prominent member. The nuclear pacifists seemed to be saying

"Better Red than dead," and the nationalists seemed to be saying "Better dead than Red." The nuclear realists were saying, or betting on "Neither dead nor Red" as their position. They argued that we should keep the nuclear weapons as a deterrent to war. But the nuclear pacifists insisted that keeping them would inevitably involve their use and the destruction of civilization.

The World Council of Churches debated the issue at the New Delhi Assembly in 1961, and the Roman Catholic Vatican II debated the issue in 1962. Both ended by allowing the *possession* of nuclear weapons but not their *use*. In my dissertation, I evaluated the arguments of both the nuclear pacifists and the nuclear realists. By the time I finished my "new" dissertation in 1966, I was a nuclear realist.

TEACHING AT BRIDGEWATER COLLEGE

When I came to Bridgewater College in 1961, William Willoughby was head of the Philosophy and Religion (P&R) Department, and David Metzler was the other full-time department member. A year later Willoughby headed to Europe for four years with Brethren Voluntary Service, and Metzler went to Boston for four years to complete a doctoral program. Bob Wagoner, who was involved in a Harvard graduate program, and William Beahm, retired dean at Bethany Theological Seminary, joined the P&R faculty. That fall, in a sidewalk conversation, Bob Wagoner said to President Warren Bowman, "When are you going to appoint McFadden as acting head of the department?" And thus I became the department's acting head.

Faculty changes, eight in all, occurred every year for the next eight years. In the fall of 1970, Steve Watson joined the Philosophy and Religion faculty, and I became department chair. For the next twenty-five years, McFadden, Metzler, and Watson formed the continuing base of this faculty. Six others worked part time during those years. Martha Thornton taught part time in the department from 1968-86.

For me, those eight years of transition, with the coming and going of faculty members, meant arranging class assignments to accommodate the changing interests of the faculty members. In 1970 Bill Willoughby moved to the University of Laverne, and Steve Watson joined the faculty. Watson taught the philosophy courses, and I focused on Old Testament studies, biblical archaeology (after Martha Thornton retired in 1986), the study of the historical Jesus, and logic. The logic course always received highly positive student evaluations. In it the students solved problems, put them on the blackboard, and had them corrected by their fellow students. It was an enjoyable experience. The last couple of years I taught five sections of Old Testament; after Metzler retired, I taught a course in general church history. Planning convocations counted as one course, and I continued in that position until two years before I retired in 1998. My nephews even honored me with a T-shirt bearing the inscription "Captain Convo!"

Planning College Convocations

For thirty-five years I was director of convocations at Bridgewater College. When I arrived on campus on Labor Day weekend in 1961, I found, in my small office on the second floor of Founders Hall a note from my predecessor: "I have scheduled President Bowman for the first chapel, Nelson T. Huffman to lead a hymn sing for the second chapel, and you for the third chapel. There is a man scheduled to come from the Richmond WCTU in October. It would be unwise to have him here." I immediately wrote to the WCTU representative that we had changed our programming and that it would no longer suit to have him on campus.

Learning that there were two chapels scheduled each week, one on Monday and the other on Wednesday, I quickly established Monday's chapel as an educational program and Wednesday's chapel as a worship service. In the spring of 1967, following a Monday morning worship chapel, the students staged a well-planned demonstration filled with signs and speeches on the campus in front of the library. One sign in big, bold letters read "Forced Prayer Unfair." In response, I changed the policy; from then on, all the programs would be educational in nature, and all of them would be known as convocations and carry credit for attendance.

As the years went by, I carried a notebook with me all year, even on vacation, keeping track of program suggestions. (My father had taught me that technique as he planned sermons.) Of course, I was planning programs during the civil rights revolution, the Vietnam

War, and the turbulent period of student demonstrations, teach-ins, and social unrest. Small four-year colleges across the country were eliminating their required chapel services. The fact that we at Bridgewater College made our convocations part of the educational program and kept them of interest to most students saved our program. The faculty allowed the convocations to be scheduled during a prime morning class hour, and that choice also made a big difference. Scheduled lyceum programs and the endowed lecturers' program carried convocation credit; their inclusion immensely enriched and enlarged the scope of the convocations.

It was not hard to find outstanding speakers. Since Washington, D.C., was not far away, speakers from there could drive to Bridgewater the night before or fly into the Shenandoah Valley airport on the day of their presentation. Many were eager to get their message across. Those who had recently retired sometimes had fascinating stories to tell. Other suggestions came from newspapers, committee members, other faculty, students, and neighboring institutions. Of course, we also had "homegrown" programs from talented faculty and students. For two convocations in the 1960s we had Robert Short present his slide show "The Gospel According to Peanuts." Twice we had Myron Augsburger, then president of Eastern Mennonite College, as a keynote speaker.

Once, when the scheduled speaker had to cancel because of illness, he suggested a person to take his place: Ted Glick, a student who had been part of the "Harrisburg Seven," who had poured blood on the Selective Service files and served time in prison. Ted was a member of the Glick clan, well known in the Shenandoah Valley. His father, Wayne Glick, was president of Keuka College in New York (and later of Bangor Theological Seminary in Maine). I thought what he had to say would interest the students and be educational.

I knew having him speak at Bridgewater College would be controversial, but I decided to go ahead. I had the announcements mimeographed first thing on Monday morning and placed in the college post office boxes. (As I remember, that particular convocation was scheduled for a Tuesday morning.) Then I went to President Geisert's office to tell him what was going to happen. He was so upset that his lower jaw trembled when he spoke, and he instructed the publicity office to provide no coverage whatsoever of the event. Then he left town for a planned meeting. We were both right. The students were quite interested in Ted's story, and some of their parents wrote letters of displeasure to Dr. Geisert.

Overall, however, I had the full support of the president. That was the only way that I could have operated. I was directly responsible to him, not to the Council on Education, the dean, the provost, or the convocations committee. Thus, I did not have to clear all the programs with another person or council or committee. Seeking clearance for twenty programs a term would have been a nightmare. Of course, we had regular convocation committee meetings, and I always sought the advice and counsel of its members.

Enjoying Educational Opportunities and Travel

Additional educational experiences were important to me throughout my teaching career. They made possible some of the articles that I wrote and some of the classes that I taught. For example, I was a member of a four-person team from Bridgewater College that participated in a summer seminar on Chinese studies at Pugwash, Nova Scotia, from August 8-18, 1965. Persons from the Chinese Studies Department at Columbia University led four teams in the ten-day seminar on classic philosophers from ancient China.

Seven years later, when Bridgewater initiated a 3-3-1-3 calendar, including an Interterm offering, I decided to offer as an Interterm course Ancient Chinese Philosophy, based on a reading of classics by Lao Tzu, Chuang Tzu, Mo Tzu, Han Fei Tzu, Confucius, Mencius, and Hsun Tzu. During the three-week interterm, seventeen students and I would meet each morning in the north end of the second floor of the library. Their grades would reflect their oral contributions to the discussions. Everyone in the class did the initial grading; I had the final say. The Pugwash conference had originally been set up to promote non-Western studies in American liberal arts colleges, and this class was my contribution to that goal.

A second major educational opportunity was a two-month trip to India (June 20-August 15, 1971) for an introduction to the cultural, political, historical, economic, and educational concerns in that country. This summer study, sponsored by the U.S. government and the Kansas City Regional Council for Higher Education, turned out to be an incredibly informative venture, which had a direct impact on convocation programming at Bridgewater College.

In 1978 I took a half-year sabbatical to spend April and May at the Tantur Ecumenical Institute, halfway between Jerusalem and Bethlehem. I followed the advice of Ursula Niebuhr, who had lived there for a while; she told me to get outside, not to spend my time in the library! I would go into East Jerusalem with the mail car after breakfast, walk in the Old City for an hour, and then go back to Tantur on the Arab bus that ran to Bethlehem. I also went on every field trip that was available.

In the summer of 1980, I was one of twelve faculty members to participate in a National Endowment for the Humanities (NEH) Seminar at Yale University: Biblical History in Its Near Eastern Setting, directed by William Hallo, Professor of Assyriology and Babylonian Literature. He was also curator of the collection of 40,000 Babylonian clay tablets at Yale. My personal project was to compare the book of the prophet Micah to the Babylonian literary sources. My completed article, "Micah and the Problem of Continuities and Discontinuities in Prophecy," compared the book of Micah with reports of the "diviners" of ancient Mesopotamia.[14]

In 1985, I again went to Jerusalem and the Holy Land as part of an Ecumenical Holy Land Seminar directed by Dr. Walt Wegner. This experience provided insights into the Holy Land and included travel to significant archaeological sites. We stayed in the residential facilities of the Patriarchate of the Greek Catholic Church in Old Jerusalem, and lectures and travel filled every day from June 18-July 10 that summer.

In the summer of 1986, I was a participant at the University Museum of the University of Pennsylvania in a six-week-long American Schools of Oriental Research (ASOR) seminar. Entitled "A Summer Institute in Near East Archaeology," it featured experts in four different areas of study. Its purpose was to provide a chronological review of how archaeology has revealed and illuminated the development of civilization in Syria-Palestine—the Ancient Near East.

Starting in 1987, I taught biblical archaeology during the Bridgewater College interterm and continued offering that interterm course until I retired in 1998. During this time, I also wrote an article that summarizes archaeological discoveries and their significance for biblical study.[15] One of the best textbooks used in this course was Keith Schoville's *Biblical Archaeology in Focus*.[16]

I have not married, but also during this period, on November 24, 1996, Glenna Wampler and I established a relationship. We have been supporting partners and special friends ever since.

REFLECTING UPON OLD TESTAMENT STUDIES

I taught Old Testament for over forty years, first at Juniata College for three years and then at Bridgewater College for thirty-seven years. The first course that I taught in the Lifelong Learning Institute (LLI) at JMU in 2000 was Introduction to the Old Testament. (Although the church of which I am a member has always claimed to be a "New Testament Church," I never thought that view limited study to the New Testament.)

Now as then, I do not approach the Old Testament by trying to explain the warfare that is part of the Scripture. I do not start with the premise that "all war is sin." Rather I start with these questions: "When is war right?" and "What is right in war?" How one views the continuing conflict that has always been a part of human history makes a difference. It is a part of biblical history as well. There are "good empires" in the Old Testament (Israel under King David, the Persian empire), and "evil empires" (both the Assyrian empire as described in Nahum and the later days of Solomon's empire as recorded in 1 and 2 Kings).

The first course I took in biblical studies was at Manchester College. Robert H. Miller used as textbooks Elmer W. K. Mould's *Essentials of Bible History*[17] and *The Bible: An American Translation*.[18] My Old Testament teacher in seminary, Floyd Mallot, took this approach: "The Old Testament is Oriental history—neither matter-of-fact history nor Oriental myth." His view grew out of his years of missionary work in Africa and his understanding of Middle Eastern thinking as opposed to Western thinking. For me, studying under such teachers, the Bible came alive and remains so.

I also read William Foxwell Albright's *From the Stone Age to Christianity*.[19] The leading archaeologist and Old Testament scholar in the United States at the time, Albright was a linguist and the founder of an American school of thought regarding the Old Testament. His students included G. Ernest Wright, who later taught at the Harvard Divinity School, where I sat in his graduate seminar for majors while I was at Boston University. A second generation of that school of thought included William Dever, one of the instructors at the ASOR seminar at the University of Pennsylvania in the summer of 1986. Richard Elliott Freedman's *Who Wrote the Bible?*[20] is a continuing exposition of that school of thought. I wrote an essay for my LLI class about what I considered to be a major focus for Old Testament study today and for the course I taught at Bridgewater College. The essay was later published as an article.[21]

CONFRONTING THE CONFLICT OVER CIVIL RIGHTS

My public high school, Van Cleve High School in Troy, Ohio, was integrated; but not everyone in Ohio, I learned, agreed with that policy. One of the band members was "Doc" Bradford, an African-American who was a trumpet player and also an outstanding football player and a track team member. I played the trumpet and sat beside "Doc." At a district band contest in Springfield, Ohio, we took our lunch break together and decided on a small restaurant. However, no one there would serve us. As we left, I told the manager that he was "not a very good American!"

At Manchester College, my senior roommate was Larry Wong, a Chinese-American who had served in World War II. He was a strong advocate of civil rights for all races. From 1958 to 1961 I did my doctoral work at Boston University School of Theology, where Martin Luther King Jr. had received his doctoral degree a few years earlier. When the Montgomery Bus Boycott occurred, everyone in that seminary community was well aware of what "their" graduate was doing! Many students and graduates, some from the south, became involved in the civil rights movement.

After arriving at Bridgewater College to teach in 1961, I continued to go back to Boston University in the summers to complete work on my dissertation. The second such summer was 1963. When I returned to Bridgewater in August, I made plans to attend the Civil Rights March for Jobs and Freedom in Washington, D.C., on Wednesday, August 28. I was aware that busloads of people from the Boston area were planning to go, including students from various universities in the city, church groups from many different denominations, labor union members, and many other groups. The demonstration was in the papers and on the radio; I knew it was planned as a peaceful demonstration.

I stopped in Harrington, Delaware, to visit a friend on Tuesday evening and went into D.C. on Wednesday. My friend, a recent graduate of Bridgewater College, had heard all the talk in the D.C. area and said she feared for my safety. Since I knew the nature of the crowd coming from Boston, I felt no such concern. Actually the event turned out to be more like a family Sunday school picnic that bore no resemblance to a violent demonstration. I parked my VW "Bug" near the Mall in a federal building's construction area south of Independence Avenue, but I saw no construction that day. I walked over to the Mall with an African-American cab driver, then to the Washington Monument, next toward the Reflecting Pool, and finally the Lincoln Memorial. At the east end of the Pool, I discovered other Church of the Brethren members who had gathered there and were holding up signs. Eventually ending up on the south side of the Reflecting Pool, I was able to hear King's famous "I Have a Dream" speech.

At Bridgewater College that fall, I scheduled a convocation titled "Report on the March for Jobs and Freedom." One other faculty member, James Stayer, a member of the history department and a graduate of Juniata College, had been at the Washington March and was well aware of its historical significance. The two of us gave our reports on October 2, 1963.

Later that month, on October 23, a talented student trio, The Round Hill Singers, challenged the campus community with their convocation program. I had suggested that they might include one or two civil rights songs that I had learned at the march. To my surprise they dedicated the entire program to songs of the civil rights movement. On their printed program they wrote this explanation:

> When we were asked to sing for Convocation, it was suggested that we might include a few of the folk songs that have come into fairly common use in the current struggle for racial equality. We decided to do a complete program around this theme, entering it as our personal protest against racial discrimination. . . . We sincerely hope that you will join us and sing out for freedom. The Roundhill Singers.

It was a fantastic contrast to the negative response that occurred when Heslip Lee was on campus for the Focus Week later that fall, November 11-13, 1963. Heslip Lee was the executive secretary for the Virginia council on Human Relations, an educational organization to promote racial integration. I could hardly believe it was the same campus. At that time, freshmen men expressed bitter hatred in a late-night dormitory discussion led by Lee. The campus reflected the deep tensions that existed in society during those years.

Considering the Concept of Limited War

In November 1967, James Ware, head of the Department of Philosophy at the State College of Arkansas at Conway and a former faculty member at Bridgewater College (1963-64), invited me to participate in an institute on limited war. I was asked to present a paper on "The Ethical Aspects of Limited War" at the Arkansas Institute on October 11, 1968. Two other papers were to be presented, one on the military aspects of limited war and one on its political aspects. The institute was to be informative in nature, not polemical as in a debate. We were instructed to treat the subject of limited war and to use Vietnam and Korea only as illustrations, not as the primary subjects of discussion. I was hesitant about being on stage with nationally known figures but finally agreed and spent summer 1968 preparing the paper at Christian Theological Seminary in Indianapolis, Indiana. Since this seminary was next to Butler University, I enjoyed the use of two libraries.

I organized my presentation around the two ethical questions posed by Paul Ramsey: "When is war right?" and "What is right in war?"[22] (An ethics professor at Princeton University, Ramsey was known for his theological support of just war theory, about which he would write more in later years.) In answer to the first, I argued that one must take into consideration the existence of nuclear weapons (which gives rise to the concept of limited war in the first place), the ideological conflict of the great powers, the revolution of rising expectations in the developing nations, and the growing body of international "common law."

In answer to the second question, I argued that the involvement of the masses of people and the obliteration of the line between combatant and non-combatant is the *common* factor in the philosophies of Gandhi and Mao Tse Tung. Despite their great differences, and contrary to (popular) American conceptual working patterns, the effectiveness of a military power is its ability to achieve political ends, or to implement political goals.[23]

I viewed my discussion as neither directly supporting the American government's policy in Vietnam nor, for that matter, directly criticizing its policy in Vietnam. Since it was not an attack on the government's policy, my lecture took the standpoint of just war doctrine, not pacifism. The other two participants on the panel were S. L. A. Marshall, a nationally known military historian, and Eugene Rostow, Undersecretary of State for Political Affairs and former dean of the Yale Law School. I presented the same lecture on four other occasions: in a Bridgewater College Faculty Forum; at the Institute on Limited War at the State College of Arkansas; at Bethany Theological Seminary (Oak Brook) in an abbreviated form; and in one of my classes on the Bridgewater College campus. The reactions in each instance were quite different from one another!

PARTICIPATING IN JMU'S LIFELONG LEARNING INSTITUTE

In the summer of 2000, I received a telephone call from Nancy Owens, Director of James Madison University's Lifelong Learning Institute. After a meeting in the RMH Hospital cafeteria, we agreed that I would teach a course that fall on the Old Testament. Such a course was my "bread and butter" at Bridgewater College, and I was more than happy to do so. Also, I was suffering from depression and illness, and teaching would give me something challenging to do.

The institute offers courses every fall and spring semester. Each course includes a two-hour session once a week for five weeks. While the instructors need to prepare for their classes, they do not assign homework, require term papers, or give tests and grades. The students, most of whom are retired senior citizens, want to be present and bring with them a wealth of experience and background.

I taught courses six different years, up until and including the fall of 2006. They were The Old Testament, The Search for the Historical Jesus, The Dead Sea Scrolls (twice), Islam and the West (twice), Early Church History, Medieval Church History, Modern Church History

(1500 to 2000), and, finally, a course in The Old Testament and Archaeology.

What a wonderful, fulfilling way for a teacher to retire!

April 2012
Revised October 2015

Robert McFadden with his grandniece, Monica McFadden

NOTES

1. Charles Culbertson, "War and Remembrance," *Bridgewater College Magazine,* 87.1 (Fall 2011): 22-25.

2. Robert McFadden, "Perspective in Pacifism," *Brethren Life and Thought* 6.2 (Spring 1961): 36-52.

3. *Minutes of the Annual Meetings of the Church of the Brethren, 1778-1909* (Elgin, Ill.: Brethren Publishing House, 1909), 10.

4. John 15:19.

5. Gordon Shull, "The Pilgrimage of an Ex-Pacifist," *Brethren Life and Thought* 5.2 (Spring 1960): 13-19.

6. Reinhold Niebuhr, *Christianity and Power Politics.* (New York: Charles Scribner's Sons, 1940). (See ch. one, "Why the Christian Church Is Not Paci-

fist," especially p. 5).

7. Robert McFadden, "The Nuclear Dilemma, with a Nod to Kierkegaard," *Theology Today* 17.4 (Jan. 1961): 505-518.

8. Soren Kierkegaard, *Fear and Trembling*, ed. C. Stephen Evans and Sylvia Walsh (New York: Cambridge University Press, 2006; first pub. Copenhagen 1843).

9. Herbert Hogan, *Gladdys E. Muir: Professor, Peacemaker, Mystic* (LaVerne, Calif.: University of LaVerne, 1998).

10. William Temple (Archbishop of Canterbury), *Nature, Man and God*, the Gifford Lectures, 1932-1933 (Edinburgh, Great Britain: H&R Clark, 1934, 1935, 1940).

11. Reinhold Niebuhr, *Christianity and Power Politics* (New York: Charles Scribner's Sons, 1940).

12. Umphrey Lee, *The Historic Church and Modern Pacifism* (Nashville, Tenn.: Abingdon-Cokesbury Press, 1943).

13. Anton T. Boisen, *Exploration of the Inner World* (Philadelphia: University of Pennsylvania Press, 1971), 9.

14. Robert McFadden, "Micah and the Problem of Continuities and Discontinuities in Prophecy" in *Scripture in Context II: More Essays on the Comparative Method*, ed. William W. Hallo (Winona Lake, Ind.: Eisenbrauns, 1983), 127-146.

15. Robert McFadden, "Notes on Archaeology in the Holy Land," *Brethren Life and Thought* 35. 4 (Autumn, 1989): 212-220.

16. Keith N. Schoville, *Biblical Archaeology in Focus* (Grand Rapids, Mich.: Baker Publishing Group, 1978).

17. Elmer W. K. Mould, *Essentials of Bible History* (New York: Thomas Nelson and Sons, 1939).

18. *The Bible: An American Translation*, Edgar J. Goodspeed and J. M. Povis Smith, eds. (Chicago: University of Chicago Press, 1931, 1935).

19. William Foxwell Albright, *From the Stone Age to Christianity* (Eugene, Ore.: Wipf & Stock Publishers, 2003; first published 1940).

20. Richard Elliott Freedman, *Who Wrote the Bible?* Riverside, New Jersey: Summit Books, a division of Simon & Schuster, Inc., 1987).

21. Robert McFadden, "The Deuteronomistic History," *Brethren Life and Thought* 55.3-4 (Summer and Fall, 2010): 68-73.

22. Paul Ramsey, *War and the Christian Conscience: How Shall Modern War Be Conducted Justly?* (Durham, N.C.: Duke University Press, 1961; pub. for the Lily Endowment Research Program in Christianity and Politics).

23. Robert McFadden, "The Ethical Aspects of Limited War," *Journal of Church and State* 13 (Winter 1971): 113-127.

Since the author presented this memoir in 2012, he has published two collections of essays, both of which are available at Amazon.com. The first was *Is the Bible Correct?: And Other Essays* (Seattle: CreateSpace Independent Publishing Platform, 2013, rev. 2014). It is a collection of essays that highlights issues in biblical interpretation (including the Flood), contains reflections on sea-going cowboy experiences and civil rights, and asks the serious question, "Is the Bible correct?" It begins with a quotation from George Fox: "The Spirit is superior to Scripture."

The second was *Collected Writings on Pacifism and Just War: War and Peace in the Nuclear Age* (Seattle: CreateSpace Independent Publishing Platform, 2015). The first essay documents the differences between nonresistance, nonviolence, and vocational pacifism. The second essay spotlights the significance of nuclear pacifism. The additional essays reflect the author's growing interest in just war traditions in the nuclear age.

Lee M. Yoder

Educator Par Excellence

Dreaming of a life of farming as a youth, Lee found success in an educational career. He became an innovative administrator at Christopher Dock High School, Eastern Mennonite College, and Bridgewater College. After a short stint in the business world, he and his wife, LaVerne Zehr, moved to Cairo, Egypt, where, as invited, he founded the Narmer American College (NAC) and LaVerne also taught. Later he became the head of the American School of Vietnam. In retirement Lee chairs the ACRS Steering Committee and also the Accreditation Validation Teams for the Middle States Association of Colleges and Schools. NAC invited him back in 2016-2017.

Photo by by Lifetouch Church Directories and Portraits Inc.

LEE M. YODER

From Farming to a
Life of Educational Leadership

From the beginning, home for me was one farm along the Belleville, Pennsylvania, Back Mountain Road and then, a year later, a second one that my dad farmed for Rudy J. and Naomi Yoder in Frog Hollow. I was born on the first farm into a family of five in 1940 as the youngest child of Jonathan Z. (1900-1989) and Barbara (Sharp) (1904-1958) Yoder. Since my two older brothers and a sister were soon living and working away from home, I and my sister, three years my senior, grew up in a small family where my parents welcomed any help I could give on the farm. To my disappointment, when I was six, my dad moved us to the town of Belleville to work for the New Holland Machine Company. On the morning of the move, I sadly milked our cow Sarah by hand by myself. I hated to leave her and the farm.

While I enjoyed my school days in the Belleville public schools and, in my senior year, Belleville Mennonite High School, the desire for the farm kept coming back to me. In the middle of my freshman year in high school, at age fourteen I jumped at the opportunity to return to the home farm of Mrs. Naomi Yoder and to work for her son Mark R. Yoder in Frog Hollow—home country for me since Mark's brother Percy S. Yoder lived on the adjoining farm where I had lived until age six.

As a teenager, I was sure that I wanted to farm for the rest of my life. During my high school sophomore year (sophomore means wise and foolish), a college representative came to the farm where I was milking cows and asked about my possible interest in attending college. I replied, "You will never catch me inside college doors!"

While my schoolwork took a downturn, my interest in dairying did the opposite. I helped to maintain dairy records for the herd of Holstein cattle. These Dairy Herd Improvement Association (DHIA) records were essential to improve milk production and to build a registered herd of the cattle. Visits to nearby Pennsylvania State University Agricultural and Dairy Facilities expanded my vision. I helped to develop the herd prefix name of "Yoderstead" for the registration and breeding records. In 1956 Mark gave me the unusual gift of a new Holstein heifer calf, which I named and registered as "Yoderstead Rishel Gracie Lou."

My schoolwork continued to take a lower priority. I filled my class schedules through Grade Eleven with home economics, bookkeeping, typing, and any subjects I could easily enjoy. Meanwhile, the more I worked on the farm, the more my responsibilities expanded. Not everything went smoothly, though. Since Mark was active in church work and missions sometimes weekends, when he was gone, I assumed responsibility for the herd.

On one occasion, I asked a friend over to help me chop grass for the cows and fix the electric fence lines. While driving out to the field, we decided to chop the grass first and to fix the fence later. A few seconds after I started the machinery, we heard a loud bang. Then I remembered. I had placed the sledgehammer on the pickup of the harvester. Now I had just run it through the harvester, causing major damage. I felt terrible. But when Mark came home, he asked me only one question, "How did it happen?" There was no scolding, no ridicule for my thoughtless actions. This was a learning experience that would be useful later.

During these high school years, I was actively involved at the Locust Grove Mennonite Church. I had become a member of the church while in the sixth grade and was received upon confession of faith with water baptism. As president of the Mennonite Youth Fellowship (MYF), I led youth programs within the Locust Grove Church and with other churches in Pennsylvania's Big Valley, helping to develop interchurch basketball and social events. These programs opened church-wide MYF opportunities, and Mark Peachey, a Conservative

Mennonite Conference member, encouraged me to write articles about organizing youth programs for the Conservative Conference's *The Missionary Messenger*.

I also served as the janitor of the church building, taking care of the ventilation and the sound system for church services. I soon learned that one could not please all of the people at the same time. One person said that when one lady reaches for her sweater and another takes out a personal fan, the temperature is just right. Later on, I found this idea worked as a concept for organizational leadership: If one goes for 80 percent, there will always be 10 percent on either side of a position or principle of policy.

My life goal of farming began to change during my high school junior year after I left Mark's and his mother's farm for my brother-in-law and sister Ivan E. and Mary C. Yoder's farm. Since Ivan had been ordained to the Christian ministry and was now extra busy, he needed my help. It was there that Ivan and others began encouraging me to pursue a college education. They pointed to a bigger picture of life than I had seen and suggested that I consider how I could best prepare to serve in it. When Ivan and Mary left the farm, they held a public auction. There I sold my registered Holstein heifer to Mark—my last act as a would-be farmer.

At this time the local public school system expanded with the joining of townships to form a new Kishacoquillas High School near Reedsville. Since my dad did not want me to attend this expanded school, he enrolled me in the nearby Belleville Mennonite High School for my senior year. However, because of my earlier focus on farming, my academic records were deficient. Thus, in the summer between my junior and senior years, Laurie Mitton, Principal of Belleville Mennonite School, tutored me in Latin. My senior year studies then included courses for a now college-bound student: more Latin, chemistry, geometry, algebra II, English literature, Modern European history and Mennonite Bible doctrine.

During this senior year, I appreciated affirmations from teachers, including Dr. Frank Brenneman, my geometry teacher (now retired math professor from Tabor College, Kansas), who ordered me in the gymnasium to "take this whistle and call this basketball game." I had never played basketball! Somehow, though, I and my referee calls survived. Indeed, during college, I not only officiated at many games but also received my official license for the Virginia High School League.

During my high school senior year, our family was saddened when my mother's diabetes worsened and she lost her eyesight. She could not attend my graduation, but she saw to it that I had a new suit of clothes for the occasion. Still, she did not change her mind about my new educational goal. She did not want me to go to college. She felt that if a person went to college, one would get a "swelled head" and then break "like a cabbage head in the garden." I stayed home after high school graduation.

On August 27, 1958, my mother died. Her funeral, which she had planned, was at the Locust Grove Mennonite Church on August 29. The service included the singing of more than eight hymns by a men's octet. After the traditional viewing of the body at the front of the church, on my own I walked up to the casket and closed it, a task usually done by the undertaker.

During the 1958-1959 school year, I also worked as the school janitor at the Belleville Mennonite School and distributed the teachers' supplies, earning a $100 per month. Actually, on the day of my mother's funeral, the new second and third grade teacher, Miss LaVerne Zehr, arrived from Lowville, New York, with her parents, Pastor Elias M. and Martha Widrick Zehr. They had stopped first at the church to inquire about the service in progress, where they learned that it was the funeral of the school janitor's mother.

That summer and into the winter, I drove a truck to haul milk from mostly Amish farmers and to deliver ice to them to cool their milk and home iceboxes. I also worked for my brother John, who, to my surprise, offered to pay for my first year of college at Eastern Mennonite College (EMC), including the tuition, room, and board for $875!

The new second and third grade teacher from upstate New York captured my interest, and I soon learned when she had a free period. That became a good time to check the furnace in her classroom building. All of my older brothers and sisters had to this point married Yoders. I decided that "new blood" was needed in the family and that I was not going to marry a Yoder! It seemed to me that someone from New York would indeed be a new person for our community, only to learn later that the Zehrs already knew all the ministers at Locust

Grove since all attended the Conservative Mennonite Conference meetings.

OFF TO COLLEGE AFTER ALL

The choice of a college to attend was easy to resolve, even if Penn State was only twenty-five miles from Belleville and Juniata College was fifteen miles away in Huntingdon. Each year many in the Belleville community went to *The Holy City* in Harrisonburg, Virginia. For many years, I wondered where this Holy City was; it sounded like such an attractive place to visit. Later I learned that it was not a place but a cantata by Alfred R. Gaul sung each spring at Eastern Mennonite College. It was Laban Peachey (whose memoir is in ACRS Memoirs, vol. 2, *Continuing the Journey: The Geography of Our Faith*, Telford, Pa.: Cascadia, 2009) who helped me to plan for attending Eastern Mennonite College in Harrisonburg.

In the fall of 1959, I was off to EMC, driving my green Oldsmobile even though freshmen were not permitted to have cars on campus. Like my mother had been, my dad was opposed to my going to college. He worked the night shift at the New Holland Machine Company in Belleville. Thus it was morning when I went to his bedside to say goodbye. "You are going without my blessing," he said. I simply replied, "See you later, Dad."

I did not know who my college roommate would be. Don Showalter (from Broadway) met me at my car when I arrived at EMC and told me that we were rooming together. Don was eager to help carry my luggage up to our room (on the south end of the third floor of the Administration Building, known as the Ad Building) because he wanted to see if I wore a "straight-cut suit." (I did not.) J. Lorne Peachey and Allen Lind were our hall managers; and I soon met our neighbors, Paul R. Yoder Jr., Bill Helmuth, Ron Swartzendruber, and Oren Horst.

I decided to study math as a major until the end of the year, when I switched to history and studied under John A. Lapp (whose memoir is also in ACRS vol. 2) and Harry A. Brunk. Lapp had such an enthusiasm for history it seemed to me that this must be the best field of study to pursue. He explained how the Hyksos came out of Asia Minor with their chariots with sharp metal like razors on the wheels, invaded the land of Palestine and went on into Egypt when Joseph was a ruler for the Pharaoh. This was an "aha" moment for me because it brought secular and biblical history together for me. Brunk had a unique way of expressing his personality. While teaching, he would call out, "Of course the answer is . . . and wait for a student to respond. He declared, "Public opinion is stronger than law," even as Don Showalter would argue to the contrary in U.S. Government. At the end of my senior year, I was pleased to accept the class history award from these professors.

Among the many other professors who influenced me, it was Myron S. Augsburger who, in my senior year Bible Doctrine course, reshaped my understanding of the Bible. The timeline that he saw in the Bible moved from the "beginning of time" to the culmination of history and the return of Christ. This timeline represented the unfolding story of God's quest for and relationship with humankind. When Christ, the Lord of history, stepped into the world, he changed the relationship between the Old and New Testaments. The Bible, I learned, was not a flat book. With this timeline Myron pointed out that the Israel of the Old Testament was not to be equated with the nation-state of Israel founded in 1948.

During my freshman year, through letters and home visits, I maintained close contact with the Belleville schoolteacher, LaVerne Zehr. We were engaged during my freshman year; in summer 1960, on August 13, we were married in Lowville, New York. We traveled through the New England states on our honeymoon, and my pocket had only fifty cents in it when we got back to Lowville!

In the fall I returned with my bride to EMC, where we lived in the EMC Trailer Park. I had borrowed $1,500 (interest free) from Percy S. Yoder in Belleville to purchase our trailer. With her two years of college and two years of teaching experience, LaVerne was nevertheless welcomed as a teacher in the Rockingham County Public Schools at Tenth Legion, and her salary was a godsend. (I also contributed to our finances by working one summer for my father-in-law on the home Zehrdale Farm in Lowville, and other summers I did painting in Harrisonburg for Luke Hurst.) Later, while talking with a neighbor in the trailer park one Sunday afternoon, LaVerne decided to resign her teaching position and finish her college work. She did so with additional summer school, and we both graduated in the class of 1963.

For my college graduation, my dad was the first to arrive. During my four years at EMC, he had done a lot of traveling and met other parents who also had children at EMC. Later, though, when I completed my master's degree, he could not comprehend why this was necessary; when I received my doctoral degree, I did not even mention it to him. Actually, of my eighty-eight first cousins, all of whom contributed much to their communities, I was one of two who went to college and pursued advanced degrees.

Opportunities at Christopher Dock High School

During my senior college year, the question was where I would teach in a secondary school. With her degree, LaVerne would be seeking an elementary teaching position. It was in one of the teaching position interviews on campus that I met Richard C. Detweiler, Supervising Principal of Christopher Dock High School, Lansdale, Pennsylvania. In response to the application that I mailed to the school, I received a handwritten postcard acknowledgement from Mr. Detweiler. I was most impressed by this personal touch. Earlier, I had applied to several schools in Lewis County, New York, and learned that there was not one single open teaching position in all of those schools.

The Christopher Dock openings included physical education, library, and social studies. I was soon happy to accept the full social studies position to teach World History to grade ten and Problems of Democracy to grade twelve, beginning September 1963. The school assignment also qualified as a 1-W Selective Service position, so my two-year assignment, which included summer school maintenance work, met the requirements of my draft board during this Vietnam War era. Our first son, Lawrence, was born in February 1965.

It was in December 1964, however, when I was twenty-four, that Supervising Principal Richard Detweiler came to our home one late afternoon. He invited me on behalf of the board of trustees to consider becoming principal of Christopher Dock School, but first I would need to take a year to get a masters' degree in 1965-1966 at Temple University in Philadelphia. The trustees would pay me the same teacher salary and all of my expenses for that year at Temple.

On July 1, 1966, at age twenty-six, I became superintendent of Christopher Dock Mennonite High School. I was really shaking in my boots! I kept asking myself if I could do this work like Richard Detweiler. He had wide rapport not only as the superintendent of the school but also as a church and conference leader. Finally, I had a freeing experience when I concluded that I was not Richard Detweiler, I would not become Richard Detweiler, and I could do this work only according to who I was.

In October 1966 our daughter, our second child, Lela Faye, was born. LaVerne and I now had two small children at home, and I, new educational challenges.

Although many of the faculty members had been with the school from its beginning, they were gracious and cooperative as I oversaw the development of in-service and orientation programs for them and new trustees, as well as a new index of faculty and administrator salary schedules, retirement and sabbatical leave programs, and policies. We soon moved to seek and receive in 1971 the first school accreditation from the Middle States Association. Meeting with the principals of other Mennonite high schools in the U.S. and Canada, I chaired the Mennonite Secondary Education Council in developing the first secondary teachers' conventions and the annual Mennonite High Schools Music Festivals. Other special events included the 1971 Bicentennial Celebration of Christopher Dock, the colonial schoolmaster, which included the production of the film *The Quiet in the Land*, by John L. Ruth and an extensive exhibit of fraktur art. Roland B. Yoder, the art teacher, designed a new school diploma as the administration and trustees sought to apply the fraktur design for all school graduates.

Then a trustee prompted me to explore the purchase of land on sale adjoining the school property, 108 acres with an asking price of one million dollars. I called together six "brethren": Norman K. Souder, Mahlon A. Souder, Raymond H. Rosenberger, Sanford A. Alderfer, Horace W. Longacre, and Ralph B. Hedrick. Their strong consensus was to pursue the purchase of the land but to do so in cooperation with the Franconia Mennonite Conference. The 1972-1974 years saw the land project become reality, and more land was added to the school's campus as well as the founding of the Dock Woods [Retirement] Community.

Our third child, second son Lawson, was born in 1968, and we moved into a new house on Clemens Road in Harleysville. Now our family mission was caring for three children under age four with LaVerne at the helm while I was fully engaged in school administration. I never knew what challenges I would face in the course of a school day. For example, Larry Godshall, head custodian, once walked into my office and said that the PTO gears were stripped on the school's tractor. With a quick flashback to my days on Mark Yoder's farm, I replied only, "How did it happen?" I did not lecture or charge negligence.

In 1972, I decided to begin doctoral studies at Temple University with a major in curriculum theory and development, taking only one course at a time through the next years.

The opportunity to work with the Christopher Dock board of trustees was a special experience since they strongly supported broad latitude in my leadership. Their comments stayed with me through my work. Some of the wisest ones were these: Sanford A. Alderfer's "half right is all wrong"; Merrill S. Moyer's "make decisions not linked to each other so that later they can be more easily changed"; Ralph B. Hedrick's "decisions come in bits and pieces"; and Floyd M. Hackman's in response to changes in the school's dress code "the apostle Paul did not say thou shalt, but he 'encouraged and admonished' believers."

THE FAMILY'S MOVE SOUTH

Meanwhile, President Myron S. Augsburger of Eastern Mennonite College and Seminary asked me several times to consider taking an administrative position at EMC. However, it was difficult to think of leaving Christopher Dock School and moving the family to Virginia. While considering this invitation, I played my phonograph recording of Stuart Hamblin's song "Teach Me Lord to Wait" over and over as I lay on the living room floor, turning one way and another and listening as the piece continued with the first part of Isaiah 40:31, "They that wait upon the Lord shall renew their strength; they shall mount up with wings as eagles." The last stanza of the song ended with "and let me be on this earth what you want me to be."

In 1974-1975, while I was on a sabbatical leave as principal to complete my doctoral course work and residence requirements at Temple University, President Augsburger and EMC became more serious in their communications with me. I played the phonograph record again and again! Finally, in the fall of 1974, I agreed to accept the EMC invitation to begin July 1, 1975, as vice-president for administrative affairs, a new position approved by the trustees. On November 10, 1974, at midnight I took two letters to the Lansdale post office; one was my resignation addressed to the Christopher Dock board of trustees, and the other was my letter of acceptance to President Augsburger at EMC.

The morning of November 11, I read in Edythe Draper's *Living Light; Daily Light in Today's Language* (Carol Stream, Ill.: Tyndale House, 1972) these words from Exodus 23:20: "I am sending my angel before you to lead you safely to the land I have prepared for you." The *Living Light* response was, "Lord, lead me as you promised me you would; otherwise my enemies will conquer me. Tell me clearly what to do, which way to turn. Oh, send out your light and your truth—-let them lead me . . . " My decision was made and affirmed.

Everything then happened quickly. I finished the course work for my doctoral program at Temple University, which also approved my dissertation proposal. While Christopher Dock's sabbatical policy stated clearly that one was required to return to the school after a sabbatical leave for at least one year, EMC generously agreed to pay Christopher Dock the total of my sabbatical funds, and the Clemmer Moving and Storage in Souderton, Pennsylvania, agreed to move our family to Harrisonbug, Virginia (as a gift to EMC) in late June 1975.

There LaVerne scouted out the schools for our children, who were ready for grades one, three, and four. Living at first in a rented house, we soon found a building lot to purchase, and LaVerne immersed herself in all the details of having our new house built. A year later in July 1976, our family moved into our new 855 Summit Avenue residence, which she had completed with the builder. Since she had planned so well, our new home not only met the various dreams of the members of our family but also provided a gracious welcome for guests. By this time LaVerne had also begun teaching in the Rockingham County public schools, first at Pleasant Valley Elementary and then at South River Elementary in Grottoes.

Challenges at Eastern Mennonite College and Seminary

Earlier, thinking about the kind of person I would like for my administrative assistant, I had written a list of the tasks I desired this person to do. LaVerne took one look and predicted, "You will be lucky to find anyone willing to do all that!" Fortunately for me, Dorothy Logan accepted the position. From July 1, 1975, my first day in office as EMC's vice president, she kept everything organized as I responded to the ongoing renovation of the chapel building. It was clear that a large amount of work needed to be done on this building before the students arrived late in August. However, everyone pulled together, and the new auditorium was ready for the opening of the new college year.

As I surveyed the campus needs, I acted to strengthen several aspects. To promote a campus community concept, I recommended that the weekly "Faculty Bulletin" be renamed and expanded to serve as the "Campus Bulletin," which was then published weekly from my office. As an administrator and associate professor of education, I took the lead in a number of changes: developed and directed a new Master of Education curriculum and program 1979-1981; developed marketing strategies, directions, and uniform graphic standards for the campus; developed personnel policies and procedures in a new personnel office; developed an indexed salary/wage schedule for faculty, administrators, and office and physical plant personnel; reviewed the purpose statement of the college, needed as part of the reaccreditation process for the Southern Association of Schools and Colleges; and taught the terminal course for education majors, Promoting Teacher Effectiveness.

At the college and seminary, in addition to being the vice president, I also served in a number of other positions, such as director of institutional advancement, director of parent and church relations, secretary of the board of trustees, interim chief executive officer (CEO) during the Augsburger to Detweiler presidential transition, chief planning officer, and director of personnel.

During my years there, the "Update for Mission" fundraising campaign exceeded its $4.5 million goal with a total of $5.3 million, the largest campaign up to that time in the history of EMC, which I conceptualized and developed. I also developed policies for endowed professorial chairs at the college and seminary and raised over two million dollars for three endowed chairs.

Further, during the years of my vice-presidency and leadership, the amount of total funds raised per year increased substantially, and I worked closely with the president and the trustees to help resolve key financial issues, such as the large $180,000 operating deficit in 1975-1976. A new Commitment Authority Policy was adopted to define exactly the budgetary responsibilities of each department head and officer throughout the organization.

During this time, I facilitated with the dean's office the application for a new Title Ill Federal Grant, which was funded and stimulated many curricular innovations, including the new General Education Global Village Curriculum, with cross-cultural study terms. Retirement policies were reviewed and set in clearly defined terms for the senior faculty members, requiring that the unfunded retirement liability, which the trustees had earlier adopted, be funded in the annual operating budget. Sabbatical leaves continued, and a retiring teacher received a gift of a chair or a trip funded by the college.

President Augsburger requested that I draft a policy statement to begin the Annual Augsburger Lectures, which he personally funded and the trustees so established. To honor President and Mrs. Augsburger upon the conclusion of their presidential leadership in 1980, Dorothy Logan and I planned a delicious dinner and special program at which the Augsburgers received a gift of sculptured art. This event was also part of the presidential transition to President Richard C. Detweiler and his spouse Mary Jane.

These were years of transition, including the separation of Eastern Mennonite High School from Eastern Mennonite College and the founding of two separate corporations. With these many changes, I sought a change of pace and diversion by resuming basketball officiating in area schools with the Virginia High School League license. President Detweiler also invited me to consider assuming the role of academic dean during these years, but I felt I had made enough changes of positions, and I respectfully declined. The presidential search committee of the Mennonite Mutual Aid Board asked if I would consider their leadership opportunity, but that I also declined.

After the 1984 administration building fire, I worked with the Mishawaka, Indiana, Troyer Group of architects to develop the concepts and key features of the new campus center building, and drafted the design statement approved by the board of trustees. The four million dollar project, including the $500,000 endowment for building maintenance, was funded by the October 11, 1986, dedication.

In August 1986, persons and offices were moved into the new campus center from their temporary quarters in the North Lawn building. This was also the time of the trustees' announcement of the next college and seminary president, Joseph L. Lapp, who, although chair of the board of trustees, had not been a member of the search committee. Having served for eleven and a half years in the administration of two EMU presidents, Augsburger and Detweiler, and now aware that the incoming president was looking for a new cabinet configuration, I resigned by the end of December 1986 for another opportunity in the world of education.

THE NEW WORLD OF EDUCATIONAL TECHNOLOGY

In January 1987, Dwight O. Wyse, president of Computer Management and Development Services, introduced me to the world of technology and invited me to accept the position of vice president of operations and client services. His company, I learned, served colleges and universities in the United States with computerized data and management systems. I would be the non-technical person who worked with client leadership persons on their satisfaction with our services.

From my earlier studies at Temple University, I was well aware that the installation of a new management information system required that all parties, including top management, be actively involved in its implementation and use. Also, this rapidly growing company needed new personnel policies and procedures and new programs for staff recognition and professional development. I personally needed to learn how to write and work differently with the advancement of technology applications on all fronts.

During this time, I also served on the (Old) Mennonite Churchwide Nominating Committee as its chair for two terms, and I developed my own consulting work for organizational leadership in what I called Shenandoah Associates. I presented workshops nationwide on the roles of trustees to help them develop clear mission and goal statements, and I demonstrated how the values of an organization when integrated with its mission could enable it to flourish.

THE CALL FROM BRIDGEWATER COLLEGE

One day the telephone rang. I learned that Bridgewater College was in search of an academic dean and that I was invited to meet with the president, provost, and faculty representatives about the needs at Bridgewate. On July 1, 1992, President Wayne Geisert appointed me dean for academic affairs and professor of education. My responsibilities included supervising the sixteen academic departments through their department heads as well as the registrar, director of the library, and director of academic computing. I helped lead twenty-five faculty members and taught IDS 101: College Seminar as part of the Freshmen Year Experience program, which created a new Professional Portfolio Program for the incoming freshmen. A faculty colleague and I presented this new program at national professional meetings.

As chief academic officer, I also provided leadership in the following ways: developed new curriculum initiatives; recruited new faculty members and reviewed faculty matters such as course evaluation instruments, workload, promotion and tenure; developed a new academic advising model based on a student's portfolio; encouraged the application of technology to teaching; and chaired lecture committees that brought to the campus such noted speakers as Cornel West, John N. Gardner, Ernest Boyer, and then Under-Secretary General of the United Nations Kofi Annan.

During this time, Phillip C. Stone succeeded Wayne Geisert as president of Bridgewater College. I continued to serve as chief academic officer, reporting directly to the president since the previous provost position was discontinued. Meanwhile, learning that I was being considered by the presidential search committee of Messiah College (and was on the "short list" of candidates), I chose not to complete all of the required doctrinal forms and withdrew my name. I felt inclined to stay at Bridgewater and support the new president. However, after I sensed that the president was seeking a candidate with a national profile for the academic dean position, I concluded my responsibilities at Bridgewater College after six years.

AN OPPORTUNITY IN CAIRO, EGYPT

A New York educational consultant, Rollin P. Baldwin, sent me an email message in late December 1999, asking "What about Egypt"? I replied, "I don't know. What about Egypt?"

In January 2000, I met him at the Union Station in Washington, D.C., and in February joined him in Boston for an international teacher and administrator recruitment fair, where I met some Egyptian leaders. In March I went to Cairo, Egypt, for a week. After meeting the Muslim owner, Mohamed El Rashidy, and his eight daughters, I signed a contract to develop a new American school there from "scratch" for grades K to twelve. It would be named Narmer American College (NAC) after Narmer, the first Egyptian king who was ruling when Lower and Upper Egypt united at about 3,500 B.C.

While in Cairo, I began to prepare the school calendar for the year to come and met with interested parents who wanted to know more about an American school program. With them I addressed the basic concepts of critical thinking, investigation, problem-solving, research, and the ways American schools function.

Early in August, LaVerne and I landed in Cairo to meet the school owner and begin our new work in a country where we would deal with challenges significantly different from anything we had met before. As the founding headmaster who was named superintendent in March 2006, I worked immediately to recruit teachers and administrators and to establish all the first policies, procedures, curriculum, parent relations, instructional materials, library, grading scales, report cards, transcripts, graduation honors and awards, attendance procedures, and student programs.

Beginning a new school is one thing, but to do so in another culture is an even greater challenge. Egyptians have a different sense of time, and it takes longer to get something done. Since planning there is not a priority, a lot of things are done at the last minute. But the Egyptian people are friendly, and they have a great sense of humor, as the following incident illustrates. The official work for the school always involved the Egyptian minister of education in varying degrees. Early in my first years, I was told that the minister did not approve of the geography text we were using from the U.S. Holt, Rinehart, and Winston Company . The minister objected to the southern border of Egypt on the maps between Egypt and Sudan. He also objected to the

Lee M. Yoder, head of the Narmer American College in Iftar in Cairo, with kindergarten students

uneven treatment of the Palestine-Israeli issue.

The compromise solution was to tear those disputed pages out of the book. My western reasoning concluded that we would need to tear these pages out from all twenty of the textbooks. "Not so," said our owner. "Only the one textbook copy that goes to the minister needs to have those pages removed. Continue to use the textbooks as you have been doing!"

I discovered that the parents, upper-middle-class professionals—lawyers, doctors, business executives, contractors, and oil executives—were willing to pay $7,000 a year for admission for their child. Eighty-one percent of the students were Egyptian. Others, including dual nationals, hailed from twenty-seven countries, including the U.S. The student enrollment went from twenty to 120 and then to 495 in grades pre-kindergarten to twelve. From 2003 through 2008, a total of 197 students graduated from this accredited American school. Students went on to study in higher education in Egypt, the U.S., Canada, Qatar, Italy, Switzerland, and the U.K.

The fifty faculty members were mostly certified U.S. teachers, as well as some from Canada, Egypt, Guatemala, Austria, Poland, and Cyprus. Because of the more than thirty nationalities in the faculty and student body, flags from each of these countries flew at the opening of school assembly and at commencement.

The school program and ways of thinking and working were all new to the students and their parents. In one of my geography classes, when we were discussing the Palestine-Israeli issues, I asked a sophomore student for his opinion.

"What? You want me to say what I think?" he responded in disbelief. "Yes, what are your own views?" I replied.

He answered, "No one ever asked me that before!"

Clearly this was a different way of learning, and the school owner wanted Egyptian students to have an opportunity to be critical thinkers, to be creative, and to develop their skills through a wide range of school activities. What made the American school approach so appealing was its contrast to the Egyptian national system, based on memorizing for a big test at the end of each school year. In Egypt, it did not matter if the student went to school, and it did not matter what the teacher said. The student just had to pass a test at the end. Further, in many schools, grades were bought and sold, which I refused to do. I said, "In the U. S . we do it the old-fashioned way: Students earn their grades and achievements." One father, a doctor, wanted to come by my office at the end of the school year to "help with his son's final grades." I told him that would not be necessary. The grades would not be changed from what the student had earned.

After the student surprised to be asked his opinion entered Cairo's Modern Sciences and Arts University, he found how really different his schooling had been at NAC. He said, "I realized how I finished tasks assigned to me without struggle, more than most people. I knew what kind of information I needed at each certain stage, and how and where to search and collect it to achieve my goals because learning in NAC is not just about academic syllabus, nor about stuffing data in one's brain." He graduated with a degree in computer graphics and was hoping to do postgraduate work in the U.S.

Young students everywhere enjoy exciting and educational events, some of which at this school took advantage of its location, like the field trips to Luxor, Aswan, the Sinai Desert, and even the

Czech Republic; and students participated in the Model United Nations programs in Qatar, Harvard, and China. At the school, middle and high school students performed such drama as *Annie, You're a Good Man, Charlie Brown,* and in my last year there, *Cats.* Elementary students contributed exceptional music programs. Everyone was involved in the athletic program, designed to teach students what it means to be team players and honor their commitments to their team. Well-done assembly programs taught students to listen quietly. A five-star hotel was the setting for the annual proms, and the colorful graduation ceremonies included a promenade to Sir Edward Elgar's "Pomp and Circumstance March No. 1" and "The Triumphal March" from Giuseppe Verde's *Aida.*

Also for the teachers, new traditions needed to be started, such as faculty recognition for years of service and an annual holiday tea, which LaVerne hosted at our apartment. The last year we had sixty-five faculty and spouses in our home for the December holiday event, and all joined in singing "Joy to the World," "We Wish You a Merry Christmas," "Upon the House Top," "Silent Night," and more, with the help of an electric keyboard.

At the school the faculty members participated in the introduction of the guidance programs, library development, and computer systems school-wide with training in the use of smart boards. In my last year the new curriculum director from the U.S. worked on curriculum refinement and mapping.

Discipline had its usual human components, but with an Egyptian flavor, a strong feeling for revenge. The question always was who started the problem. I would ask the involved students in my office how long this revenge should continue. Until bones are broken? Until there is blood? "Will we have peace or war?" I would ask. I had many peacemaking sessions in my office, after which the students would shake hands and walk out with their arms around each other. In her kindergarten, LaVerne would use conflict management skills with her students. She would have them sit down together and seek to solve their issues. These concepts were also applied at the middle and high school levels.

One day, however, a student grabbed the tie of the Arabic teacher. The student was becoming violent, so I walked him to the front gate and told him he was finished at this school. My owners were surprised since the minister of education usually required students to remain in a school all year. I did not know that and had expelled the student on the spot.

The owners of the school, students, and parents provided great cooperation, and I took a "firm but fair" approach. However, the teachers always needed to be alert for cheating on homework and exams. One day the first grade teacher told me that she believed that one of her students had changed the grades on his report card before his parents received it. I expected the parent to say, "Not my child. I know my child, and he would not do that." When I had the student in my office for a while, he kept denying his acts, which seemed very clear. Finally he needed to go to the restroom, but I made him wait a little longer, thinking that the biological forces of the body would soon be apparent. They were, and the child finally said he did not change the grades but his cousin did. Nice try! His mother said that because of this she would not be speaking to her son for a week. Giving threats over and over was a common parental response. I asked if the child lived at home and if she really would not speak to her child for seven days. I said, "I know you will, and hereafter do not say something that you will not carry out!"

As the school developed, many positive events cheered everyone. In 2004, the Narmer School Board proceeded with plans to construct a new campus for the school and import the furniture from America. Stone setting and groundbreaking ceremonies occurred in October 2005. Our actions for accreditation culminated in June 2006, when the school became a candidate for accreditation by the Middle States Association, Philadelphia, Pennsylvania. By the 2006-2007 academic year, 470+ students met in classrooms on a totally new campus in New Cairo City.

I did take time out, however, at the Ohio State University Medical Center on January 5, 2005, for heart surgery to repair my mitral-valve prolapse. LaVerne, there with me, returned to Cairo on January 31, and I was back at the end of February.

Each year, a two-week orientation with workdays was planned to welcome new faculty and to help all persons to sense the spirit of the school and its mission. At my last faculty orientation session in August 2007, I stated to all that we had stood together, Muslim and Christian, to develop this new American school in this land of the ancients, this cradle of world civilization. I joined hands with our owner and invited all faculty to join hands with us, just like brothers Isaac and Ishmael standing side by side at the burial of their father Abraham in Hebron, Palestine.

Rich in history, Egypt holds eighty percent of the world's antiquities. Our school was an American one, yes, but one with a global emphasis. When the U.S. invaded Iraq in 2003, it did not provide a good model because of how it was done without regard for Iraq's culture and history. Democracy cannot be shipped into another country. On the day of this invasion, NAC was still on the same campus as the national school. That school had a march protesting the war and the U.S. However, NAC had an assembly program to comment on the war and to encourage discussions in the classrooms led by the faculty to introduce program content on peace and global understanding.

After the new campus was completed, Mr. Mohamed El Rashidy became ill with Alzheimers disease and then died on June 10, 2009. The 2007-2008 year became a period of transition for the school; it was time, after eight years, for LaVerne and me to return to Harrisonburg to our families. With the expense of an American school and the new campus, the school owners were beginning to look for lower-cost approaches, including more local Egyptian teachers. LaVerne and I shall always be grateful to God for this wonderful experience that was ours to live and work as educators in a cross-cultural land.

The American School of Vietnam

The phone rang in the middle of night, 1:00 a.m., on February 2, 2012, Groundhog Day in the United States. The caller was Phil Nguyen, owner of The American School in Vietnam (TAS), founded in Ho Chi Minh City in 2010. He had just dismissed his second head of school, whose short tenure had been October 2011-February 2012, and was now inviting me to be the third person to accept that position.

Developing this almost new American school in Vietnam would be no small task, but I was immediately intrigued. Recalling my experiences in Egypt. I knew the essentials for a thriving school: leadership continuity, vision, and team building. Although I also knew about the differences one faces in another country in language, housing, food, transportation, and customs, I felt ready for this new challenge.

After LaVerne and I discussed this invitation, we decided that I would leave as soon as possible for Vietnam and LaVerne would follow in about two weeks. Managing in the next several days to secure a final contract, the other needed documents, and airline reservations, as well as to pack, I found myself landing in Ho Chi Minh City on February 14. The very next day I met Phil Nguyen and my efficient administrative assistant Ms. Hang, toured both the elementary and the secondary schools, and met their principals, teachers, and as many students as possible. I saw attractive classrooms, the library, art rooms, and a canteen area.

The following day I had a good interchange with the secondary faculty during a short twenty-minute meeting in the library. They seemed pleased to have an opportunity to voice their views. Clearly

The American School of Vietnam (PK-12) in Ho Chi Minh City

they were talented, experienced, and able teachers. They were also excited about field trips, Opera House programs, the student production of *The Sound of Music,* and extensive art shows; and the experienced coaches had launched the first athletic program for students in Vietnam.

That first week, the numerous issues I had needed to address at the school in Egypt and now here in Vietnam became clear. Several of these tasks had to do with the next academic year: securing software to do student class scheduling; ordering textbooks; finding the needed qualified teachers and being able to offer them a faculty handbook, contracts based on clear faculty loads and assignments, and a teacher salary scale and benefits. I also wanted to prepare a mission and core values statement.

In addition, the school needed to be ready for the mid-March visit by Marilyn George from the Western Association of Schools and Colleges (WASC) regarding our next steps in seeking school accreditation. With this challenge in mind, I wrote to California to get permission to use that state's standards and benchmarks in our program and curricula. Another immediate task was to prepare for faculty and administrator meetings.

Perhaps one of the most valuable changes I was able to bring about during my time at the school was the new dual-enrollment plan. This enabled students in the grade eleven English course to earn three undergraduate university credits at Missouri State University (MSU) in Springfield, Missouri, for only a $300 fee to MSU. The arrangement happened through my nephew, Lester J. Yoder, who, while working at Jenkins Diesel Power in Springfield, overheard a university representative talking with the owner about a desire to add more Asian international students to the university. My nephew then explained that his uncle was the head of an American school in Vietnam. Everything came together for this special opportunity and, indeed, became a first for many international schools.

AS I LOOK BACK

As an educator, I have tried to enable students and all who served them with me to accept or move on to the kind of work for which they were best qualified; and I have been grateful for those who did the same for me. Although I never became a farmer, the rewards of hard work in my early rural history shaped the educator I became when I moved into my true calling. In relating to people in other cultures, I saw how their experiences shaped their perceptions of their world and mine and better understood the sources of my views. As a school founder and leader, I learned the necessity for clear written policies and the need for sensitive supervision.

From my birth onward through the unfolding stages to follow, my journey was prompted by many voices of affirmation from my parents, siblings, spouse, children, family, employers, professional colleagues, teachers and professors, trustees, peers, and community and church leaders. These persons provided words and expressions that were in tune with the Lord God of the Universe, who has led me on this way through these years.

February 2011
Revised October 2015

PART III

Making a Difference
... Through Leadership Abroad

Douglas (Doug) Hostetter

His "Neighbors" Live in War Zones

Seen above, Doug is speaking at the UN in his present role as the director of MCC's UN Office in New York City. In his youthful first MCC assignment in a battle area in South Vietnam, he experienced an eye-opening Good Samaritan event when a young Buddhist monk provided needed help for the children and welcomed him as a brother. Through the years since, he has worked as a humanitarian and peace activist with major organizations and is today also peace pastor at Evanston (Ill.) Mennonite Church.

Photo courtesy of MCC

DOUGLAS (DOUG) HOSTETTER

My God Was Too Small:
GOD IS BIGGER THAN WE THINK

I was born the son and grandson of Mennonite ministers and raised in the Virginia Conference of what was known as the Old Mennonite Church. When I was growing up in the 1950s, we were very sure that we were followers of Jesus and the people of God. As a matter of fact, we suspected that we were the only people of God. As a youth I was certain that all non-Mennonites would not be going to heaven—they were doing all sorts of things that I as a Mennonite understood were prohibited. In fact it wasn't even clear to me whether many of the other Mennonites were going to heaven since Mennonites themselves were, as they are now, a very diverse community.

We in the Virginia Conference considered ourselves a very "godly" group who followed all of God's teaching and principles. We were God's people. We were "in the world" but certainly not "of the world"; as instructed in Romans 12:2, we were "not conformed to the world" around us in any aspect. Our Mennonite women were not allowed to cut their hair, in accordance with chapter 11 of the apostle Paul's first letter to the Corinthians. Our Mennonite men were instructed not to wear neckties, in accordance with a simple lifestyle. It was quite clear to me that the church buildings with stained glass windows were in violation of the second commandment, which prohibited "graven images." Of course, with regard to members of churches that had statues or crucifixes or things like that, it was clear that these were not God's people. How could they be God's people? They were unambiguously violating God's second commandment.

In many ways, it may be surprising now to believe, I had a very comfortable childhood. Although in the 1950s we Virginia Mennonites were different and other people often looked at us strangely because of our behavior and dress, this was a small price to us to pay to be true followers of God's commandments in all aspects of life and, of course, to inherit Eternal Life.

My first experience of living outside a Mennonite community, aside from a few weeks as a counselor at an evangelical Christian summer camp during my college years, was while I was working in Việt Nam. After I had graduated from Eastern Mennonite College in 1966, just as the U.S. war in Việt Nam was expanding, I immediately became draft eligible. I applied for and received conscientious objection status. My conviction to serve as a conscientious objector was not because I was frightened of combat but because I truly believed that Jesus taught that we were to love our enemies. Thus, for me the godly way of relating to the Vietnamese was not to kill them with guns and bombs as was being done by the U.S. military at the time. Rather, since I knew that young men of my generation were being sent against their will to fight in Việt Nam, I felt that as a pacifist I could do no less than to go to Việt Nam to serve God and the people of Việt Nam.

I was surprised to learn that the Mennonite Central Committee (MCC)—the relief, development, and peace agency of the Mennonite and Brethren in Christ churches of North America—was working in Việt Nam in a coalition with two non-Mennonite organizations, Church World Service and Lutheran World Relief in an organization called Việt Nam Christian Service (VNCS). MCC was linking up with people from other organizations who claimed to be Christians, but who, I knew, weren't really following all of Jesus' teachings. Some of the VNCS volunteers in Việt Nam smoked, drank, and danced while a few even felt God condoned killing if done in combat in a "just war." I was sure they were not followers of Jesus as we Mennonites were; and here we were, working side by side in Việt Nam!

Atlee Beechy, the director of the Việt Nam Christian Service at the time I arrived, was a Mennonite; but he was from the Midwest, where the Mennonites were much more liberal than we Virginia Conference Mennonites. Some of my Mennonite friends in Harrisonburg had hinted darkly that it was not certain that many of the Midwest Mennonites would make it into heaven since they allowed their women to cut their hair and most of their women did not even wear the prayer covering. I had also been told that some of their women wore makeup and jewelry—things that we knew were clearly against biblical teaching. Most of the Mennonite men in the Midwest wore neckties, and I had heard that it was often difficult to tell a Midwestern Mennonite from a non-Mennonite.

However, although Atlee Beechy was an Indiana Mennonite, I welcomed him into my Mennonite Community in Việt Nam. I was halfway around the world with few Mennonites of any flavor in sight, and I desperately needed a Mennonite community. It was Atlee, then, who gently began to urge me to expand my understanding of the Christian community even beyond Midwestern Mennonites to include Presbyterians, Lutherans, Methodists, and Disciples of Christ, all of whom participated in Việt Nam Christian Service.

Later, after my six weeks of language study in Saigon, Atlee encouraged me to expand my understanding of God's community even further. "Doug, you will be going up to a small village in Central Việt Nam. There are no Mennonites in Tam Ky, but there is a Vietnamese Christian congregation there. [The Vietnamese Protestant Church was started a century ago by Christian and Missionary Alliance missionaries.] It is called the Tin Lành Church, which means "good news" in Vietnamese. They will be different from the Mennonites of Virginia, but you need to accept them as your Christian brothers and sisters. God has a bigger and a wider family than you may have known."

Tam Ky was in Quang Tín (now Quang Nam) Province in the northern part of South Việt Nam, called "I Corps" by the military as it was the first and northern-most military zone in South Việt Nam. It was in the middle of the heavy combat area about 150 miles below the Demilitarized Zone that divided South from North Việt Nam. I was the first Mennonite volunteer to go into that area. My initial task was to try to find out what the local people needed and to see how MCC might help them. I was surprised to learn that most of the villagers felt that education for their children was their most pressing concern.

The refugees had come from the rural areas of Quang Tín Province. The rural areas of the Quang Tín had been lost by the U.S. and Saigon government forces two years before I arrived and were then largely controlled by the Vietnamese National Liberation Front (the NLF, which the Americans called the Việt Cộng or VC). When the U.S. lost control in that area, the armed forces responded as militaries usually do in situations like this; they bombed the infrastructure in the enemy-controlled area: schools, clinics, and marketplaces. The refugees streaming into Tam Ky in 1967 had already lived for two years without schools in their rural areas. Parents of children who were age six to eight years old were particularly concerned that they had missed the first two years of school. They were desperate to find someone to help their children learn to read and write.

I understood immediately that literacy would be important work, but I also realized that it would be ludicrous for an American just learning to speak Vietnamese to try to teach Vietnamese children to read and write their own language. Since I desperately needed help, I turned to the Vietnamese Christians of Tam Ky. I went to the pastor of the Tin Lành (Protestant) Church and asked if he would allow the Protestant youth group to work with me on weekends in a literacy program in the Tu Hiệp Refugee camp at the edge of the village. The thousands of refugee children in that camp were very eager to learn to read and write.

The pastor reflected awhile and then responded, "We already go out to the Tu Hiệp Refugee Camp every Sunday after our morning worship service. The youth group sings gospel songs, and I go along and preach God's Word. Many people come, hear the gospel, and give their hearts to Jesus. The fields are 'ripe for harvest'; we must concentrate on what is most important. I'm sorry, but we will not be able to help with your literacy classes."

I found his reply devastating. Most of the refugees with whom I had spoken had pleaded for education for their children; not one had asked for evangelism. They had desperately hoped that I could find a way to help their children learn how to read and write.

I knew I couldn't teach Vietnamese myself, and the Protestant youth group was unavailable; so after weeks of procrastination I worked up my nerve and went to speak to the Catholics. Father Tri was a young Catholic priest associated with the large Catholic church in town, but he was both the principal of the Catholic high school where I taught English and also the leader of the Catholic youth group.

When I asked him if I could use the young people from the Catholic youth group to teach literacy to refugee children, Father Tri responded, "Yes, just show me which are the Catholic children. We will be glad to teach the Catholic children how to read and write!"

His offer would be a help because about ten percent of the children in Tu Hiêp were from Catholic families. However, it left out the ninety percent of the children who were Buddhist, Taoist, Cao Dài, or Confucianist.

For several more months I struggled with the dilemma of how to help the non-Catholic children in the Tu Hiêp Refugee Camp. I had been taught growing up that Buddhists were heathen. I remembered the stories of the returned missionaries from China, Burma, and India of how the people in those countries burned incense, bowed down before, and chanted prayers to idols. I shuddered at the thought of even entering a pagoda. But I was desperate. There were thousands of children in the Tu Hiêp camp, and only a few score were being helped by the Catholic youth group.

Again working up my nerve, I entered the pagoda where I could meet the young monk, Thích Hanh Doc, who was in charge of the Buddhist youth group. His response was immediate, "Yes, we will be glad to come to Tu Hiêp to teach the children." He didn't ask which of the children were Buddhist, which were Catholic, or who was Confucianist. He said they would be happy to teach any of the children. He also invited me to teach English in the Buddhist high school!

I was already teaching English in the public high school, a Catholic high school, but I would never have dreamed of teaching in a Buddhist school. I remembered my days at Eastern Mennonite High School. Although we would occasionally have chapel speakers who were missionaries who had served in Buddhist countries, I knew that we would have never allowed a Buddhist to teach at Eastern Mennonite High School; thus I hardly expected Buddhists to allow a Christian to teach in theirs.

I will never forget my first class at the Bô Dê High School. Thich Hanh Doc introduced me by my Vietnamese name, which was easier to pronounce than my American name. "This is Nguyên Anh Tuân. He is a Christian from the United States. We are Buddhists. Buddha is not God but is a finger pointing the way to God. I know very little about Christianity, but I have heard that perhaps Jesus Christ is also a finger pointing the way to God. Tuân is our brother. He is here to help you learn English."

I was absolutely astounded. I had been welcomed warmly, and throughout my time there I was invited to the Pagoda to enjoy their vegetarian feasts in celebrations of Buddha's birthday, the lunar New Year, and other Buddhist holidays. I was always welcomed as a brother and received as an honored guest.

I spent three years in Tam Ky during the height of the war. The village was heavily fought over, and many friends were killed during that period of time. Tam Ky was actually taken over by the National Liberation Front, though usually only for a few period of hours in the middle of the night, about a dozen times while I lived there. During Tết 1968, however, the NLF (with the help of North Vietnamese soldiers) overran Tam Ky, holding the Provincial Headquarters and the airport for more than a week—but I was cared for and protected by my Vietnamese friends.

I was very careful not to be involved politically with either side, and my efforts to educate all of the children were appreciated by the people of Tam Ky regardless of their political leanings. Eventually I was able to set up schools in villages in the areas controlled by the Saigon government and in nearby villages controlled by the National Liberation Front. I had friends on both sides, and most Vietnamese on either side who knew me appreciated my work. With God's help I was able to befriend and work with people on both sides for almost three years amid a bitter war.

War helps you see many things more clearly. A person's true character seems to display itself in a wartime situation, when you don't know if you will live to see the next day. In the life and death of war in the small village of Tam Ky, I began to realize that the people of God—people whose lives exhibit the "fruit of the Spirit [which] is love, joy, peace, longsuffering, gentleness, goodness, faith, meekness, temperance" (Gal. 5:22-23 KJV)—did not all come from the Mennonite church. In fact, many of these people were not even Christians. Many of the profoundly spiritual people and the most faithful pacifists I met during my three years in Việt Nam were Buddhists!

One of my closest friends in Tam Ky was Hanh Dc, the young monk who worked with the Buddhist Youth Group. I knew him for more than two years before I learned that his mother had been killed in front of him, her legs blown off by an American bomb. I had been taught that only Mennonites (and a few Quakers who were pacifists) actually practiced the teachings of Jesus to love your enemies. I remember wondering how many Virginia Mennonites I knew who could have befriended a Russian in the middle of a war after the Soviet military had killed their mothers. Could Mennonites in the Shenandoah Valley have lived God's love and forgiveness to the degree I had seen in some of the Vietnamese Buddhists with whom I was living in Tam Ky? I experienced people who had never heard of Christ but who were living godly lives: something I had thought impossible.

I was working in Tam Ky with the Mennonite Central Committee (MCC). MCC is not a missionary society but a Mennonite relief, service, and peace organization set up to convey God's love through service to people in need, especially in times of war. Though my responsibility in Việt Nam was in the area of service, I had also hoped, as a Christian, to personally lead some Vietnamese to Christ. I procrastinated many months, but I knew that it was important not to shirk from my duty of Christian witness.

One day with about half a dozen Vietnamese high school students with me in my room, I decided that it was about time to teach these people about Christ, the Mennonites, and our faith and traditions. I was not quite sure how to start. It seemed a bit hard to start with the Virginia Conference of the Old Mennonite Church or even the early Mennonite leader, Menno Simons, so I decided to go back to basics. I would start with Abraham and the Jews and work my way through the Old Testament up to Christ and the early Church, and then we could proceed to the Reformation, the Anabaptists, and Menno Simons and end up with the Virginia Conference of the Old Mennonite Church.

Before the conversations started, I had looked up the Vietnamese word for *Jew*. I then proceeded to tell the students about Abraham, the Jews, and the early Bible stories. The students all looked confused. Not one of the high school juniors and seniors in the room had ever heard the Vietnamese word for *Jew*! I realized that this was going to be hard. How was I going to help them to become Christians, as I knew Christianity, when they did not even know the word for Jew? I realized that it would be a task that would take many years, maybe even decades.

Some of the evangelical missionaries in Viêt Nam, however, had learned a few shortcuts. They would simply teach Vietnamese who wanted to become Christians John 3:16, the Lord's Prayer, and a few other favorite Scriptures. Once the candidates had memorized these Scriptures in English or in Vietnamese, the missionary would ask them if they wanted to give their lives to Jesus. If the answer was "Yes," they were baptized as Christians. Many of the Christians whom I met in Tam Ky had taken this short route to Christianity; and although they knew some Christian language and a few verses, often they seemed mostly interested in the relief supplies or job offers that were available from missionaries or military chaplains.

There is a Vietnamese saying: "*Hêt gao, lây dao, nuôi con.*" This aphorism, which entered the Vietnamese language during the French colonial era, translates roughly as, "If your rice bag is empty, adapt your religion, and feed your children." In the French era it meant, "If your children are hungry, convert to Catholicism and work for the French." During the American war, it meant, "If you want help from the chaplains and the missionaries, become Protestant and your children will benefit." In an earlier era of missionary work in China, converts like these were called "rice Christians."

A person's true character tends to emerge when the bullets are flying and mortars are falling. It was instructive to see who helped their neighbors and who merely cared for themselves and their families. I guess I should not have been surprised to learn that many of the Vietnamese who converted to Christianity for the economic advantages were also opportunistic and self-centered. Happily there were exceptions to that tendency. But I was astounded to see that many of the most caring and "godly" citizens of Tam Ky were people who had never met Christ or knew anything about Christianity.

Theologians have struggled for centuries to try to find the right words to talk about God. If it is difficult to discuss God with people from your own culture in your native language, you can imagine trying to describe God in a culture and language quite alien from your own. My challenge in Vietnam was enormous. The Vietnamese words for the Christian God are *Duc Chúa Troi*. The problem of talking about Duc Chúa Troi (the Christian God) was that it was the French colonialists who introduced Duc Chúa Troi to the Vietnamese. The first shelling of Saigon by the French navy was done in the name of Duc

Chúa Troi. The Treaty of Saigon, which was signed by Vietnamese and French authorities after the destruction and submission of the city, guaranteed French missionaries the rights to evangelize for Duc Chúa Troi in the southern part of Viêt Nam and granted Vietnamese converts to Christianity the legal right to practice their faith in Viêt Nam.

Thus I suddenly realized that it was not Duc Chúa Troi whom I worshiped; Duc Chúa Troi was a colonial western militarist. Duc Chúa Troi was a French god that used the French Navy to enforce special religious rights for Christians in Viêt Nam. The U.S. military chaplains also worshiped Duc Chúa Troi and with his name blessed the pilots, their bombs, and the U.S. infantry that was destroying the villages and farmland in Viêt Nam. This was certainly not the God I worshiped. But Duc Chúa Troi was Vietnamese for the God of Christians.

I concluded that the alternative to using language to describe God was to use my life to convey an understanding of God—one that had nothing in common with the colonial god of the French who blessed their conquest nor with the militaristic god of the American chaplains who sanctioned the destruction of the Vietnamese people's homeland. I stopped talking about God and started trying to live my understanding of God. This was a formidable challenge, in many ways much more difficult than speaking; it required me to try practicing my faith through the things I did and my interactions with the people around me.

I learned many things while trying to live my faith rather than preach my religion. Words are frequently misunderstood between people of the same language and culture but are often even more confusing in a cross-cultural setting. Yet the integrity of a sincerely lived life is almost always understood, even between people of widely disparate cultures and languages. When words are completely incomprehensible, intention and meaning are often *read* by a careful observer. The contrasting emotions of love or hatred, trust or fear, are intuitively understood by children and animals even when there are elaborate attempts to disguise them. Pre-verbal children and animals are almost always better judges of the character of the people with whom they interact than the verbal adults around them who are deceived by the words.

When I loved the people of Tam Ky and tried to live my understanding of God in their community, they loved and accepted me in return. They did not need words—my words led only to confusion—but they did understand my life, and they understood it in their own culture.

When I was leaving, one of my best friends wrote a long poem for me. He ended the poem with, "You have been like a tear in the eye of Buddha, crying for the suffering of the people of Tam Ky." I was deeply touched. I realized that the young schoolteacher had seen God's compassion in my life and had expressed that in his own language and understanding. I knew his poem would have been misunderstood by my Sunday school class back home; but my friend had sensed that my love and compassion were of God, the God that he believed Buddha was pointing toward.

Conversations with My Father

I was a changed person when I came back to the States after my three years in Việt Nam. God and God's family were much bigger than I had ever suspected while growing up in the Shenandoah Valley. I had personally encountered members of God's family in places I would never have suspected. I knew in the depths of my soul that they were my sisters and brothers. I had watched them carefully as we lived, worked, and nearly died together in the most difficult of circumstances. They were godly people in the most profound sense of those words. I knew that the spirit that we shared could have come only from God.

My sister Pat was in Việt Nam with MCC during the same time I was, living in Quang Ngãi, about thirty miles south of Tam Ky. We got together whenever possible. She had also discovered that God's children existed in places she had never suspected. On returning home, we attended graduate schools on different sides of the U.S, but we still met on holidays back at our parents' home in Virginia.

I will never forget the evening we got into a heavy theological discussion with my father, a Mennonite minister. Pat and I both told of living with Vietnamese who we knew were definitely people of God. They were godly individuals who embodied the "fruits of the Spirit" but who were not Mennonites—in fact, most were not even Christians. The discussion went very late into the night, but we could not resolve the differences between our experiences and Dad's theology.

Finally Dad got up and walked over and put his hands on a Bible and said, "I have been a minister of the gospel for over twenty years now. The Bible says there is only one way to God, and that is through Jesus Christ. That has been the foundation of my faith from the very beginning; I can't begin to start to question that now."

Pat and I talked afterwards, and we realized that Dad had been totally candid with us; he had gone as far as he could go. He could not comprehend that there could be people of God from outside our Christian tradition. Dad's theology had already grown enormously during his lifetime. After Dad and Mother moved to Virginia when I was very young, he had started preaching on the Mennonite Hour radio broadcast while the ministers of his home congregation in Manheim, Pennsylvania, still taught that it was a sin to own or listen to a radio.

While Pat and I were in Việt Nam, Dad had returned to study theology at an American Baptist seminary where he had worked closely with Christians outside the Mennonite tradition. Dad had moved very far from the theology of the small Mennonite congregation in which he had grown up and been ordained, and he was frankly telling us that he believed that God's spirit could reside only authentically in Christians. It was unthinkable to him even to consider a family of God bigger than the evangelical Christian church.

On another holiday visit home I learned that Dad and Mother had been asked by the Mennonite Board of Missions to go to Africa to set up a seminary for the Church of the Lord Alladura, an independent African Christian church. During my time with MCC in Việt Nam, I had seen how many of the evangelical Christian missionaries had been insensitive to Vietnamese culture and traditions. They seemed oblivious to the way in which God was already working among the people of Việt Nam.

I wanted my father to understand the broader possibilities of God as he left to help a Nigeria church. "Dad," I asked, "how long have missionaries been in Africa?"

He responded, "I guess it's been a hundred or a hundred and fifty years since the British missionaries brought Christianity to Nigeria."

"And how long do you think God has been in Africa?" I asked.

Dad responded, "Of course God has been in Africa as long as people have been in Africa and even long before that I suppose."

"When you go to Africa," I said, "it would be interesting to try to discover what God had taught the Africans before the Christian missionaries arrived."

I could tell that Dad was uncomfortable with that question, but he responded, "Why would I try to find that out? Anything that God had taught the African people in the pre-colonial era had to be far inferior, far less complete than what they learned after the Christian missionaries arrived."

Ten years after returning to the U.S., I met and fell in love with a young Jewish woman. I remember the long discussions with my grandfather and my father after Bobbie and I were engaged.

"Bobbie, who is Jewish, is going to remain Jewish while I, who am Mennonite, am going to remain Mennonite. Actually it is not a problem," I explained, "since Bobbie and I both worship the same God and share the same moral and ethical values. We do not feel that it will be difficult to raise children together since our God is the same and our values are shared."

My father and grandfather both found this to be incomprehensible (as did Bobbie's father). Although we discussed and re-discussed this issue over many months, we could never reach a theological understanding. I went on to marry Bobbie, who has been my wife now for more than three decades. We have had many fights over our thirty years of married life and the parenthood of two boys, but Bobbie has always said that my major problem is not that I am a Mennonite, but that I am a male.

Dad and Mother were not able to attend our wedding since they were in Nigeria on mission work at the time. Since we have been married, however, they have totally accepted Bobbie as part of our large family. Dad always loved and included Bobbie in our family. He knew that she was not a Christian and, from his theological perspective, not part of God's family, yet he always made it clear that she was part of his family—that she was loved and accepted just as were his five other daughters-in-law, who were Mennonite.

My father and grandfather were both prominent ministers in the Mennonite church. They were known for their strong convictions, clear voices, and articulate sermons. My parents had always hoped that their oldest son would continue the family tradition, but when I returned from Viêt Nam, my interests and convictions led me to work on the issues of peace and justice. I had been profoundly affected by my experiences during the war and felt called to struggle against the unspeakable evils of war and injustice wherever they were found. I have spent much of my adult life working either in war zones around the world or in this country, struggling against militarism and injustice.

Doug Hostetter with trucks as they were arriving in Takhar Province with supplies for displaced persons in the camps there, who had fled U.S. bombing in Afghanistan and fighting with the Taliban at the front lines about ten kilometers south of the camps.

The B. Charles Hostetter family has always been close, getting together for family reunions at least once every year. Over the years Dad and I have had many discussions about my life and my work. Dad would often say, "Doug, you have a good vocation: you are working for peace, justice, prevention of war and, when war breaks out, helping to heal the wounds of war. This is good work, but it is not the best work. The best work is to bring people to a personal encounter with Jesus Christ. For people to be 'born again,' is the most important of God's work. You have chosen a good work but not God's best work." This was always painful to hear. I knew that Dad loved me, despite the fact that my vocation had not followed his and our theological differences remained unresolved. Still I yearned for his full approval.

Some years ago Dad had a serious stroke while traveling by car to a church meeting in Virginia. I was visiting him in the hospital a few days after his stroke when he told me about this incredible place where he had been several days earlier. "It was so pleasant, so full of light, and so comfortable."

Curiously I asked him, "Are you talking about the hospital in the small town where you were first taken the first evening, right after the stroke?"

"No," he said, "that was awful and very uncomfortable."

"Was it the room you were brought to in Roanoke before they did all of the tests?"

"No, these hospital beds have all been very uncomfortable. It was that first night after the stroke before we got to the hospital. It was such a comfortable, wonderful, and beautiful place. It was almost like lying on clouds. I want to go back there and take Grace [my mother] with me."

I came to believe that Dad, in his near-death experience, had had a glimpse into the other side. I don't completely understand what happened to Dad that night, but to me and others in the family, he was a changed man.

We were all very fortunate. Dad lived for six weeks after the stroke, and all of his children got a chance to spend time with him. Dad was quite lucid until near the end, but his speech was slurred from the effects of the stroke except when he was in prayer. When Dad was in prayer, the slur was gone, and his thoughts and speech were crystal clear. As he prayed, we heard the Dad we had always known, praying to the God he had served his entire life, praying for the people and communities he loved.

We took turns within the family staying with Dad during those final weeks of his life. After my initial visit with Dad in the hospital, I had returned to my work in New York. One evening, about a week after the stroke, I called Dad's room in the hospital to see how he was doing. My sister Miriam answered the phone by the bed and informed me that Dad was in prayer. Dad had always felt it was important for the family to pray together; after the stroke he very much enjoyed praying with family when they were with him in the hospital room.

"I'll just put the phone down so you can hear Dad praying," Miriam said, "and when his prayer is finished, I'll tell him you are on the phone to talk to him." She lowered the phone to Dad's bed so I could hear the beautiful cadence and resonance of his communication with God.

When he had finished. Miriam told him I was on the phone. My sister told me later that Dad never left his prayer mode but took the phone to deliver, in clear un-slurred speech, an incredible blessing that I could hardly believe I was hearing over the phone. He expressed how my life had been a blessing to him, the family, and the world and that Bobbie [my Jewish wife] had been a blessing to me and to our children and the entire family. He observed that God had used both Bobbie and me in very profound ways to work out his will in this world. He went on for quite some time, never leaving his prayer mode, with a totally unreserved blessing of me, my work, my wife, and my children.

When Dad stopped, Miriam got back on the phone and said, "I hope you heard every word. That was an amazing blessing."

I don't know what happened to Dad during his near-death experience, but Dad came back a different person. I believe he returned from that experience with an understanding that God's people and God's work are much broader that he had ever known before.

In Orthodox Judaism it is forbidden to write or to say the word *God*. G-d is infinite and we are mortal. If we write or say the word G-d, we are committing idolatry. Idolatry is holding up something that is less than G-d for worship. When we attempt to put the infinite and immortal G-d into the finite box of the human intellect and language, be it English, Hebrew, Greek or Aramaic, we have made G-d into a human mold, an idol.

I wonder if many of us as Christians are guilty of idolatry. We have worshiped a god about whose boundaries we presume to know. To understand G-d through our human intellect, we have forced G-d into the small boxes that we can comprehend—our language, our culture, and our religious traditions. We have worshiped this small immature, undeveloped reflection of the true almighty and infinite G-d.

My God was far too small. With every day and every year that I live, I keep discovering that G-d is much bigger, more infinite, more powerful, and much more wise and just than I could have ever imagined.

October 2012
Revised August 2015

Doug Hostetter standing in the rubble of the El-Wafa Rehabilitation Hospital in Gaza, the only rehabilitation hospital in Gaza, which was destroyed by Israeli forces in July 2015. He is looking at a patient file that he found the rubble.

Paul Swarr

Laborer for God in Israel

Paul and his family served as Christian missionaries in Jerusalem during the thirty years from 1957 to 1987, which included the Six Day War. Clearly his most rewarding time there was when he pastored the Anglican Beit Immanuel congregation, largely composed of messianic Jewish believers—a group close to his heart—and he and his wife Bertha saw the congregation grow "from about twenty-five to ... about 140." In his memoir Paul offers timely advice in the section "Lessons God Taught Us."

Photo by Ken Layman

PAUL SWARR

Laborers Together with God

My first trip abroad occurred at the end of World War II, on January 18, 1947, when I joined the twenty-nine other volunteers aboard the S.S. *Woodstock Victory* leaving the port of Norfolk, Virginia, with 600 mules on board on a trip sponsored by the Brethren Service Committee. Our destination was Patras, on the western shore of Greece. For the next two weeks we fed and tended the mules as we sailed across the Atlantic Ocean and past Gibraltar to Greece. About twenty of us, mostly farm lads, were Mennonites from Kansas, Indiana, Ontario, and Pennsylvania.

After unloading the mules at Patras, some of us took a fourteen-hour bus journey across the war-tattered countryside to Athens, to view the Acropolis and imagine Paul preaching boldly there. This was my first taste of the international world to which God was introducing me.

On the return voyage from Greece to the port of New York, our ship, now empty of its cargo, was hit mid-Atlantic by an eighty-five mile gale that caused it to list forty degrees as sixty-foot waves crashed over the empty mule stalls on the top deck. I hung onto the rods of my triple-decker bunk, not to sleep, but to ride out the storm for a day and a half. Was God preparing me for several more trans-Atlantic ocean journeys? I could not foresee then that to my wife and me, the white buildings and busy streets and alleys of Jerusalem would become as familiar to us in our thirty years of ministry there as our past homes and school areas in Pennsylvania and Virginia.

Preparation Years (1927-1944)

In 1927 I was born to Mennonite farmer parents in what was fondly called "The Garden Spot of America," Lancaster County, Pennsylvania. This was the era of the Great Depression, and I distinctly remember my grandfather, Milton L. Swarr, reminding us frequently, "Waste not, want not!" He also urged us to save electricity by switching off unnecessary light bulbs with the query: "Why burn a hole in the daylight?"

From the perspective of eighty-plus years, I now look back with much gratitude toward a heavenly Father who granted me a rich heritage. My brother Mark and I were the eighth generation of the Swarr family living on a tract of farmland west of Lancaster, which ancestor Peter Schwahr, a first-generation German settler, bought from William Penn in the 1720s. Our brick farmhouse was reportedly built by Hessian soldiers, conscripted by the British at the time of the Revolutionary War.

My father, Harry C. Swarr, was born to a Mennonite father and a Church of the Brethren mother, Minnie Cassel, who joined her husband Milton as a member of East Petersburg Mennonite Church, just five miles north of Lancaster. This became my boyhood congregation.

My father took a two-year agriculture course at Penn State College, a training somewhat unusual for the Mennonite community of his day. Like most of his neighbors, my grandfather raised tobacco as his main cash crop. However, my father reasoned that if he did not want his sons to smoke tobacco, he could not grow that weed. Therefore, he fed beef cattle and made potatoes his cash crop. He transformed the big tobacco shed, using the upper level for farm equipment and the lower level for a potato cellar. I frequently helped my father on his weekly truck trip taking sixty-pound bushels of potatoes into Lancaster. There he had a regular route delivering potatoes to fifteen or twenty grocery stores, plus to the cafeterias of businesses such as the Hamilton Watch Factory and the Lancaster General Hospital. Dad always insisted that we give a good full weight (more than sixty pounds) to every bushel of potatoes that we sold.

Father was active in our church congregation, both as a song leader and as a Sunday school teacher. He subscribed to the *Sunday School Times*, published out of Philadelphia, in addition to the Scottdale Mennonite Publishing House materials, to enrich his teaching. I often imagined that my dad could have been a schoolteacher or a bank clerk if he had not chosen to be a farmer. In his retirement years he became an active member of the board of Phil Haven Hospital, established by Lancaster Mennonite Conference to meet the needs of emotionally handicapped persons.

My Mother, Kathryn Leaman, was the daughter of Nathaniel Leaman and Annie Risser, of Lititz, Pennsylvania. The fifth of twelve children, she lived for a time with an older brother in California. Among her dear friends were Elta Wolf, who later became Mrs. Orie Miller, and Martha Eby, who became the wife of Clayton (C. F.) Yake, editor of the *Youth's Christian Companion*, published in Scottdale, Pennsylvania. Thus, the Miller and Yake children related to us like cousins during our growing up years, and several of the Yake boys came to work on our farm during the summer harvest seasons.

Although they were active church participants, my parents did not approve of all of edicts of the Lancaster Conference leaders. For many years my dad, like Orie Miller, wore a long tie under his "plain coat." Also, we had both a piano and a radio, and our family would gather around the piano to sing on a Sunday evening. My father was a good pianist, even as a farmer, inspiring me to take piano lessons for about four years in my early teens. Dad sang bass solos, never at church, but often in our home and family gatherings.

But home life soon changed. When I was only eight, my dad shared the news that Mother had breast cancer. She was in and out of the hospital several times in the next three years and went to be with her Lord when I was eleven. The next several years were difficult, with various housekeepers helping in our home. Also, Dad developed Parkinson's disease, which stayed with him the rest of his life.

In November 1941, my father married Katharine Hostetter from Mt. Joy, Pennsylvania, who, as our second mother, brought healing and hope back into our family. She stepped into the role of mother in such a beautiful way that we never thought of making stepmother jokes. She helped to shepherd me through my teen struggles and became the only grandma that our children ever knew.

Apart from my parental home, another spiritual influence during my boyhood was Sunday school. I was fortunate to be part of a boys' Sunday school class who had Irvin Kreider as the teacher for eight or ten years. Irvin, the father of Roy, who eventually became my dear colleague in Israel, took a personal interest in each of his students, and we enjoyed discussing the practical implications of our Bible stories together. Several of those fellows are still my dear friends.

I remember very little about the worship services, except that we usually knelt for prayer times, turning and facing the church benches. Later I was to discover in Israel that kneeling for prayer was a good Anglican practice, except that their churches had cushions upon which one knelt!

EDUCATION AWAY FROM HOME (1944-1952)

Life for me at Hempfield High School in Landisville, Pennsylvania, during the early years of World War II was not easy. I disappointed my teacher and fellow students as the only one in my classroom who did not salute the flag or buy war bonds. My homeroom teacher had so desired 100 percent patriotic participation by her whole class.

Thus I welcomed my parents' encouragement in 1944 to take my senior high school year at Eastern Mennonite School (EMS) in the Shenandoah Valley of Virginia. Studying at EMS became a life-changing experience for me. I met fellow Mennonite young people from Ohio and Michigan, from Iowa and Oregon, and from Kentucky and Mississippi. In our 1945 EMHS graduating class of ninety-five students, many later moved into church ministries. These included Dan Baer, Dan Reinford, John W. Miller, Harold Housman, Evelyn Landis Shenk, Thelma Ketterman Brunk, Ralph Malin, Eugene Souder, Barbara Keener Shenk, Henry (Hank) Weaver, Don Jacobs, Robert Alger, and Nathan Hege.

In autumn 1947 I enrolled at Eastern Mennonite College (EMC), expecting to major in math. Midway through my freshman year, however, I felt nudged by the Holy Spirit to pursue a Bible and theology major in the next four years, with possible pastoral work in my future. In this program, the professors deeply influenced me not only by their teaching but also by their going out to preach in the hills of Virginia and West Virginia on weekends. Also, the Young People's Christian Association (YPCA) opened doors for students' creative participation in Saturday evening street meetings, church planting in downtown Harrisonburg, or gospel teams to Kentucky and Tennessee. My spiritual growth took place as much outside as inside the classroom.

Among the spiritual highlights was the Spiritual Renewal Week in autumn of 1948, my sophomore year. A time of public confession broke out during one morning chapel, and soon students were waiting in line to come to the microphone to bare their hearts and ask for forgiveness. Faculty leaders had the spiritual discernment not to hinder what the Holy Spirit was initiating and therefore canceled classes for a day or two. It was a holy moment. Later we heard that similar student initiated renewals had happened on the campuses of Asbury College, Kentucky, and Wheaton College, Illinois.

At the same time, a cluster of male students began meeting regularly for deeper sharing and intercession in the prayer room above the men's third floor dorm in the Administration Building. This became a true "upper room," where we shared and upheld one another, were knit together as brothers, and gained more vision for future ministries. Many of that group sensed a call to pastoral work or to foreign missions. The political world of nations was just starting to recover from the tragedies and trauma of World War II. Doors were opening, and the Lord of the Harvest was clearly beckoning many of us to leave the North American shores.

MUSIC AND MARRIAGE (1947-1955)

Meanwhile, another privilege of being on the EMU campus was the way music permeated so much of our lives. As well as experiencing the lovely a cappella singing in the daily chapel worship hour, I had the joy of participating in the Mixed Chorus and also the Touring Choir under the direction of J. Mark Stauffer. But the unique privilege for me was becoming the baritone member of the Crusader Quartet, who stayed together as close-knit brothers during our four years of college, 1947-1951.

I had sung in a men's quartet in my home congregation and during my senior year at EMS. But this was different. Aaron King, Roy Kreider, Eugene Souder, and I, all Pennsylvania lads at this Virginia college, teamed together for the sake of ministry through music. We sang from the balcony in chapel services, in street meetings in Mt. Jackson, on Gospel Teams to Kentucky, for Summer Bible school and at evening evangelistic meetings in Vermont. A truly special opportunity come our way when B. Charles Hostetter, the campus pastor, invited us after our sophomore year to join his team in leading summer evangelistic tent meetings in Hannibal, Missouri; the invitation had come from Nelson Kauffman, the local coordinator. Milton Brackbill and, also from EMC, a ladies quartet, and several other students were part of the team. The campaign in Hannibal, sponsored inter-denominationally, opened rich new vistas of opportunity before our eyes. Our quiet Shenandoah Valley views were shaken to the core!

"Charlie," as we loved to call him, invited our quartet to travel with him from Hannibal for additional weeks of ministry in Montana and Alberta, Canada. Our tasks included teaching daytime Bible school classes and singing at the evening evangelistic meetings in churches as far north as Blue Sky, Alberta. In late August, when Charlie needed to fly back to Harrisonburg for faculty meetings, we drove his car back with some evening services enroute in Saskatchewan, Michigan, and Ohio. We joyfully participated in the Tent Campaigns in Hannibal for two more summers with Kenneth Good as evangelist.

Another unusual opportunity for our quartet came via Earl Witmer. (He and Harold Housman were my roommates in an off-campus basement during my freshman year.) Earl had a vision to involve Lancaster Conference youth in breaking ground evangelistically in the huge metropolis of New York City. We traveled with Earl in his car with a loudspeaker mounted on the roof. This speaker made possible the public meetings held on streets and in parks in Manhattan and the Bronx. Earl did most of the preaching while our quartet sang, gave personal testimonies, and spoke with interested people after the public meetings. We cooperated with similar groups to impact this city with the good news of Jesus.

An unusual and unexpected door opened for our quartet in our senior year, 1950-51. In Hannibal, Missouri, radios were used as a way to attract listeners to attend the public outdoor meetings. At that time Virginia Mennonite Conference did not sanction radios. However, radio station WSVA in Harrisonburg offered us fifteen free minutes on Saturday mornings. Norman Derstine agreed to be the announcer for this music program, and we felt inspired by the Holy Spirit to accept this challenge, which then opened the way for the development of The Mennonite Hour broadcast one year later, after our quartet had disbanded. We recorded six 78-rpm records (three at two different times) of our Crusader Quartet music. (In 2009, these were transposed into contemporary CDs, and eleven songs made available along with the booklet *He Keeps Me Singing: A Four-Year Journey with the Crusader Men's Quartet 1947-1951, Eastern Mennonite College* by Roy H. Kreider and Eugene Souder. (Note: Roy's last name is misspelled on the cover as "Dreider.")

It was during the summer of 1949, at the evangelistic meetings in Hannibal that I first met Bertha Carolyn Wenger, a student at Hesston College, Kansas. Bertha and her parents had traveled from Versailles, in central Missouri near the Ozarks, to attend the tent meetings in Hannibal. Two years later, when I transferred from EMC to Goshen Biblical Seminary for a one-year bachelor of theology degree, Bertha was at Goshen College in the elementary education program; and we got acquainted. An excellent typist, she even typed several of my seminary term papers. I never dreamed then, however, that she would become my lifetime secretary! Besides getting a BS in elementary education at Goshen, Bertha stayed for an extra year in the seminary for a bachelor of religious education degree. She reports that often she was the only woman in her seminary classes.

Following seminary, I served as the youth pastor at St Jacobs, Ontario, for two years, 1952-54, under the tutelage of Roy Koch. Among other activities I led a youth choir for Christmas and Easter programs and helped in a Sunday afternoon church planting effort in Hamilton, Ontario. In the summer of 1954, I had the joy of inviting Bertha to join me on the staff of the summer camp program at Chesley Lake, Ontario. It was there that I proposed to her, and she cheered my heart with an affirmative reply. For the next year our courtship took the form of airmail correspondence.

On May 8, 1955, we were married at Bertha's home congregation of Mt. Zion Mennonite Church in Versailles, Missouri. Since this was a busy rural community, we decided on a Sunday morning wedding so farming families could attend. Bertha made the wedding cake herself with our life motto, "Laborers Together with God" (1 Cor. 3:9, KJV) inscribed on it. Nelson Kauffman from our Hannibal days was the pastor who officiated. Bertha and I sang a wedding duet, "With Thy Spirit Fill Us," not realizing the rich significance of that prayer for our future ministry.

Our first home was in Middletown, Connecticut. Why? For the two-year period 1954-56, I served under Lancaster Mennonite Conference as a roving pastor to men serving in 1-W service as an alternative to military service. These 1-W units were located at what were then called "mental hospitals," scattered along the Atlantic coast from Delaware up to Connecticut. I made regular pastoral visits and also spoke at unit meetings. Bertha joined me in making a room and a half apartment into our first home in Middletown, Connecticut. She also soon became the editor of our monthly 1-W newssheet, "The Coastal Compass." Those were the days when we mimeographed copies to mail to the hundreds of unit members. After the Middletown unit closed, we moved to Norristown, Pennsuylvania, where more than 150 men were serving. It was there that our son David was born.

OUR CALL TO ISRAEL (1955-1957)

Within the first year of our married life, Orie O. Miller challenged us to consider an overseas assignment in either Vietnam or Israel, under the Eastern Missions Board of the Mennonite Church (EMBMC). My cattle boat experience had opened my eyes to such a possibility. Bertha remembered that as a young lass in Missouri, while walking the farm lanes, she sensed that farming was a right vocation for her four brothers but not for her. She dreamed of following the camels in her childhood Bible storybooks. We sensed God's Spirit telling us to say yes to an Israel assignment.

Then a beautiful thing happened. We learned that three Mennonite mission agencies were interested in beginning work in Israel! J. D. Graber, the overseas director of the Elkhart, Indiana, Mennonite Board of Missions and Charities (MBMC); Orie Miller representing EMBMC, Salunga, Pennsylvania; and Harold Eshleman of the Virginia Mennonite Board of Missions (VMBM) had met and chosen to unify their efforts. They agreed to send missionaries under the administration of the MBMC but with the support of Salunga and Harrisonburg.

Roy and Florence Kreider had been sent in 1953 as the first workers. I was ordained in the summer of 1956 at my home congregation of East Petersburg, Pennsylvania. Then the world political situation slowed us down. President Nassar of Egypt nationalized the Suez Canal, and war broke out between Egypt, Britain, and France. Therefore, the Elkhart Board sent us to be house parents for the nearly twenty volunteer (VS) workers at the La Junta General Hospital in Colorado, for six months.

However, in June 1957 we sailed from the New York harbor on the *Queen Frederica* steamship bound for the Middle East—and quite a few challenges. By this time, David was an active fifteen-month-old boy, and Bertha was pregnant with our second child, Evelyn Ruth, later born at the Assuta Hospital in Tel Aviv. Roy and Florence warmly welcomed us to their home in Tel Aviv, but their welcome was short lived. Visa difficulties forced them to leave within two weeks of our arrival. Thus we had a rather lonely fifteen months (until the Kreiders returned) of adjustment to our new homeland. At that time we had no idea whether our stay would be three months (because of visa difficulties), three years, or thirty years. However, we had entered this assignment with a clear sense of a long-term commitment.

OUR MINISTRY YEARS IN ISRAEL (1957-1987)

First impressions

We soon sensed the enthusiasm of the birth years of a new nation, similar perhaps to the hopes of the thirteen American colonies in the 1780s. Now 1957 was just nine years after the 1948 founding of this new Jewish state, with immigrants from all six continents flooding her shores. Excitement was in the air after two millennia of dispersion among the nations.

On the street where we lived, we were the only known Gentiles, and we soon joined with many Jewish immigrants in making the learning of Hebrew our first goal. (Hebrew had been revived as the new national language after centuries of use only in synagogue worship.) Sitting in language class with many immigrants was a quick way to make discoveries about them. Some were headed for life on a kibbutz settlement to help develop the agricultural life of the nation. Those coming from Eastern Europe were already accustomed to the communal life style of the kibbutz and the socialist pattern of national government; and most of them were idealists, expecting that living under a Jewish government would solve all the problems they had faced when dispersed in the many nations of the world.

In the hot summer weather we soon noticed the many who had been branded like cattle with tattooed numbers on their arms, a bitter reminder that they were among the few who had escaped from Auschwitz or another of Hitler's concentration camps. Many of them considered Hitler to be a Christian—what else, since he was not a Jew or Muslim? How could we share our Christian faith with these refugees from Nazi Europe?

Then came another early discovery. We had come to the Holy Land, hadn't we? Yet only about fifteen percent were Orthodox Jews who regularly attended synagogue. The majority were as secular as their cousins in southern California who went to the beach on the Sabbath. The halo over this land totally disappeared for us when some years later thieves ransacked our home in suburban Tel Aviv. We might as well have been living in Chicago or Richmond!

Yes, we visited the sacred sites of Jerusalem, Bethlehem, and Nazareth. We reveled in the calm beauty of the Sea of Galilee. We had come to the Land of the Book, were studying the language of the Book, meeting the people of the Book. But where was the God of the Book in this secular Jewish nation? We were permitted a visa as American Gentile tourists but certainly not as Christian missionaries. How were we to begin to share the message of the only true Messiah in this historic land?

An outline of our ministry years (1957-1987)

God kept us in Israel for thirty years, but we were always considered tourists or temporary residents by the government. The challenge of gaining a visa always stared us in the face. After the first long months of intensive Hebrew language study, the next twenty years broke down into three seven-year segments, with some overlap.

Dr. Robert (Bob) Lindsey, chair of the Southern Baptist work in the land, graciously offered to support our visa appeal if I would teach in their school at Baptist Village near Tel Aviv. This was a school begun for Arab orphan children plus some Baptist missionary children. For a block of about six years, I taught Bible and math there at a secondary school level.

Meanwhile, Menno Travel Service had hoped to open an office in Israel, but because they already had offices in Beirut and Alexandria, the current Arab boycott did not permit a location in Israel. Therefore, local representatives of the Nazareth Hospital of Lutherans, Baptists, and Mennonites formed a board to establish Sharon Tours, which catered especially to Christian pilgrim groups desiring to visit biblical sites. I did some tour guiding as well as office work at Sharon Tours, whose office was just several blocks from our home. This work served as a valid business reason to secure an Israeli visa.

During those first fifteen years, we hosted many Bible studies in our home as well as shared with individual seekers. In addition, we attended services in local congregations established by Anglicans, Plymouth Brethren, and Baptists. I was invited to serve as secretary of the United Christian Council in Israel (UCCI), which gave us visa security for about six years in the 1970s. The UCCI was a fellowship of Protestant churches and agencies, ranging from Anglican to Pentecostal and including groups from Europe, Scandinavia, the United Kingdom (U.K.) and the U.S. Whereas Catholic and Eastern Orthodox churches had existed in the Middle East for centuries before the state of Israel and therefore had legal rights, no Protestant denominations (other than Anglican) were recognized by the Israeli government. Thus, the UCCI was a way of having a unified Protestant voice to the government.

In 1977 I was invited by the Anglicans to serve as pastor of the Beit Immanuel congregation when the previous pastor, Henry Knight, needed to return to the U.K. for health reasons. Henry, himself a messianic Jew, had transformed the Immanuel House ministry away from being mainly the expatriate church for the British Ambassador to being a local assembly for messianic Jewish believers and seekers. To this vision I felt called. Those ten years of pastoring (1977-1987) were the most fulfilling of our thirty years of ministry in Israel. God wondrously blessed those years with growth from a nucleus of about twenty-five to an assembly of about 140 by the time we left Israel in 1987. Those attending were mostly messianic Jewish believers, but some were Arab Christians, and a few of us were Gentile believers.

Some lessons God taught us in Israel

I would like to share ten of the spiritual principles or lessons that we believe God taught us during our thirty years in the Holy Land.

1. Identify locally. Early on we noted how embassy families and even some missionaries transported house furnishings to Israel so that they could live as nearly as possible as they did in, say, Nashville or Omaha. How thankful we were that the Elkhart staff had counseled us to buy furniture and clothing mainly in Tel Aviv so as to identify with the local customs, not import American culture. Speaking and reading Hebrew was also a basic way to identify with our neighbors. Ours was the challenge to adjust. I, a farm lad, needed to settle into life in a metropolis of half a million.

2. Be teachable. How were we to know what would be acceptable to share with new Israeli neighbors? I went to Israel as a young ordained Mennonite pastor who had been taught in seminary to preach and teach others, but no congregation awaited me. Someone else did, however: an Austrian gardener who became our friend and frequently came to visit us on a Sabbath evening. Shimon confronted me: "Where were you when my family was perishing in Hitler's ovens?" I pleaded teenage innocence. "So where were your parents?"

His conversation revealed a vast knowledge of the crusades, pogroms, ghettoes, and holocaust woven into Jewish history; I soon recognized that I was not an expert with all the answers to complex world problems. I clearly needed to take time to listen to Holocaust victims with tattooed numbers singed on their arms if I would ever have the right to share my witness regarding Jesus. I needed to be teachable before I could teach others—and listen to their hearts.

3. Be flexible. Many adjustments caught us unaware. As Americans we expected every family to have a car, but in Tel Aviv in the 1960s only the wealthy minority could afford one. Thus, for our first eight years there, we rode the public buses like almost everyone else. We also learned to plan for no public transportation from sundown Friday to sundown Saturday in honor of the Sabbath. When our children attended public school, their week began on Sunday and ended Friday afternoon. We asked ourselves, "Was not the biblical principle that of sanctifying one day out of seven?" Most evangelical churches in Jewish areas of the land chose to worship on Friday evening or

Saturday morning, and a few on Saturday evening. However, Arab Christians chose to worship usually on Sunday.

Flexibility was also a necessity in messianic Jewish worship. In the 1950s, expatriate missionaries had established most of the congregations, using their own languages and traditional liturgies; one could hear translations in various corners of the worship rooms. However, young Israeli believers now demanded that the services be led in their national language. Also, they were not comfortable with the organs and pianos of western worshipers or the translated Western hymns. They were not rejecting us, just our Western cultural elements. In 1980 a group of young believers from various congregations met at *Beit Immanuel* to share some of the new Hebraic melodies they had composed to the words of the Psalms or vignettes from the Gospels. Soon worship teams in many Hebrew speaking congregations were using flutes, guitars, and drums. The Spirit said to us, "Be flexible!"

4. *Ask forgiveness.* Many others like our gardener friend, Shimon, were bitter about the centuries of Christian persecution. That six million Jews perished during the Second World War was burned into their souls. To them the number was more than a statistic. Most of the European Jewish immigrants to Israel had lost at least some of their family members. I learned what I had to do. As a Western Christian Gentile, I needed to get on my knees and ask forgiveness for what my people had done to Shimon's people.

Several decades later, in 1996, I was thrilled when a Reconciliation Walk was organized for Christian pilgrims to follow the trail of the first Crusades of nine centuries earlier, in 1096, from France and Germany across Europe, Turkey, and Syria to Jerusalem. The purpose? All along the pilgrimage, the walkers requested forgiveness from Jews and Muslims, whose ancestors had suffered or died at the hands of the crusaders.

5. *Be aware of the family's role.* J. D. Graber had told us that one of our first tasks would be to be "a house by the side of the road" (Sam Walter Foss, 1858-1911, "The House by the Side of the Road"). For us, that happened literally. Our children were touching the lives of those of their friends on our street as they all played together and went to school together. For a time Bertha led a (Sabbath) Children's Club in our home, sharing the gospel by using strictly First Covenant stories

that would be acceptable. Relating to adults, Bertha taught English lessons to those who were willing to use "The Bible in Basic English" (1000 words) as the textbook. Meanwhile, I was pastoring a scattered congregation, one person by one person in a sort of house church approach.

Also, for quite a few years, everyone in our family was involved in being hospitable to various international students. For example, Adebisi from Nigeria spent a summer with us, and Hazel from Australia stayed a full nine months. Roni, a new local Jewish believer, came in and out of our home like a daughter. Stewart, whose father lived in California, came to the American International School almost like an orphan. Our two older children were the ones who requested us to take him in like their brother.

(When we traveled in America, we spoke in churches as a family, sharing testimonies and singing as a group. I look back with amazement and intense gratitude to God that each of our children values those years in Israel as a time when we were responding to God's call to us as a family.)

6. *Look for spiritual renewal.* A rainbow often shines the brightest against a dark cloud. Sometimes we could see only the dark clouds. We had expected the Jews to be excited to discover their true Messiah, but for many Jesus had become a Gentile god. In our first half dozen years, there had been only one baptism. We felt desperately dry. So did others. Out of mutual desperation, about six of us interdenominational couples (Baptist, Pentecostal, CEF, and Mennonite) chose to meet together on our knees. Those weekly prayer gatherings quickly became more precious to us than the larger Sabbath service at Baptist Village, which most of us attended.

With us one day was a dear seventy-year-old British lady, Mary Smith, who, because she had a calcified back, could sit only stiffly in worship services. That afternoon we felt strongly impressed to pray for her. Almost immediately she jumped up, touched the floor with the palms of her hands, and shouted: "I'm healed!" News of her healing stunned believers throughout the land. She was quick to declare, "This miracle was not just for my comfort, but for the building of the faith of believers throughout Israel!"

Some weeks later, Bertha felt strongly impressed one morning to lay aside the glasses she had worn for twenty years. Subsequently, her optometrist confirmed that she had regained 20/20 vision. (That healing continued for the next twenty years until old age brought on the need for magnifying lenses.) What a way to restore a faith that had almost dried up! So what was God's Spirit teaching us at this time? Was he not demonstrating that Jesus' authority to do miracles had not ended with the New Testament era? We recognized that secular Jewish unbelief had invaded our hearts and minds. Apart from a deep spiritual renewal in our hearts, we had little to tell our Israeli friends! (For more of our story of spiritual renewal in the 1970s, see *My Personal Pentecost,* ed. Roy Koch, Scottdale, Pa.: Herald Press, 1977.)

7. *Learn to cooperate.* One of the crucial results of the spiritual renewal that swept across Israel in the 1970s was a longing for more cooperation and less competition. There was less of the flying of the flags of separate denominations and more willingness to join efforts for the sake of kingdom goals. The renewal had first impacted the expatriate community, but soon touched local believers, both Arab Christians and messianic Jews. When I became general secretary of the UCCI, the chair was a messianic Jew and the vice chair an Arab pastor. Roy Kreider had already served as chair, and Joe Haines became secretary after me. Meanwhile, Bertha served as editor of the forty-page quarterly UCCI News magazine for about a dozen years. After we left Israel, Bob and Nancy Martin each had important roles in the UCCI.

As a relatively small group in the UCCI, we Mennos were likely less threatening than some of the larger groups. The conviction grew that our task was not to add to the multiplicity of denominations and agencies at work in this tiny land. Local believers were confused by the call to give allegiance to the Dutch Reformed or Scottish Presbyterians or Finnish Lutherans or Southern Baptists! We felt Spirit led to support the growing number of local assemblies worshiping in Hebrew and Arabic and to prepare for indigenous leadership. When the Anglicans invited us to join such an effort at Beit Immanuel, we sensed this as God's call.

8. *Work for peace and reconciliation.* Early on we had discovered that Israel was similar in size and shape to the state of New Jersey, which made it quite vulnerable in times of conflict. We faced the agony of stuffing our family into a basement room during the Six Day War. The children experienced the trauma of diving off a school bus into a nar-

row ravine when Iraqi planes flew over. Later came the Yom Kippur War and the war with Lebanon. Meanwhile, I taught Arab orphans at the Baptist Village school, worked with Muslim hotel owners while with Sharon Tours, and continued my interracial work in the UCCI and at Beit Immanuel.

Then came Wajdi, a devout Muslim *kadi* (judge and counselor) who had attended services at Beit Immanuel frequently as part of his spiritual search. He asked for baptism. Now I had baptized numbers of messianic Jews by that time, and each of our three children had been baptized in the Sea of Galilee. But Wajdi was different. He asked for the privilege to immerse himself in the baptismal pool of a local church in a private ceremony. That way no one could accuse a foreign pastor of bribing him. He subsequently continued his work as a Muslim kadi but told us that he used principles from the Sermon on the Mount in his counseling work without labeling them. We saw him as a messianic Muslim like the messianic Jews we served.

After the Six Day War, it was possible for the MCC (Akron) workers in Old Jerusalem to join with the MBM (Elkhart) staff, who were serving in Nazareth, Haifa, and Tel Aviv, for an annual retreat. On these occasions we could share our stories, our ministries, and our lives with each other. By his Spirit, God was teaching us to refrain from complicating the political issues of being pro-Jew or pro-Arab but rather choosing to be pro-people. Jesus taught that the field is the world. Jesus was calling us to a two-eyed vision for the Middle East.

9. *Welcome the transformed*. In the first two decades of our ministry in Israel, relatively few made public decisions for Christ in the Holocaust generation of immigrants coming from Europe. The breakthrough came in the 1970s and 1980s. The *Sabra* (native-born) generation of those born in Israel began to travel abroad after their three-year required army service. The bubble of the Zionistic idealism of their grandparents was bursting, and they eagerly traveled abroad to find larger answers.

Reuven, the son of Russian immigrants, went to study at the University of Arizona in Phoenix. To earn extra cash, he advertised Hebrew language lessons, and his best student was a vibrant Gentile believer. Reuven puzzled over how this Gentile knew his *Tanach* (Old Testament) better than he did as a secular Jew. Finally one night he walked out under the stars and cried heavenward, "God, must *Yeshua* be part of this equation?" In his heart he sensed the answer and returned to Tel Aviv, searching for other young Israelis who believed as he now did. He discovered the Beit Immanuel congregation, and we joined the search together. Later on, Reuven became an active deacon among us.

Reuven was not alone in his search. The congregation at Beit Immanuel grew as young Jewish believers began to share their messianic faith with their friends. This was no longer an ethnic religion (like Judaism) but a universal message. They were glad to be known as messianic Jews, that is, young Israelis who had discovered that Yeshua was Jewish after all, and the Messiah for Jew and Gentile alike. The name *Yeshua* (Savior) became precious to all our ears, for in Him we were bonded together. This was true spiritual transformation that only the Spirit of God could accomplish!

10. Mentor the leaders. With the influx of young Israelis into the body of messianic Jews in the Land, many expatriate missionaries sensed the urgent need to do more discipling and training. At Beit Immanuel one weekend we had the wonderful joy of chartering a bus to take the 150-kilometer journey to baptize seventeen new believers in the Sea of Galilee. What a thrill!!

Roy Kreider had the vision to begin a Study Center at Beit Immanuel to offer evening classes for Bible training for young believers. Salim Munayer, a young Arab Christian leader in the congregation, continued that vision when Roy left Israel in 1985. Salim later became the dean at Bethlehem Bible College. He also initiated Musalakha, a venture to bring together both evangelical Arab Christian and messianic Jewish pastors and leaders for a three-or-four-day-retreat in an isolated location, where they could learn to know, respect, love, and bond together as spiritual brothers with the same kingdom goals. Roy and Florence, along with Bertha and myself, had the privilege of offering premarital counseling as well as leading messianic weddings for about a dozen couples in our last eight to ten years. Several of those weddings became strong witness magnets to the secular relatives who attended.

It became increasingly clear to me that God was asking me to release my pastoral leadership to local citizens. I preached and taught in American Hebrew, but they could preach and lead in Israeli Hebrew. In the summer of 1985 on our furlough, I shared with Ron Yoder and

A beautiful rainbow over a fishing boat on the Sea of Galilea lends special symbolism to Paul and Bertha Swarr's lifetime call to be fishers of women and men.

the Elkhart leadership my request to return to Israel for a final two years to mentor young Israeli leaders. By the spring of 1987 we had installed four young men, most in their thirties, as the team of elders at Beit Immanuel, along with two mature women as deaconesses. When we had arrived in Israel in 1957, there might have been fifteen or twenty Hebrew-speaking messianic Jewish congregations in the land. By 1987, more than 100 such congregations were led mainly by local indigenous citizens. All glory to God: Abba Father, Incarnate Yeshua, and the inspiration of *Ruach HaKodesh* (Holy Spirit)!

(For a more complete account of the Mennonite presence and ministry in Israel, see Roy Kreider's book, *Land of Revelation: A Reconciling Presence in Israel,* Scottdale, Pa: Herald Press, 2004.)

MINISTRY AND RETIREMENT IN THE U.S. (1987-2013)

Powhatan Mennonite Church (1987-1990)

Already before leaving Israel, I had received an invitation to serve as pastor of Powhatan Mennonite Church, thirty miles west of Richmond, Virginia. This was especially attractive to Bertha and me since all three of our married children lived in the Powhatan and Richmond area. However, the transition from being an urban international and interdenominational pastor in Tel Aviv to being the leader of a rural Virginia Mennonite congregation proved to be somewhat of a mismatch, though we continue to have many dear friends in Powhatan.

Hope Christian Fellowship (1990-1999)

The Virginia Mennonite Mission Board came to my rescue with an offer to support us in an effort to plant a new congregation in the west end of Richmond. We formed a team of seven or eight couples and families who sensed the same call and met in a daycare center first and later in an elementary school auditorium. Local families joined Hope Christian Fellowship so that by the mid-1990s around eighty were attending. Because we emphasized the cell church model, we became part of the Cornerstone District of Virginia Conference. I gladly released leadership to them in the mid-1990s. We then spent a number of years involved at First Mennonite Church in Richmond.

Warwick District overseer (1993-2000)

During the twenty years that we lived and served in the greater Richmond area (including Powhatan), all three congregations were part of the Warwick District of Virginia Mennonite Conference. The Moses who gave gracious and clear leadership to these Warwick churches was Lloyd Weaver. His wisdom and vision shone through at district meetings. Lloyd also had a special gift for discovering and releasing young people into ministry, which affected our family in an unexpected way.

Already in 1995 while we were yet in Tel Aviv, Lloyd had ordained our son David for his role in youth ministries in Virginia Conference. David was also an elder in the Powhatan congregation. Then in the early 1990s, Lloyd ordained Jay Hostetter, our daughter Evelyn's husband, to be part of the active leadership of Hope Christian Fellowship. About the same time Carl Stauffer, our daughter Carolyn's husband, was ordained to the team leadership of the Jubilee Christian Fellowship, a new interracial congregation in eastern Richmond. All three men and their families have continued to be active in teaching and discipling ministries: David and Sharon in Richmond and Israel; Jay and Evie in Powhatan and Fredericksburg; and Carl and Carolyn in South Africa and now at EMU. I stand amazed at the abundance of God's grace at work in unexpected ways!

In 1993, Lloyd retired from his bishop role, and it took four others to attempt to fill his shoes: Leslie Francisco, Gordon Zook, Stan Maclin, and myself. For seven years, 1993-2000, I served as overseer for three congregations: Powhatan; First Mennonite in Richmond; and Warwick in Newport News. However, I never felt as content or successful in this administrative role as in my pastoral and teaching ministry.

Richmond and Harrisonburg (2000-2013)

In these years, it was our privilege to serve in supportive roles. From 2000 to 2008 we were active at First Mennonite congregation in Richmond, with Barry Loop as pastor. There I did some teaching, played the organ, and served several years on the eldership team.

However, when Bertha unexpectedly experienced a stroke in April 2008, we were stopped in our tracks. God had granted her excellent health for seventy-six years. Now the stroke affected her walk-

Paul Swarr leading the baptism of grandchildren at First Mennonite Church in Richmond, Virginia, in 2001.

ing and gave her short-term memory loss. Thus, we knew it was time for an anticipated move to Harrisonburg, which was recommended by our children. How delightful now to be renting from James and Ruth Stauffer, with whom we have mutual grandchildren. Ridgeway Mennonite congregation has become our church family, along with associate membership in Family of Hope, a house church. We are thankful also to live next door to the Virginia Mennonite Retirement Community with its Wellness Center and many pleasant facilities and activities.

Youth with a Mission Agency (YWAM, 1987-2008)

Parallel to the various church activities here in Virginia was our fairly major involvement in Youth With A Mission. We first discovered YWAM in Israel in the early 1970s when Darrel Hostetter, a son of B. Charles and Grace Hostetter, stopped in and reported on his YWAM experiences in West Africa, where his parents were then serving. Subsequently our David and Evelyn went to a School of Evangelism (SOE) in Lausanne, Switzerland, and then joined outreach teams in the Communist nations of Eastern Europe and also in the Middle East. Later Carolyn went to a Discipleship Training School (DTS) in Heidebeek, Holland, with outreach in Amsterdam. We soon sensed that all of our children had put their roots down deeply into a strong living faith before heading into the challenge of academic and university studies in America. We stood back in awe and honored Yeshua!

By the time we arrived in America in 1987, YWAM had a strong program going at what had been a Catholic girl's school called Rock Castle near Powhatan. Two years later, David became the leader of a YWAM base in Richmond and served there for ten years before returning to Israel for ministry. YWAM International has three basic areas of service: evangelism, discipleship, and mercy ministries (the latter is somewhat similar to MCC). The discipleship department, known as University of the Nations, has locations in all six continents and a multitude of nations. Bertha had the privilege of serving as registrar for this program in Richmond for about fifteen years. There she corresponded with many international students, helping them to secure U.S. visas, and becoming the first face of YWAM Richmond to these newcomers. Together we served as leaders at the School of Church Planting and Leadership for nearly ten years.

A special privilege was beginning a School of Jewish Studies, which had not existed previously anywhere in YWAM. This attracted many international students, including some messianic Jewish believers. We sensed that God had opened the door of YWAM to us, for it seemed related to our experience of working internationally and interdenominationally with young people in Israel!

Another similarity to our latter years in Israel was the privilege of discipling relatively new believers, teaching the basics of biblical truth, and mentoring young people for leadership roles. Also, as at Beit Immanuel, we had the joy of doing premarital counseling and officiating at weddings of persons as diverse as a Colombian bride and American husband and a Brazilian bride and a German groom.

In the last several years with YWAM Richmond, Bertha and I served with a Korean woman in a pastoral ministry to the staff persons of the base. When we made plans to move from Richmond to Harrisonburg, about thirty of the YWAM staff came to help empty the house, load the truck, wash the windows, and dispose of the trash.

Then the reality hit my stomach. What an irony that at age eighty, I was still accepted and respected enough to be on the staff of an effective mission agency named Youth With A Mission! But then I knew. If God could use Moses at age eighty to liberate a nation from slavery, or use Caleb to claim his inheritance in the Promised Land, or grant children to barren elderly women like Sarah or Elizabeth, perhaps age is not a big factor. Is it not availability to the gracious purposes of the Lord at whatever stage of life we are in? And so I pray, "*Adon Yeshua* [Lord Jesus], grant us the Holy Spirit discernment never to miss your clear signals in each phase of our journey!"

March 2012
Revised November 2015

Richard (Rick) Yoder

Leader of Solutions That Worked

From EMC student days, observations during years in MCC's international programs, and the completion of a doctoral degree, Rick entered a career of international development work at the national public policy level. In some fifteen countries—his examples are Swaziland, Bangladesh, Kenya, Nepal, and Armenia—he put to use huge government, UN, and World Bank funds in areas like microfinance and health reform. Few have made greater life-saving differences for so many than have Rick and his wife Carolyn, a counseling psychologist—abroad, in Harrisonburg, and at EMU as faculty.

Photo by Carolyn Yoder

RICHARD (RICK) YODER

Redeeming the Assets of the Empire

INTRODUCTION

My wife Carolyn says that I was born on "third base" and have had a charmed life. Compared to the people she has worked with in her private counseling practice and her psychosocial trauma work overseas, plus the many people we have seen and worked with in nearly twenty years of living in some of the world's poorest countries, I am certainly fortunate. I have had no major disease, injury, or psychological/emotional problems. I grew up in a caring, loving, and supportive family and now have a wonderful wife, three daughters, two sons-in-law, and two grandchildren, all of whom love being together. I have enjoyed many educational opportunities and advantages. I somehow even managed to attain two master's degrees and a PhD, despite twice being ineligible to play in a high school football game because of low grades. I must confess I continued that pattern as an Eastern Mennonite College (EMC) student by getting a D in both History of Western Civilization and Statistics! Yet I eventually returned to my alma mater as a faculty member who taught Statistics. So in many ways I have had a charmed life indeed.

But some of the world's sages claim that "a crack in the wall is what lets the light in." They maintain that misfortune and adversity are the primary sources of insight and wisdom. Has then my life really been charmed? Perhaps I have yet to experience life. On the other hand, I might also ask what kind of cruel God would say that a full and authentic life comes only after experiencing much pain and suffering.

My comments in this essay focus on those significant events that have shaped my life; they are organized around my growing up years, my international development work, and my academic life as an EMU faculty member. Four themes emerge as I consider these events: (1) having had a charmed life, as Carolyn claims, (2) working with the world's bottom quintile from a macro public policy perspective, (3) experiencing a restlessness, and (4) having a degree of unawareness or "cluelessness."

My Early Years

I spent the first ten years of my life growing up on a dairy farm near Elverson, Pennsylvania. My father had finished high school, and my mother had completed the eighth grade. I was the third of four rather competitive brothers. Give us a ball, and to this day we will start some kind of competitive game. A dairy farmer typically had little money; however, Dad and Mom helped support a missionary family in Puerto Rico even though they more than once had to borrow money to pay their bills.

When I was in the fourth grade, my parents responded to a call for Dad to pastor Huber Mennonite Church near Dayton, Ohio. It had about twenty-five members, most of whom belonged to one extended family. The MYF consisted of the Yoder boys! Dad sold vacuum cleaners to support his family and was very successful at his job. Mom was a self-described "helpmeet" who was totally devoted to her husband and sons. After around ten years, Dad wanted more education to be a better pastor. Being committed to his church, he asked the members not for financial aid but simply for their blessing for him to attend EMC and get a college degree, after which he would return if they desired. The church refused, so he did not go.

Two factors are significant for me from these very early years. First, moving to Ohio was like moving to a foreign land for my parents. They left behind their family, friends, and community. As difficult as that probably was for them, it was in my opinion among the best decisions of their lives because it opened new worlds to all of us.

Second, borrowing money to support missionaries in foreign lands, along with asking the church's blessing on their desire to get a college degree, demonstrated a commitment to the church and its values that has stayed with me.

Also, my parents took the Bible seriously, but they were not particularly conservative. For example, Carolyn and I had a conversation about homosexuality with Dad a year or two before he died. He said, "You know, I have a lot of discomfort with this issue; but if I'm going to err, it's going to be on the side of grace and love." I hope I can model such grace and openness to change when I reach that age. I was clearly taught the message of peace and nonviolence, but more by deed than by word.

During my teenage years, I spent most of my time playing sports and being outdoors, exploring the world. Dad never missed any of my athletic events and would organize his schedule to attend them. Mom made sure I had a steak dinner before all my games. Education was certainly encouraged by my parents, but apparently not at the expense of sports. Academics were low on my agenda. And while it was embarrassing to stand on the sidelines of the football field two Friday nights because of low grades, it was not so embarrassing that it increased the amount of time I spent studying. The college basketball recruiter who came to my house soon lost interest when I told him my GPA. However, I always felt enormous love and support from my parents, and that was a foundational part of being born on third base.

TURNING POINTS

My belief that life was too short to study too much continued at EMC, particularly during my first two years. But somewhere along the way, I became more serious, and my priorities changed. Perhaps the deep thoughts of my fellow college students challenged me, or my inability to participate in their analytical conversations shamed me. Perhaps I was changed by going to Washington, D.C., to join antiwar and civil rights demonstrations. Or maybe I became inspired when classmate Ken Lehman and I connected with an African-American lawyer and organized EMC students to go to southside Virginia to register voters in that African-American community. Or perhaps the really interesting speakers at Peace Fellowship meetings that filled the Science Center auditorium captured my attention. The 1960s were heady times with huge amounts of learning taking place. How could one not be influenced?

In 1968 I participated in a cross-cultural program in Colombia, South America, through Bluffton College. (This was before EMC had its own cross-cultural program). This experience laid the foundation for my interest in liberation theology and its preferential option for the poor. The Colombian family I was living with wanted to hear an evangelist preach at a large soccer stadium, so I went along. As we were walking toward the entrance of the stadium, the evangelist arrived in her red Cadillac convertible. She was a well-dressed bleached blonde bedecked with expensive jewelry. Her message to the thousands of mostly low-income people in that soccer stadium was an otherworldly one: "Don't worry; if you accept Jesus, your rewards will come in the next life where heaven, with its streets of gold, will satisfy all your longings." In my awakening consciousness, something about that message did not seem right.

After graduating from EMC in 1969, I went to Jordan and then Afghanistan with the Mennonite Central Committee (MCC). It is hard to convey the enormous significance of the nearly four years I spent in those areas of the world. Two events exemplify the importance of that time. First, in Jordan it was the events surrounding "Black September," the Jordanian civil war of 1970. During this time, partly due to my own curiosity, I was shot at and held hostage by members of the Palestine Liberation Organization (PLO), the largest guerilla group in that area. Fortuitously, the commander who interrogated me in their base camp had earned a PhD in journalism from Harvard and knew about Mennonites and their views on the Middle East conflict. That is perhaps why he decided to release me.

It was at this time that I faced the first major ethical dilemma that still impacts my faith and life. The PLO, the Jordanian army, and several embassies were negotiating a way to provide foreigners a secure way to reach the airport and be evacuated. Meanwhile, the U.S. Sixth Fleet had moved into the eastern Mediterranean Sea and was prepared to fly helicopters over Israel into Jordan to pick up Americans and take them to safety if the negotiating parties failed to reach an agreement. What should I, a conscientious objector to war, do? Could I let a military force I could not join and whose methods I could not condone protect me in such a direct way? I decided I could not get on those helicopters if they came. I would choose to remain in Jordan. Eventually the negotiating parties agreed on a plan, and we were safely evacuated to Athens. I never had to implement my decision. But this experience led me to return my partly burned draft card to the Selective Service System. Along with other events, it also led me to be a war tax resister, a position Carolyn and I hold to this day.

For a variety of reasons, MCC decided not to reopen its office in Jordan immediately and reassigned me to work in Afghanistan seconded to the Medical Assistance Program. It was my experiences there that would lead me into a career of international development work at the national public policy level. A fellow worker who had enormous influence on me was Dan Terry, a young college graduate like me and a Methodist missionary kid who had grown up in India. Dan's love of that part of the world spilled over on me; and in the years we worked together, he influenced my life in a unique way. Dan, along with his family, spent nearly his whole adult life in Afghanistan until his tragic death, along with those of nine other humanitarian aid workers, at the hands of the Taliban in 2010.

In Afghanistan, I worked as a jack-of-all-trades in a fifteen-bed hospital in the Hindu Kush Mountains. In this incredibly mystical place, we lived at 9,000 feet and were surrounded by 17,000-foot mountains, where the temperature dropped to forty degrees below zero in the winter. We were mud- or snowbound four months of the year, so the project had a Cessna 185 aircraft equipped with snow skis to ferry people and supplies in and out. What twenty-three-year-old would not be enthralled by such an environment?

My workplace was also an environment unlike any I had experienced before. At this hospital we treated many children with intravenous fluids because they were dehydrated from diarrheal diseases. After some time I began to notice that the same children kept coming back with the same type of diarrhea problems, and we kept treating them with intravenous fluids. I wondered why this pattern persisted.

Although I was not yet able to articulate my thoughts, I later came to realize that we were "ambulance driving." In other words, we were treating the symptoms rather than the causes of diarrhea. A better solution lay in the realm of sound national public policies and actions, like building pit latrines and digging wells so that people would not need to use for drinking and cooking the same river water into which human and animal feces flowed whenever it rained. I also realized later that instead of spending today's equivalent of over $1 million on building that fifteen-bed hospital, it would have been better to spend that money building those wells and pit latrines or immunizing 75,000 infants and children. Such measures would have saved many more lives. This was my first lesson on how *not* to do development and on the value of sound public policies.

As I recall this formative period of my life, it is clearly evident that events during the '60s along with my MCC experiences were opportunities for enormous learning and personal growth. What are those events today that generate such learning? In the absence of a military draft that led conscientious objectors to war to do alternative service, why have not the American wars in Iraq and Afghanistan, along with climate change, rising inequality, and the American plutocracy put people on the streets? Why is the Mennonite church not at the front of the line, asking these and other critical questions and generating alternative options?

PREPARATION FOR THE FUTURE

After my experiences in Jordan and Afghanistan, I returned to the U.S. and enrolled in a graduate program at the University of Pittsburgh. Some may wonder why a graduate school would accept someone with an academic record like mine. For that, I must thank my MCC experience, not only for getting me into graduate school but also for providing me a full scholarship for all my graduate work. As a now highly motivated student, I earned master's degrees in public health and in public and international affairs. I continued my studies for an interdisciplinary PhD that focused on economic and social development, public policy, and public administration. During those years, I learned about national and international systems, structures, and policies (those "principalities and powers" Paul refers to in Ephesians) that, for good or ill, reach all the way down to the children I saw in that little hospital in Afghanistan.

In 1975, during our time in graduate school, Carolyn, also an EMC graduate and a Yoder-Yoder, and I were married; she had just returned from two years in Egypt with MCC. She went on to complete a master's degree in linguistics and then taught at the university while I completed my PhD. Let me say I found in Carolyn a real partner in what would turn out to be a wild, stimulating, and challenging ride (yes, a calling) that we have shared. She has been a partner in not only a relational sense but also in a mutually rewarding professional sense. We get stressed out together, review and critique each other's work, test out ideas on each other, and have wonderful conversations every day. Carolyn is a gift and a treasure whose presence brings joy to the journey.

During our five years in Pittsburgh, Carolyn and I participated in a Quaker meeting. It was there that I learned about the value of being silent, listening, and waiting for the "inner light" to emerge, along with "seeing that of God in every person." Each of these characteristics and practices is critical to healthy interaction with creation, including people, particularly those different from ourselves—a goal to which I still aspire.

INTERNATIONAL DEVELOPMENT AND PUBLIC POLICY

Armed with my degrees and some grassroots development experience, it was time to go change the world—and that was my vision! Although that vision may have been a little ambitious, I offer no apology because I think everyone needs a vision for his or her life. Of course, visions will be modified along the way, but too many people have either no vision or one that is too small. As Nelson Mandela said, we do no one a favor by thinking small, a trait I would suggest Mennonites too often cultivate.

The biggest share of my international work has been on projects financed by large donors such as the United States Agency for International Development (USAID), the Department for International Development (DfID, the British development agency), United Nations, and the World Bank. Although the funds typically came from governments, empires if you will, it was my hope to use them in a redemptive way. In the course of my career, I have worked on extended projects in some fifteen countries. We always lived overseas as a family until our daughters entered college. Carolyn was generally able to find meaningful activities: teaching English, earning a second master's degree in counseling psychology, and doing psycho-social trauma work in Kenya, Jordan, and Armenia. She also did private counseling in person and via Skype in various countries.

The two areas in which I have worked were microfinance and health reform. I did not focus on the clinical aspects of course but on ways to organize and finance a country's healthcare system so it leads to better quality, at a lower cost and with improved access and equity, especially for the poorest populations. The size of the projects ranged from as little as $2 million to as much as $100 million. I will give examples of several of these projects to add context to my reflections.

In Swaziland, with USAID funding, our task was to work with government officials in reorienting the country's health care system away from an urban and hospital-based curative system toward a rural, preventive, and community-based health care system. When I returned to Swaziland ten years later to help prepare another five-year national health strategy, I learned that the reforms we introduced had been institutionalized, leading to significant reductions in the burden of disease.

In Bangladesh, I worked on a United Nations-financed project designed to strengthen the planning, management, and research skills of some 10,000 government officials, with the research findings used to develop health policy. The goal was to improve health, especially maternal and child health, and reduce rates of population growth. Although for many years I considered this project to be one that had minimal value, I learned several years ago that the government training institution where the project was based is now granting master's degrees in public health.

In Kenya, I was head of a $15 million USAID- and Ford Foundation-financed microfinance program that gave small loans of $300-$400 to *jua kali* (under the hot sun) businesses designed to create jobs and increase incomes. Its current status? From what I hear, it is alive and well—despite predictions that, when the foreigner (I) left, the organization would collapse due to corruption and mismanagement. Someone told me some years back that this program had become one of Africa's largest and most cost-effective microfinance organizations. If true, it is significant only to the extent to which it has provided jobs, higher incomes, and better quality of life for lots of people.

Nepal was a $100 million DfID/World Bank-financed health reform project designed to make the health care system more effective, more efficient, and more equitable. Armenia was another health reform project with similar objectives. The Armenian project and the one in Swaziland are probably the two that have brought me the greatest satisfaction, particularly in terms of "making a difference" and believing that the whole country is better off, not just a few people or a few communities. I know I am not supposed to say such things because it is "un-Mennonite," even though the evidence supports these assertions.

Has my work in international development at the national public policy level met my original vision? Responses to such a question can be detailed and complex, so I will just give some summary reflections. Working at macro public policy levels has certainly been challenging, rewarding, and stressful; but I would argue that it has been a redemptive use of the empires' money, and I would do it again. Positive change does happen at the national level. I have provided only a few examples of projects in which I have been part. But when these efforts are combined with those of many people doing similar projects around the world, they have global impact.

In low-income countries there have been dramatic improvements in health status indicators. For example, maternal mortality has gone down some fifty percent over the last twenty years, and infant and child mortality has declined by a similar percentage. (That is an enormous improvement, especially if one of these statistics is your child, mother, or wife.) Life expectancy has gone up; malaria has declined by fifty percent in ten years; HIV/AIDS has reached its peak and is on the decline.

Obviously, many factors have contributed to these improvements and result from the work of many committed people around the world. But certainly a significant share of these improvements can be attributed to structural and systemic changes made at the national level of countries. Yes, some projects have wasted money and done poorly, and it is these we hear about most frequently. But that has not been my personal experience.

For me, access to health care has always been a justice issue, one of those "necessary but not sufficient conditions" for building peace. It is just as important as other basic needs such as food, water, housing, or education. For justice to mean anything, it must be operationalized into concrete policies and programs.

Mennonites are fond of saying that it is more important to be faithful than effective. While I agree with that assertion on certain issues, such as withholding payment of war taxes, I also think such a perspective can lead to small thinking and sloppy work. It should be both/and; faithfulness and effectiveness are not mutually exclusive.

Another observation is that perspectives change when a person gets an inside view of a situation, with those views often becoming more nuanced, balanced, and realistic. For example, as a longtime critic of aspects of the World Bank, I was surprised to see that in Nepal the World Bank was leading the initiative in supporting the government's policy of "social inclusion"—that is, reversing the cultural practice whereby Dalits (Untouchables) and women are excluded from access to resources, opportunities, and voice. In rural Nepal, high-caste Brahmin doctors would often not examine or treat low-caste Dalits, especially Dalit women. Although I am a firm believer in cultural sensitivity, this cultural practice could not be condoned. I was impressed by the World Bank's stance on this issue.

Also, since I was usually the head of the projects on which I was working, I was often invited to cocktail parties and other official functions of the larger donors. I never felt quite at home at these events. I could make conversation with the people I met, and I even enjoyed many of these occasions; after all, people are interesting! And I could use these functions to make important connections with key people who advanced the project. But I never felt comfortable with treating people as having "instrumental value" over "creation value." Nor did I feel at home in the diplomatic culture where pursuit of national strategic interests rather than the common good was the underlying objective. Another familiar adage applies: "You can take the Mennonite out of his or her subculture, but you cannot take the subculture out of the Mennonite."

A fair amount of my work has been dominated by ambiguities and paradoxes related to issues such as having more income than we needed and enjoying better housing than many around us. I was bothered by the material disparities between my local counterparts and me. How does one live in this reality while remaining committed to Anabaptist values of simplicity, community, justice, and equity? I was also uncomfortable because of disparities in power. How does one maintain a servant perspective while having control over substantial sums of project money? Whose interests are being served—those of the rich and powerful, or those of the poor and weak?

I have fewer answers and more questions than I once did. My work has made me increasingly aware of the complexity of doing development work, partly because it is so multi-dimensional. Of necessity, my answers have become more nuanced. On a recent trip to Uganda, I remember seeing once again what we see all over the world: people sitting on the sidewalk and selling cigarettes, candy, used books, or house wares spread out on a cloth. They are just trying to earn a living, but I automatically think, How does one respond to this?

On one of my recent trips to Zambia, I read Adam Hochschild's *King Leopold's Ghost* (Buena Vista, Va.: Mariner Books, 1998), which traces the history of the Congo as far back as the fifteenth century. It is a dark and awful account of plunder, terror, and greed—a common story of the "center and periphery" around the world, even though the "center" and the "periphery" change over time. It struck me, as I was reading, that this story is really about extraction: extraction of raw materials, extraction of souls by the missionaries, extraction of human beings not only by slave traders but also by missionaries who could not resist the lure of great profits. (I should also say that missionaries were among those who later internationally publicized these atrocities.) But then it also struck me: Am I part of this extraction through the development work that I have done during my career? Do I extract more value than I create and leave behind?

One final observation is that at EMU I felt a mixed reception over the fact that I had worked at a policy level, mostly because I had worked with the U.S. government, the empire, often on USAID contracts. I understand this attitude not only because government forces chopped off the heads of Anabaptists back in the sixteenth century, but also because the American government, past and present, has been the heart of the beast. Along with the good it has done, it has caused great harm around the world.

Could I have worked on a USAID contract in Southeast Asia during the Vietnam War? No. Could I now? Yes. The same is true about working in Central America during the Contra war. I am glad that EMU through the Center for Justice and Peacebuilding (CJP) is using USAID and other government money in a positive way in several locations. I would like to see more of such work, especially at a policy level where the sphere of influence can be substantial.

Given this rather upbeat perspective, we cannot forget that for most rich donor countries, official development assistance is a part of promoting national strategic interests; and resource allocation is justified on that basis and channeled toward that interest, even though this aid may or may not overlap with the interests of the host country. There is great need for making the case that promotion of the common good and global interests is, in the long run, the most effective way for the U.S. to reduce the threat of terrorism and promote its national interests.

I will end this part of my story by quoting Jason Elliot, a writer who spent some years in Afghanistan in the 1990s. This excerpt from his book *An Unexpected Light: Travels in Afghanistan* (New York: Picador, 2001) exemplifies the pull, the attraction, for doing international development work and living abroad that is still with Carolyn and me:

> From the beginning I felt the touch of the land and people, which came to form the backdrop of my feelings and broke into my life in unexpected ways. It threw everything into sharper focus and brought such immediacy to the present that the world of home took on at times a dreamlike quality. It pushed my feelings into unchartered orbits and challenged my ordinary logic in ways that would have been easier to ignore. Like vines that prosper on the slopes of a volcano I thrived nonetheless under its influence until I felt the whole of life more keenly, both its joys and its sorrows. I found luxury in small things and in friendships discovered bonds I felt would last for life.

TEACHING AND RESEARCH AT EMC/EMU

In general, my work experience has alternated, in three- to five-year blocks, between working on projects overseas and teaching at EMU. In 1985, after five years of development work in Bangladesh and Swaziland, we felt it was time to return to the U.S. By that time we had three daughters, with the youngest having been born in Swaziland. I had job offers at both EMC and Penn State and, after some gut-wrenching processing, chose EMC.

Why EMC? During our time overseas, I had come to realize more clearly the "value of Anabaptist values," not only the values of justice and peace through nonviolence, but also those of community, service, and others. I also saw the need for these values to become part of society's public policy dialogue. Thus, in the late 1980s, when we were living amid ongoing tribal conflicts in Kenya, I wrote a letter to President Joe Lapp, suggesting that "the little Mennonite Peace College in Virginia" (as some people called it) start a peacebuilding master's degree program comprised of an academic arm, a research arm, and a practice arm. Let me quickly note that, unlike Al Gore's saying he created the Internet, I am making no claim for "inventing" CJP; unbeknown to me, I was just one of several people with this dream. So one factor in my 1985 decision to return to EMC was my desire to be part of an institution that promoted these values and encouraged students to think seriously about them. I wanted to help students see the "value of these values," learn how distinctive they were, and find ways to carry them out in their personal and professional lives.

But when I came to EMU for the first time as a faculty member, I was rather disappointed to find that many Mennonite students, particularly those who had attended Mennonite high schools, had a blasé attitude toward these values. Why was this, I wondered?

When students would ask me about how to enter development work, my oversimplified response began to sound like a broken record: You should complete a double major, one in peace and justice and another in business and economics. The peace and justice studies will give you the perspective you need, while business and economics classes will give you the tools you need. After college, join an agency like MCC for several years to gain first-hand experience at the grassroots. Then go on to earn a PhD in an area related to development, and take jobs that will eventually lead you into positions of public policy.

Although students would ask me for advice, it still seemed difficult for them to think seriously about seeking public policy positions. I say this partly because a number of the development organizations I have worked with over the years have said that they would be happy to consider any of my strong students as interns. Although I have had many such students, only one took advantage of this opportunity. While I do not know the specific reasons, I suspect that at least two factors are relevant: (a) we have few models of Mennonites engaged in public policy work; and (b) the traditional Mennonite interpretation of service and servanthood can limit us. We are taught to be humble, to avoid having too high a view of ourselves, and to identify with vulnerable people who live at the margin. In other words, as Donald B. Kraybill has articulated so eloquently in *The Upside-Down Kingdom* (Harrisonburg, Va.: Herald Press, latest rev. ed., 2011), we are to have upside-down kingdom values. The interpretation we have placed on implementing these values has frequently encouraged ambulance-driving professions, in which Mennonites do small-scale relief or curative work, putting band-aids on societies' ills and injustices.

Of course, we need ambulance drivers. But I want to broaden the traditional definition of service to include public policy work so that our values and voices become part of the process of creating more peaceful, just, and equitable systems and structures at national and international levels. In that way, we can help prevent things from falling apart and thus reduce the need for ambulance driving. I think this approach is slowly being adopted, but there are many missed opportunities. Of course we will make mistakes. But through broad-based reflection and analysis, we can continue learning, and the next generation can build upon the knowledge we have gained.

Between 1985 and 2006, I spent seventeen years at EMU, though not consecutively. These were times of great satisfaction, stimulation, and reward. Of the many factors that stand out, I will mention eight:

(1) It was a gift working with an organization where there is relative value congruence.

(2) There was no need to worry about people stabbing one another in the back. It may happen, as in any organization, but at EMU this behavior was more often unconsciously passive-aggressive than intentional.

(3) Being exposed to and discussing new ideas across disciplines was always stimulating.

(4) It was highly gratifying to work with other faculty and administrators to develop new programs and initiatives. For example, we established "for the common good" as the orientation to the business and economics department. We also made these classes more rigorous so that it was no longer the major to which weak students gravitated. We instituted and developed the MBA program and several

new majors. Over time, we shifted faculty promotion policy from a seniority-based system to a merit- based system that rewarded not just good teaching but also research and publishing. Our faculty consequently became knowledge producers rather than just knowledge consumers; moreover, through publishing, they were able to introduce Anabaptist values into the public arena. Also, my colleague Roman Miller and I were able to get time built into faculty loads for research purposes, a provision that continues today.

(5) I loved teaching and interacting with students, helping them separate fact from fiction, jointly preparing and presenting papers at conferences, and publishing articles in professional journals with student co-authors. It was exciting to teach students how to use the tools of economic analysis to get at the big issues of our time, such as poverty, inequality, unemployment, environmental protection, the nature of work, leadership, debts and deficits, and the role of government. Ironically, my lack of emphasis on academics in high school and early college years helped me become a better teacher. They made me much more empathetic, particularly with the weaker students who, like me, probably should have delayed their college experience a few years.

(6) It was quite fulfilling to see some of our graduates get full scholarships for PhD programs in economics at major universities.

(7) Perhaps because of an over-emphasis on sports in my high school years, I felt EMU spent too many resources on athletics.

(8) Last, while living overseas, we needed a place we could consider our community, one that would welcome us back physically and psychologically. For us as a family, we found that sense of rootedness at EMU, Community Mennonite Church, and the broader Harrisonburg community.

Despite the satisfaction of working at EMU, after a few years Carolyn and I would get restless and go back overseas for a two- to four-year period. Then in 2006, I decided to take early retirement from teaching at age fifty-nine. Besides getting restless again, I looked at my increasing age and realized that it might decrease my attractiveness to international development organizations. I decided that if I did not go overseas at that point, there might not be a chance later on.

Perhaps more importantly, as much as I liked being at EMU, I felt that it would be difficult to stay another ten years or so and have my

Rick Yoder in a rural clinic in Nepal discussing health system organization and financing issues with a Nepali health worker, 2008

spirit not just live but also flourish. In addition, Carolyn was feeling burned out as the director of Strategies for Trauma Awareness and Resilience (STAR) at EMU and was ready for a change. So when an ideal job offer arose in Nepal, all the stars seemed aligned and we could not say no. It was after Nepal that we went to Armenia for three years until 2010. Since 2013 I have been semi-retired and still do short-term consulting overseas up to a self-imposed ceiling of twenty percent of my time.

As I look back over my life, it seems that I have had some attraction to controversy, especially when it relates to inequity, misuse of power, or injustice. However, plain old curiosity often played a role. For instance, while living overseas, we would sometimes get calls from the American Embassy warning us not to go downtown because of demonstrations or some other form of unrest. For me, that was always an excellent reason to go downtown, talk with people, and understand what was happening.

At EMU, it was controversy surrounding whether the news program *Democracy Now!* ought to be taken off WEMC because, as one donor felt, it was not consistent with EMU's values. Others of us felt it was a breath of fresh air and an important source of non-mainstream media news. The seminary was another issue in that some of us felt it was getting a disproportionate share of the university's resources at the expense of other departments and programs. As someone put it, the seminary had become EMU's Pentagon, even among its loyal supporters, in that you could never spend too much money on it.

Another example: When I was chair of the Harrisonburg City School Bboard, I tackled military recruitment and the issue of Junior Reserve Officer Training Corps (JROTC), because I felt such programs did not belong in our schools. I knew the moral argument would never work in this politically conservative area, but I thought the high cost argument might work. Therefore, I did a small study that empirically demonstrated that the taxpayer cost per JROTC student was something like ten times higher than the cost of a math or English student. We had public hearings; only two Mennonites came and testified. Although invited, Virginia Mennonite Conference leaders were not among those who testified, nor were they willing to write a letter to the school board. Meanwhile, the two Department of Defense-paid directors of JROTC had all fifty or so JROTC students testify at the hearing. My efforts were unsuccessful, but the hearings generated some heat and maybe some light in the local newspaper.

As with any controversial issue, these initiatives all brought grief to some and delight to others. And just to be clear: I do not raise these issues now because I have an axe to grind. Rather, I see such happenings as part of our history that we can learn from and move on.

RELIGION, FAITH, AND SPIRITUALITY

Some ask how living in places with other religious traditions for so many years has affected my views on religion, faith and spirituality. I will provide a brief rumination in response to that question. Fundamentally, I believe having a sense of peace with one's self and life is important. I think you know when you have that peace and also when you do not.

Throughout history, religion (all forms of which claim to be the truth) has done great good and caused great harm. I am not sure how the good and the harm balance out. Dr. Amir Akrami (visiting Muslim scholar from Iran at EMU) and Dr. Yehezkel Landau (associate professor of interfaith relations at Hartford Seminary) and others speak of the "particularistic and the universal"; they advocate honoring and valuing one's own tradition while respecting and learning from other traditions within the context of the universal human story.

That view resonates with me. I often consider how to make sense of the various religious traditions, especially Hinduism and Buddhism, which are so different from the monotheistic tradition of Christianity, Islam, and Judaism. I wonder if Christianity is as difficult to figure out for Buddhists and Hindus as Buddhism and Hinduism are for Christians. I cannot help seeing Anabaptist rituals such as foot washing through the eyes of people we know around the world and wonder how they would understand them.

I also ponder the images portrayed in the words of songs we sing. Put yourself in the place of visiting Iraqi or Afghan Muslims hearing "Onward Christian Soldiers" in one of our churches while American troops and weapons systems are trying to "save" their countries. It is certainly true, as Dom Helder Camara, former archbishop of Recife, Brazil, has stated, that religious traditions are sacred ground where one needs to tread softly, for God has already walked there.

Seeing the Bible and other sacred texts more as metaphor than a set of rules has allowed me to focus on the commonality of religious traditions instead of worrying about doctrinal issues or deciding how many angels can dance on the head of a pin. Jesus' statement in Matthew 7:16, "You will know them by their fruits" (NRSV) has taken on significant meaning for me in sorting out the different traditions. Love, joy, and peace are key examples of those fruits and are found in all major religious traditions. Ethics are more important than doctrines. The concept of original blessing fits my understanding of God much better than an emphasis on original sin.

Omar Eby's *Mill Creek*, which describes Lancaster Mennonite High School in the 1950s, is not only hilariously funny, it also reminds me that bishops, church leaders, school administrators, and our parents did the best they knew how, just as I do the best I know how. They needed grace just as I need grace. I wonder how my children and subsequent generations will look back on what I did and how I did it.

Conclusion

Here I will return to some of my opening themes and end with what I call my "lawn mower question," which is my term for those subconscious thoughts that come to the surface when we are doing mindless activities, such as mowing the lawn.

First, have I been confronted by any of those cracks in the wall that supposedly provide insight? My biggest crack in the wall happened nearly twenty-one years ago, when Carolyn was diagnosed with multiple sclerosis just as I was leaving for a two-week consultancy to Somaliland. That was a very big crack: I feared I would lose her through debilitation or even death.

But in true Carolyn fashion, after learning rather quickly that mainstream medicine offered little hope, she found alternative methods of treatment, and she is fully herself. While we were living in Jordan, she wrote a book on these alternative treatments that is ninety-five percent finished; it probably will remain unfinished, she says.

Another crack in the wall occurred in Armenia. As I mentioned before, this project brought me a great deal of satisfaction. It was also one that provided a lot of stress during its final year or so. For the first time in my career, I was unable to build a positive relationship with the new USAID person who began overseeing the project during the last year. He happened to be Armenian; while my view of development fully supports having host country nationals in charge, theory does not always work out so neatly in practice. He was my supervisor but personally insecure and technically weak and made decisions that negatively impacted outcomes. (This was my view, of course, but also that of many others.) So I chose to confront him rather than just doing what he said. Nothing seemed to work: neither presentation of empirical evidence nor charm nor anything in between.

This experience raised lots of questions for me, but two were especially challenging. The first was, Why is emotional detachment from this situation so hard? The second was, Is he my mirror? Am I seeing in him a reflection of my own weakness and ego? I continue to ponder both these questions.

As for being born on third base, I have trouble buying into the Horatio Alger, pull-yourself-up-by-the-boot-strap, stories. Certainly that type of success does happen. But cross-country research shows that social mobility in the U.S. is among the lowest of the rich, industrialized countries, even lower than "socialist" France! I suspect that most people who make the rags-to-riches claim have actually been born on second or third base and possess limited understanding of what it is really like to be born on first base, or before. I certainly do not know what that would be like.

And that leads to my "lawn mower question": How do I live responsibly in a world of enormous need? Thanks to my early years of growing up, my faith, and my over-exposure to poverty and injustice, I really cannot separate my own lifestyle from that available to the bottom quintile and the majority of the rest of the world—and I am glad for that inability. As my friend Dan Terry has said, we are all knotted into the same carpet.

March 11, 2013
Revised June 2015

Yoder sitting on a destroyed Soviet anti-aircraft gun on the back of a truck while in post-Taliban Afghanistan in 2002 as part of a team rebuilding Afghanistan's national health system.

PART IV

Making a Difference ... Through Leadership in Unexpected Ways

Richard (Dick) Benner

Man of Faith in the Media

Journalists of integrity do not always live safe, comfortable lives. As a truth-telling owner and editor of a free Pennsylvania newspaper, Dick found he needed national intervention for his family and himself. Later, as editor and publisher of Canadian Mennonite, *he received a warning from Ottawa to rein in political partisan comments. Dick highlights stories "that were and are the most faith-forming, resolve-testing of my seventy-plus years."*

Photo by Lisa Kazcmarek

RICHARD (DICK) BENNER

Moments of Grace

On the grounds of the Loyola Jesuit Retreat Center near Guelph, Ontario, about a twenty-minute drive east of Waterloo, there is a labyrinth of panels in the center of a green garden. Designed to tell the story of time, it begins some 4.5 billion years ago. The panels divide the development of the universe into periods such as Homo Sapiens, Aboriginals and Primal Worship, Agricultural Societies, the Industrial Revolution, and Human Induced Extinction of Species. The last panel calls our time This Present Age of Grace. I found that description, in the purview of time, to be an odd, almost contrarian perception of our troubled age. What about the span of my three-score-and-ten years could possibly be considered a time of grace?

That span includes the following troubling and often tragic events: two world wars, three regional wars, the prospect of an Arab Spring seeming to risk bringing on World War III with an enormous loss of blood and treasure; global political upheavals; a culture of consumerism like never before in our history; the unconscionable degradation of the environment; the warring of nature in tsunamis, earthquakes, hurricanes, floods; the dumbing down increased coarseness of our discourse through the Internet; the poisoning of our body politic through polarization; the marginalization of Christianity worldwide; and the rise of religious extremism shaking places like the Middle East; growing militarism; and the criminalization of an immigrant population once welcomed to strengthen our fabric of what came to be called the "greatest nation on earth."

What about any of this could be remotely described as the Age of Grace? Had these Jesuits been cloistered too long in the garden to know what swirling realities of violence and degradation were happening outside their silent retreats, blossoming apple orchards, and verdant organic gardens? Had their liberation theology skewered their grip on reality? Or was this parody a kind of cosmic joke being played on unsuspecting attendees seeking refuge from a noisy, greed-driven, ecology-ignoring place outside these environs? Was the onlooker being welcomed into some kind of escape so cynical as to bring on fits of laughter?

The more I pondered this seemingly stark and contradictory label, the more I settled into quiet reflection and meditation. Then new reality hit me. Yes, in comparison to all of the groans of creation of those past epochs of time, our time of development—though seeming at times to tear us apart as a civilization and a people of faith—could be considered quiet. It could be a time of unusual blessing and shalom. In fact, it dawned on me that for me as a person of faith, this is exactly what my life has been, even with all its tumult and drama, all of its questions, its periods of doubt, its stresses, and seemingly insurmountable challenges. When taken in total (which is the redemption of creating one's memoir!), things take on a different perspective.

Thus I would like to summarize my story with a series of vignettes about persons and events that shaped me, forming a narrative that is winding and perhaps "wealthy" in scope. Since my profession has been largely that of a journalist, I have developed the art of storytelling in many different venues. As I review my life then with a few chosen narratives, nothing will be more descriptive of it than Alfred Lord Tennyson's oft-quoted line in Ulysses: "I am a part of all that I have met."

I want to warn you, though: Some of my stories could be disturbing since I heeded John Lapp's wish, in his introduction to volume 2 of these ACRS Memoirs, that the authors would have expressed "more freely and openly the frustrations they surely felt along the way." He observed, also, that he found "little if any anger expressed" in those stories (p. 2).

First, a Quick Biographical Sketch

I have never been a pastor. I have never attended seminary. I have never worked overseas under Mennonite Central Committee or a mission board. I have not written any religious books. I have published a collection of my newspaper editorials and columns after a mid-life break from building up a newspaper enterprise with the help of my spouse, Marlene Keller Benner, in central Pennsylvania during the 1970s and 1980s. I also compiled a book on the lives of my parents-in-law, Frank and Sue Keller, on the occasion of their sixtieth wedding anniversary.

I come from a family of Swiss/German Mennonites who settled about eight generations ago near the port of entry at Philadelphia, Pennsylvania. My father was a tradesman (a hosiery knitter) and a deacon in a small mission church. My mother's family came from a long line of farmers and merchants in farm-related businesses.

I have been in the communication field all of my life. I was educated in Mennonite schools from grade school through college. I have worked in Mennonite institutions. As an adult editor at Mennonite Board of Missions in Elkhart, Indiana, my first journalistic assignment was to ship off six pages of "Mission News" every Friday afternoon to be placed in the *Gospel Herald*, which was produced and printed in Scottdale, Pennsylvania. I set up a five-member development staff at what was then EMC (Eastern Mennonite College) at the request of President Myron Augsburger during the early 1970s and later taught journalism for eight years (1999 to 2008). During my staff years at EMC, I also set up alumni chapters nationwide and in southeastern Ontario and started an alumni newsletter.

But I was always restless inside the walls of these institutions. I learned to know many noteworthy people there: J. D. Graber, who headed overseas missions at Elkhart; John Howard Yoder, who doubled as Graber's assistant and was a Bible professor at Goshen College at that time; and Dorsa Mishler, the patient and wise human resources director. However, I always felt that my experience was too narrow, my worldview too parochial, and my social networks mostly confined to persons with whom I shared that worldview.

While I couldn't articulate it then, my lifetime reflection now tells me that my youthful idealism was anxious to put shoe leather on what I had learned from such early teachers as I. B. Horst, John A.

Lapp, and Hubert Pellman. To borrow the language of Richard Rohrer, the Franciscan mystic, in describing what he calls the "first journey of life," I was trying to find the "starting gate."

At one point early in my career, in one year I received multiple invitations that would have involved career changes: Ernest Bennett wanted me to head the information services in Elkhart; Ellrose Zook wanted me to come to Scottdale as assistant editor of the *Gospel Herald*; and Myron Augsburger wanted me at EMC to establish a development division for public relations and fund-raising. I turned them all down on the premise that I hadn't had enough life experience, was too provincial in my outlook. I needed more seasoning, more roughing up, in a changing world.

Instead, I opted for the position offered to me by Ralph Hernley, who had just left the Mennonite Publishing House in Scottdale to purchase three community newspapers in several small Pennsylvania towns close by. He wanted me to be the editor of the one in Ligonier, the bedroom community of the wealthy Mellon family of Pittsburgh and the home of the now-retired Arnold Palmer, the famous golfer who had built his own golf course there. On the competing Mellon golf course it was reported that 75 per cent of the corporate business deals in America were made on those greens. At that time the Mellon family group, who were primarily bankers, had controlling interests in many of the major corporations of America—Chrysler, Gulf Oil, ALCOA, and others.

This experience was an eye-opener for someone who had grown up in the small town/rural enclaves of Mennonite communities. There was no middle class here. Nearly everyone who was not a member of the Rolling Rock Club, an exclusive social network of all those second-level management people in the Mellon family business, worked for them in all of the service businesses in town. Ligonier was thus dominated by the wealthy, who had lives of leisure, while the working class served their every need from hardware to housing.

That was only the beginning of my working intermittently inside, then outside, the institutions. At one point, I left EMC to buy a local weekly newspaper in central Pennsylvania. Marlene and I built that paper into a three-newspaper enterprise with thirty-one full time employees, a weekly distribution of 50,000 in two counties with a delivery system of 200 carriers, and annual advertising sales of $1.3 million. After an incredibly difficult and even dangerous sequence of experiences there—to be recounted later in detail, Marlene and I left for Phoenix, Arizona.

While in that city, during a four-year break, I earned my master's degree in mass communication, and Marlene took graduate courses in family systems. Then it was back to Virginia to be close to our children and aging parents. In Charlottesville we set up a small printing business, which is presently in the hands of our youngest daughter, Lisa, and her husband, Tim.

Where we are living now in southern Ontario, Canada, I am having the time of my life in the work I enjoy most—writing, editing, and managing a national church publication, an enterprise that has a firm footing among a Mennonite population comprised of second- and third-generation Russian refugees mostly in central and western Canada and those of Swiss/German descent in eastern Canada. It has been stimulating and instructive to live and work among cultural Mennonites with a completely different historical narrative.

Well into retirement age, I am too stubborn to quit working—*so* not ready to join the ranks of those who run off to a warmer climate in the winter and a lakeside cottage in the summer. I would rather "wear out" than "rust out," to use a well-worn cliché. I am having too much fun for those retirement activities. I have battled cancer on three different occasions, always coming out the survivor, and have four stents in my heart that keep the blood flowing. Every day is borrowed time, a gift of life and health for which I thank my Maker.

I turn now to several stories, personality profiles, and events that shaped my life. With these narratives I offer a glimpse of the struggle, the ethical dilemmas, and the growth spurts that formed my character, birthed an ethos that served as a guiding star in many a tight spot, and continues to inform my decisions and judgment as I work every day "in the vineyard."

Horace Longacre

A big man with a magnanimous spirit to match his 300-pound frame, my maternal grandfather, a cattle dealer, seemed to pick me as his favorite from the get-go. I can still hear the gears grinding in his big Chevy cattle truck when he picked me up at the house of my birthplace on Adams Avenue in Souderton, Pennsylvania, to go with him to buy cows at the Perkiomenville sale barn. I was only three years old. He would sit me on his large knees as he called out the best bovine circling the ring.

He hated farming, my dad told me later when I, at age forty, persuaded him to tell me the whole family story, warts and all, which ended with Grandfather Longacre's fall from grace in his proud, powerful faith family. He was so good at judging cows that all the local farmers in the Spring City area would commission him to buy their cows for them. However, his in-laws excommunicated him from the church because he was running with the wrong crowd and passing bad checks before the days of overdraft protection. In the words of his brother-in-law—a powerful patriarchal bishop in the local 275-year-old Mennonite congregation—he was increasingly an embarrassment to the family and church.

Dad recounted a story about him once as we sped down Interstate 81 in my sporty 280Z. Pop-Pop Longacre, he said, had had to be bailed out of jail by his brothers in Harrisonburg after passing a bad check for the cattle he had bought at the local stockyard for the local farmers in the Shenandoah Valley. (That's how far his reputation for buying cows had spread.) My dad had accompanied his brothers from eastern Pennsylvania to Harrisonburg in a car he described as being full of angry and judgmental men. They had reluctantly bailed out my grandfather, but not until they had severely lectured him about his bad business ethics. Their lack of grace for him was so stark that his brother-in-law, then President of Eastern Mennonite College (now University) John L. Stauffer, had intervened with words of mercy and forgiveness.

All of this, of course, escaped me as a beloved grandson. To me, Pop-Pop Longacre was a hero. I can't help but think now that some of his rebellion and free spirit infected my own genes as I faced tough situations in my own journey. Dying of a massive heart attack at the young age of fifty-seven while living alone in a hotel room, separated from my grandmother at the time, he came to a sad end.

Was his special affection for me a projection of the love he found lacking in his own family and faith community? Has he been channeling me in some of my own struggles, especially with church authority and political figures? Does some of my own righteous anger have its roots in an attempt to avenge the unfair treatment by his own kin and faith community? Considering anger a gift, not a curse, is this, in the broadest sense, a gift of grace passed on from generation to generation? Can grace once again abound?

Marlene Keller

The contributions our spouses make to our success are far too seldom acknowledged. Thus in the lineup of persons helping to shape me I want to give tribute to my bride of fifty-plus years. At a celebration in June 2012, I read a tribute that I had written to her on her fortieth birthday and printed in my newspaper column "Behind the Scenes." Here is part of that tribute.

> From you I have drawn mammoth strength. When the decisions were tough, the problems insurmountable, you had faith that things would work out. Though cautious at times, you were always optimistic.
>
> I have come to rely on your keen instincts. Sometimes blinded by logic, I often miss the spiritual dimension. On that you have a monopoly. I don't know how you keep your senses so sharp, but they are always operative, always on tap to point the direction.
>
> Your sense of fairness has helped us build good customer-employee relations. From you I have learned that being fair spares you the pain of always being right, a refreshing balm when life, with all its inequities and injustices, seems too harsh.
>
> Your unselfishness has often baffled me. Giving up a teaching career to rear a family and develop our business is not an option for the selfish. Although wincing from time to time under the stress of it all, you never threw in the rag and called it quits. That is not in your nature.
>
> Towering above all other qualities, however, is your spiritual strength. Possessing a quiet but pervasive faith in God, you rely most heavily on that connection for all that life, with its persistent unpredictability, brings to you.

There's more, but you get the point: Teaming up with Marlene Keller was a moment of grace in my life.

Frank and Sue Keller, My In-Laws

When I married Marlene, I married into a loving family. The qualities I found in my life-partner were rooted and nurtured, I was soon to learn, in her parental home. At their sixtieth wedding anniversary in 1985, I paid tribute to the strength of their marriage, the influence of their lived Christian faith, their fair business relationships, and after retirement their joining Voluntary Service for the Mennonite Board of Missions. Becoming part of the hospitable, loving Keller family provided for me many moments of grace.

Uncle Eddie

I had to shout above the clangor of the conveyor belt at Landis Block and Concrete in Souderton, Pennsylvania, where my Uncle Eddie, the second oldest of eight, had held a job for forty years. It was a monotonous grunt job that involved moving concrete blocks off a long conveyor belt and placing them on wooden skids for the forklift to load them onto trucks for delivery. He had not taken up the family trade of knitting hosiery at the Granite Hosiery Mill. Instead, because he was hearty and strong, he was better suited for this work that didn't require skills of running complex machines, spinning out the silk stockings of the era.

Exposed over the years to the loud industrial noise, Eddie had become hard of hearing and was a bit socially challenged. Never marrying, he lived with his parents, Charles and Leanna Benner, in their large Dutch-gabled house on Chestnut Street. He had few living expenses beyond that of a car. A man of simple tastes, he could put most of his earnings in the bank.

"I'm buying a newspaper and need some down money," I shouted. "Could you loan me $25,000?"

He stopped the conveyor and looked down as if to study the question. "Where?" he asked.

"In central Pennsylvania. I'll pay you the going interest rate," I said, trying to add to the appeal and to convincing him that I was not looking for a handout.

He paused for what seemed a full minute, looking down at the ground as if he were intent on studying this unusual and unexpected proposal. Then he lifted his head and broke into one of his rare smiles

As editor/publisher of a chain of weekly newspapers in central Pennsylvania, Dick Benner is conversing with the National Guard during a truckers' strike in Breezewood, Pennsylvania, in the late 1970s.

and simply said, "Yes, I think I can do that. When do you want the money?"

There was no business plan, no elaborate spread sheet of ten-year projections, not even a discussion of the length of the term, whether five, ten, fifteen, or twenty years. When getting into the details later, I told him I would pay him six percent, which was just a little under the market for business loans at the bank. I drew up a simple demand note, and he wrote a check. He knew nothing about the newspaper business, didn't ask for any kind of collateral. The deal was sealed totally on trust between family members. Never misplacing that trust, I made monthly interest payments. When we sold the newspaper in 1984, guess whom was paid off first.

Ed Hendricks, the Porn King

Self-described as an independent pornography king, Ed Hendricks was used to getting his way. Square-jawed with piercing brown eyes and locks of black, wavy hair, he was a handsome hulk of a man, all muscle and no fat at 240 pounds.

Driven and mean-spirited, he was questioned by the police in several armed robbery cases and a murder case but never charged. It was all a charade, anyway, according to my source, because he had the local and state police paid off. The ones who should have charged him spent their New Year's Eves watching rollicking skin flicks in the den of Hendricks' large, stone ranch house near Doylestown, Pennsylvania.

Hendricks had a first-name relationship with the governor of the state, calling him with a negotiated payoff every time an obscenity bill reached the governor's desk, according to telephone conversations monitored by my source For somewhere between two and five million dollars, the bill was sure to get the governor's veto.

Hendricks' mentor was John Krasner, the so-called "Prince of Porn" from Harvey's Lake. In January 1975 Krasner was fined $4,000 and sentenced to two years in prison for the sale and exhibition of obscene materials in Montgomery County.

The two, who made quite a pair, headed up the Raintree Corporation, a ring of independent porn dealers operating outside Pennsylvania's large cities of Pittsburgh, Harrisburg, and Philadelphia. Since the Mafia had a lock on pornography distribution in those cities, independents were forced to operate in the hinterlands—where competition became so fierce among them, I learned from a reporter at the *Philadelphia Inquirer*, that they began to kill each other over territories.

Finally a truce was declared, and the territory was divided along the main highways—Route 6 (now Interstate 80) in northern Pennsylvania and Route 30 along the southern path. Hendrick's and Krasner's territory was named the Raintree Corporation. The fact that Hendricks was the primary operator on Route 30 put our small town of Everett in his path.

Raintree Corporation, it turned out, was a dummy corporation so named to throw off the press and the courts. Soon after I ran this fictitious corporation story as the beginning of a series of front-page stories in our weekly newspaper, a highly placed source in the Hendricks' family became the "Deep Throat" of my ongoing investigation. Her daughter was unhappily married to Ed; her name was Rose.

Like the Deep Throat—who undercover gave the facts of the Watergate story to Bob Woodward and Carl Bernstein of the Washington

Post, facts that brought down a sitting president—my Deep Throat, too, had first-hand knowledge but also had to keep well hidden in self-defense.

The motive of my Deep Throat, unlike those of Woodward and Bernstein, was abundantly clear. Having witnessed the domestic violence inflicted by Hendricks on his immediate family, Rose wanted him locked up for life. She would do anything to aid the press in bringing his clandestine operations out into the open.

Having checked with the local Catholic priest for my take on Hendricks, Rose placed a call early on, identifying herself, saying she had the first-hand knowledge I needed to tell the story. She was so distraught in those early conversations that I was dubious about everything she said. But believing she had valuable information, I tried to slow down the rush of emotion coming over the phone to get to the salient facts. I feared some of what I was hearing was too laden with paranoia to be completely reliable.

At some point I knew we had to meet and talk face-to-face, free from the fear of having our phones tapped. Pressed for an opportunity to meet, she finally thought of the perfect setting—the basement of the local Catholic church in Doylestown, Pennsylvania, where her eleven-year-old grandson was to be confirmed on a Saturday afternoon.

I enlisted the services of a local Catholic volunteer nicknamed Neptune, a retired antiques dealer considered by the townspeople to be "a lush" and a little crazy. He offered to take his own car for the three-hour trip to the eastern part of the state to keep my identity under wraps and to serve as my bodyguard during the basement interview. Visiting my office often during the organized picketing by concerned citizens of the town, he became my unofficial protector, constantly urging me to carry a gun for self-protection.

The idea of guns frightened me more than these violent characters. Not doubting for a minute that they would "waste" me if given the opportunity, I considered that I had a more powerful weapon in my pen and printing press. In addition, my faith told me that the providence of God was more powerful than all the guns in the world, a concept totally escaping my protector when hearing those words. He just shook his head in disbelief: How could someone be so naive?

The meeting with Deep Throat was productive. The light, airy basement of the massive stone Catholic Church felt comfortable and safe. My source was not exactly as I had envisioned. A short Italian woman with thinning sandy hair turning grey, she was intense and nervous, not sure if her son-in-law was following her or was having one of his bouncers watching her every move, even to the inner sanctums of the church.

She seemed pleased to meet me but wanted to get right down to business. As she had on the phone, she talked excitedly and fast, leaving huge gaps in the necessary facts I needed to document any illegalities in Ed's dealings. As a harassed mother of her only daughter, Ed's wife, she wanted only to get the gory story out. As a professional journalist, I needed all this deep background, yes, but enough facts to go public with a credible story.

She told me of the armed robberies in which Hendricks was involved and the regular beatings of his wife to "keep her quiet" about the business. At one of the beatings, he left her in a pool of blood and "went fishing," she said.

The citizens of Everett, once informed through my front-page stories, were enraged. The Catholics, a religious minority in town, were especially offended. Their priest, Father Robine of St. John the Evangelist Catholic Church, a young and gentle man of the cloth, was determined to put shoe leather on an organized protest. He convinced others of the heavily Protestant ministerial association to organize more than 100 picketers to carry protest signs in front of the store from 10 a.m. to 10 p.m.

One of the more dedicated ones, Diane Godwin, the boisterous daughter of my unofficial bodyguard, Neptune, would regularly give six hours a day on the line, taking down the names of persons patronizing the store. She took great glee in reporting two of the town fathers, middle-aged businessmen on the town council who were both actively involved in their churches. While they were trying to be discreet, their attendance hadn't escaped the keen eye of Ms. Godwin, who was sure that, although publicly on record as protesting the enterprise, these men were privately delighting in this newest business venture in town. Indeed, they turned out to be regular customers.

I took the liberty of publishing their visits without their names in my ongoing front-page series of stories on the porn operation. One story did it. There were no more visits to the store by these dirty old men whom the protesters considered hypocrites.

With the sustained picketing and my weekly reporting on the porn operation, business dropped off drastically at the bookstore. Hendricks, according to Deep Throat, would come home to Doylestown carrying a copy of our paper and throwing it down in disgust, issuing a volley of profanities about "that god-dam paper in Everett."

It was late one morning when I got a call from the secretary at the elementary school where our youngest daughter, Lisa, was a third-grader. "Did you call in today asking your daughter not to get on the school bus this afternoon, but to wait for you to pick her up?" she asked innocently.

"No, I did not," came my startled reply. "Why?"

"Well, I was just double-checking because a man called this morning with that message, identifying himself as Lisa's father, but it didn't sound like you," she said.

My blood pressure started to rise as I suddenly realized that the battle had gotten up close and personal. Hand-to-hand combat. This was an attempted abduction of my child. Thanking the secretary for her diligence, I told her firmly that no, I wasn't the one who had called, but that I had a suspicion who might have. "Tell Lisa," I said, "not to take the bus this afternoon. I will be there; you bet I will be there."

Shocked at this raw grab for revenge, I muttered to myself that Hendricks really was all and more that Deep Throat had described. He would stop at nothing. Failing to intimidate me in any other way, he was now resorting to the nearest and dearest of my heart. A bully knows the soft spot.

I went at least fifteen minutes early to the front of the school where the buses were soon to line up for their young passengers. Surveying the activity and other cars, I discovered nothing. Lisa followed my instructions and got into the car. I hugged her close and told her I loved her. I didn't tell her the story right then, but later explained to her and the rest of the family that we had to be very careful about our goings and comings.

Perhaps it was only a scare; perhaps it wasn't. Either way, this was a stark warning that the battle had now moved to a deeper, more dangerous level.

One evening a man appeared in our neighborhood, driving a beat-up, black Plymouth with a huge German shepherd on the passenger's side. The driver had long greasy hair. The license plate was from New York, our watchful neighbor told us. He circled the house several times just before dark on a Saturday night.

The local police confirmed the neighbor's report. Late Saturday night they had stopped a man from the Bronx, New York City, accompanied by a large guard dog. The man was carrying a weapon and a small amount of drugs. They questioned him but found nothing with which to charge him. Giving him a warning, they told him to "get out of town."

I should have known. The noose was tightening. The threat of the abduction of our daughter was the first warning. Now came the death threat. Deep Throat had actually given me advance notice. Calling, all excited, she warned me in hushed tones to be careful.

Her daughter had listened in on another one of Hendricks's phone calls. This time it was to a person named Michael. He was apparently a hit man for the Mafia who, for $500, would get me out of the way. His next phone call was to one of his contacts at the Harrisburg headquarters of the Pennsylvania State Police.

"I've just put out a contract on Dick Benner," he told the paid-off insider. "There will soon be a homicide in Everett, and you know what you have to do to cover it up."

Providence sent us out of town for the weekend, but I knew that I would have to move very carefully in the next weeks and months. Hendricks would stop at nothing. The conflict had now moved from removing obstacles in a business venture to a battle of the egos. It had become extremely personal between Ed Hendricks and me.

Not fearful nor easily intimidated by nature, I was nevertheless not foolish. The stakes were high and I knew it. Looking over my shoulder, checking for bombs under the hoods of our car and business vehicles on a daily basis were not acts of paranoia; they were for the sake of survival.

I called Father Robine late Monday afternoon after getting the full picture of the attempt on my life. Since the church was in the next block from our offices and home, he was there in five minutes, calling the family together and saying a rosary for our safety. He assured us that we would be in his prayers every hour of the day.

Divine protection was great, I thought; but this porn huckster, with his clammy reach into local and state officialdom, could snake his way through layers of bureaucracy with his dastardly deeds and not get caught. Deep Throat had told me as much. She was part of his family and knew the daily operations. No one else was paying that close attention. "He was involved, but never charged," kept ringing in my ears.

After Father Robine left, I knew I had to take this story to higher political levels. On a first name basis with our local U.S. Congressman, Bud Shuster, I called his assistant, Ann Eppard, on her direct line in Washington, D.C., and gave her the highlights.

"This is serious," she said. "We will get you the protection you need."

I asked if the FBI would get involved.

"Yes," she said, "that's the way we'll work this. As soon as I hang up, I will call the FBI agent in Johnstown (whose jurisdiction included our small town of Everett); and he will, in turn, immediately notify the local state police in Bedford, and they, in turn, will advise the local Everett police."

Despite the risks, Marlene and I, partners in every venture of our lives, tried our best to live life as normally as possible. We did not want to live in fear, nor did we want our two daughters, aged eight and eleven, to begin living life in an oyster shell. That would be precisely what Ed Hendricks, with all his perverseness, would want.

More Moments of Grace

The air was tense in Attorney Gutnik's office in downtown Pittsburgh. It was time for a mid-morning break as the two sides met for discovery in the anti-trust lawsuit that we had brought against the *Altoona Mirror*, the lead newspaper that we contended had colluded with six other area newspapers to counter our successful free newspaper. We could offer more circulation to area advertisers than all of them combined. They were selling advertising at half our rates in an attempt to take away our business.

"The petal is off the rose," their attorney had just said with an audacious sneer and the intimidating condescension he was hired to inflict on us in this David vs. Goliath legal joust. From a high profile law firm in Philadelphia, the third law firm the competition had hired to put us out of the way so that they could consummate a sale to Thomson Newspapers, this debonair, aggressive legal beagle was doing all he could to devalue our newspaper enterprise.

What he meant was that though free newspapers like ours had in recent years sprung up all over the country, challenging the monopolistic hold many one-newspaper towns like Altoona had on their markets, these free papers were a fly by-night predatory phenomenon that was fading and soon to be gone.

I felt the blood rising to my temples. How well I knew how hard we had worked for over thirteen years, growing our newspaper enterprise to take a fresh journalistic approach that often challenged the established order. At the same time, we were working at building a solid advertising base that gave a greater marketing reach to major retailers like J. C. Penney, Sears, and Murphy Mart. We were also building a classified ad section that gave the little guy the same 50,000 household market by which to sell household as well as other personal items. We were doing something this sleepy, rural Pennsylvania area had not seen in a hundred years.

However, the attorney was playing the game well and ruthlessly—with all the arrogance and chutzpah he could muster. The newspapers he represented, most of them in the same family for three generations, had become complacent with their operations, cozy with local and state politicians, and not very attuned to the changing times and demographics in their communities. This was their first serious competition. They reacted as they always had when confronted with a challenge such as we posed: They turned to the use of any means to destroy the competition, whether or not their actions were ethical or even legal.

We were told of secret meetings they had had with the seven newspapers in our market covering three counties—Blair, Bedford, Cambria, and Huntingdon—by one of the seven who was developing qualms of conscience. Thus, we knew we were on solid ground in going ahead with a lawsuit against them. Copping out of the group, he said he would testify to the facts.

But we were having our own qualms of conscience. After all, we had grown up with the biblical imperative that if someone takes your coat, give him your cloak also. In expanding on Mosaic law, Jesus had issued a new standard of justice that reversed the old law of "an eye for an eye and a tooth for a tooth." The courts were not the place to resolve differences. Rather, as Jesus' followers, we were to settle our differences in more redemptive ways, like standing personal—or, in this case financial—injury on its head and giving back more than was expected. How could we dodge this biblical standard?

We struggled with the ethics of this dilemma. Somehow the agrarian setting of ancient Palestine didn't quite fit the complexities of our situation. This was twentieth century America with a developed economy. Our financial survival was at stake. We had thirty-one employees whose wages were necessary for their making mortgage and car payments, putting food on the table, and saving money for the college education of their children. It seemed irresponsible to apply the literal statements of Jesus to our dilemma. How could we contextualize them?

We consulted our theological friends. One of them was Eastern Mennonite University Professor Ray Gingerich. "How do we fit the biblical mandate to our situation?" we posed. "Is it right for us to sue in this case? What kind of witness will this be? What is our responsibility to the larger community of faith?"

The answers came back, clearly stated. "These are injunctions for the household of faith," Ray said, "and it is not clear that they apply to your situation." Others agreed. There seemed to be a consensus. We moved ahead with a clear conscience.

I remembered, too, when a couple of my faith brothers of means in Harrisonburg had co-signed a note with a Harrisonburg bank that allowed us to expand our operations for a greater reach in circulation. Both theologians and businesspersons had helped us achieve success in our newspaper operations.

All of this came rushing into my mind as I was being hustled in Attorney Gutnik's office. My attorney, a high-profile Jewish professional who had settled many a labor dispute, called for a timeout.

As we recessed behind the closed door of his office, he warned me: "I know how angry you are with these guys, but zip your mouth. Don't say a word. Let me do the talking for you."

Reluctantly I took his advice.

We went back into session; and our attorney did a marvelous job of countering their bluster with the facts of our strategic building of a solid enterprise, challenging the weakness of their own marketing efforts, and quietly negotiating a sale (with our agreement to Thomson Newspapers based in Canada) that took the lawsuit off the court agenda. It was another moment of grace, this from unlikely sources.

Following the settlement of the lawsuit, we lived for some time in Harrisonburg, Virginia, and then moved to Phoenix, Arizona, for a much-needed mid-life rest.

SILENCING OUR VOICE IN CANADA

Fast forward to my present position of editor and publisher of the *Canadian Mennonite*, the fifty-some-year-old bi-weekly news journal for the Swiss-German "Old" Mennonites of eastern Ontario and the Russian Mennonites in the formerly General Conference churches of the central and western provinces. The search committee who had interviewed me told me that they were looking for someone with "a more prophetic voice with an edge."

Dick Benner, editor/publisher of the Canadian Mennonite, *converses with Don Regier, a reader of that publication at the 2016 annual board meeting in Rosthern, Saskatchewan.*

"Well, they got both in Dick Benner," a young pastor told Marlene at a round table discussion at a MEDA (Mennonite Economic Development Associates) workshop in Niagara Falls, bringing both a smile and a sigh from her as she told me—with probably more sigh than smile! Nonetheless, I am proud to be in the lineage of the founding editor of *Canadian Mennonite*, Frank H. Epp, one of Canada's foremost and most outspoken churchmen as a newspaper reporter, radio broadcaster, church pastor, and university professor and president.

While I thoroughly enjoy this work as a kind of crowning glory to my career as a journalist in both secular and church venues with a great deal of freedom from my employers, I must say that it is a challenge in a theologically diverse universe and among Mennonites with different historical narratives. Trying to lead the conversation and form a common Anabaptist ethos with this constituency is not easy.

It was a slow summer day one July when the mail carrier delivered a registered letter from the Canada Revenue Agency, Canada's equivalent of the IRS in the United States. "It has come to our attention," the audit officer wrote, "that recent issues of the organization's monthly periodical, entitled 'Canadian Mennonite' have contained editorials and/or articles that appear to promote opposition to a political party, or for candidates for public office." The letter referred me to the section of the income tax law that prohibits what is defined as "partisan comment" under political advocacy laws.

In my conversation with the audit officer, he cited two of my editorials and four other pieces, most of which were in our new section called "Young Voices," all of them appearing around our national election time in Canada in 2011.

Shocked and angry, I told the officer I thought this was, first and foremost, an infringement on "speech," even though we enjoyed charitable status as a publication. I was asking our faith community to remember their core Anabaptist beliefs when entering the voting booth, beliefs that we had held for 500 years. I was not championing any candidate or political party but did reference eighteen different bills dealing with issues aligned with our faith beliefs as listed on the Mennonite Central Committee's Ottawa website.

I had also lamented that the political voice of Vic Toews (Canada's Public Safety minister who had grown up in Paraguay as the son of a Mennonite refugee family) had succumbed "to the fear-mongering of this present (Conservative) government by postponing a bill that would provide safe haven for refugees and not return them to their country of origin. Instead," I wrote, "Toews has called the Tamils (an ethnic immigrant group from Sri Lanka) who came to our shores last year 'terrorists.'"

I had further challenged Harold Albrecht (the local Conservative Member of Parliament (MP) from Kitchener-Waterloo) for distancing himself from the Mennonites in the defunding of Kairos by the government for what it said were its pro-Palestinian views.

Kairos is a church-based aid group in which the Mennonite Central Committee is a partner. Andre Gingerich Stoner in his later article, "A Moment of Truth" (*Mennonite World Review*, April 13, 2015, p. 5), further defines Kairos:

> In 1985, black South African theologians released the Kairos Document, a condemnation of Christian support for apartheid policies. In December 2009, Palestinian Christian leaders issued Kairos Palestine. The full title for this 12-page statement is "A Moment of Truth: A Word of Faith, Hope and Love from the Heart of Palestinian Suffering."

In another editorial after the election of the Conservatives to a majority, I had lamented the much-celebrated killing of Osama bin Laden by Obama's military and our Canadian government's increasing militarism under Prime Minister Harper, symbolized by what I considered the totally unnecessary purchase of sixty-five F-35 stealth bombers for national security at a cost of an estimated 30 billion dollars (an estimate of $1,000 for every man, woman, and child in Canada). "This only plunges the world more deeply into a 'cycle of hate,'" I wrote, quoting one of our columnists, Will Braun, in that same issue.

So what to do with this unprecedented move on us by the government? Frustrated, I decided to sit on the incident for several months, consulting those in what I called a "leadership circle": first, my own executive board members and then MCC Canada and the Ottawa office of Mennonite Church Canada. There was a consistent gut reaction of anger and resentment from all of these organizations. The advice I received was that where I saw it as necessary, I was to continue with my critique without naming politicians or parties.

The one journalist on our board's executive committee, Carl De-Gurse, who worked as an editor for the *Winnipeg Free Press*, insisted that the story be shared with our readers so that they could weigh in on the issue. He thought it was a matter of faith, as well as professional integrity, not to keep this situation to ourselves.

Thus in our November 12, 2012, edition, we ran a story under Carl's byline. Also, my editorial in that issue related how it affected me in my work—first, as a lifelong journalist trained to shine the light in dark places and, second, as a spokesperson for our faith community.

I had no idea that this story would grow the legs it did. Within twenty-four hours after both the story and my editorial had been posted on our website, the public media weighed in. Suddenly I was conducting interviews: first with the national press (CBC News) and then on the local TV station. The newspaper of Parliament Hill in Ottawa (*The Hill Times*) ran an editorial called "The Big Chill." Apparently, the story had struck a nerve about government interference that went way beyond our small circulation to 33,000 Mennonites. The Internet lit up with responses to these pieces with some 169 comments on the CBC story alone.

While most of the responses in the public media were favorable and the *Canadian Mennonite*'s readers supportive, not all were so kind. Michael Coren, a right-wing blogger in the *Toronto Sun* (Canada's Fox News) and a columnist for the *Catholic Register*, wrote this:

> While the Mennonites are divided and do contain many fine people, their left wing is powerful and, if you'll forgive the phrase, aggressively pacifist. This alleged pacifism—itself a misunderstanding of Christ's teaching—translates less to deploring violence than to opposing the United States, capitalism, the West, and more recently Israel. They're intensely political and they detest the Conservative government.

The conversation became so heated at times, even with the comments on our website, that I had to call for peace among our readers, asking all "to guard our speech when expressing our displeasure. These persons, and government, with whom we disagree," I wrote, "should be considered our friends, our fellow citizens on a journey in that centuries-old experiment of democracy where all voices need to be heard. Let's not demonize each other."

I was invited to a faculty round-table luncheon by the Peace and Conflict Studies department at Conrad Grebel University College. The group was encouraging but asked to know how this governmental action also applied to their political commentary in the classroom. Academic Dean Jim Pankratz saw it as opening up a wider denominational discussion that would revisit our core beliefs and the ways we witness to government.

As to the final outcome of this skirmish with the government, there were no negative consequences for the magazine—no lifting of our non-profit status, no fines and no withdrawal of our annual government grant. It was only a "reminder," a warning to rein in any "partisan" political comment—a chill, to be sure, but no punishment.

STILL MORE MOMENTS OF GRACE

These, then, are a few snapshots of my life. Absent are stories of grace from other segments, such as these: my stint as the first director of development at EMC (Eastern Mennonite College, now University); a harsh church experience in Phoenix, Arizona, where we had gone for a mid-life break and where we both pursued graduate studies; my work as director of the Shalom Foundation in the Shenandoah Valley of Virginia; and my eight years as an adjunct professor in communications at EMC. Not that these absent stories are unimportant—but what I have chosen to highlight here were and are the most faith-forming, resolve-testing of my seventy-plus years.

December 2012
Revised April 2015

Lawrence H. (Larry) Hoover Jr.

Virginia's Premier Mediator

As a young attorney, Larry, moved by President Kennedy's challenge to serve one's country, did just that in the Philippines, Switzerland, and later India. In Virginia he joined his father's law practice and then began to promote mediation and alternative dispute resolution. Locally he helped to found Gemeinshaft Home and the first mediation center in Virginia (known today as the Fairfield Center) and also, in Richmond, the Department of Dispute Resolution Services within the Supreme Court of Virginia. Honored with many awards, Larry received another one in Harrisonburg when the city named April 23, 2016, "Larry Hoover Day."

LAWRENCE H. (LARRY) HOOVER JR.

Mediation and Peacebuilding: Ways to Make a Difference

As I began to sift through my memories, I decided to start with events from the late 1950s and 1960s. During those years, I started to depart from the path many people expected me to follow in life; instead, I began to explore new roads that led into a larger world. What everyone expected was that I would go to law school at the University of Virginia as my father had. I did just that. After graduation in 1959, I fulfilled further expectations by returning to the family law practice in Harrisonburg, where I worked for three years.

Then along came a new frontier. The challenging words of John Fitzgerald Kennedy really spoke to me at a deep level, so I decided that I should do what I could to follow his instructions: "Ask not what your country can do for you—ask what you can do for your country."

I went to Washington and started knocking on doors, looking for a job in government. I ended up at the State Department, which was really a fortunate choice, for I had a sincere interest in international relations. I obtained a position in the office of the Legal Advisor for the State Department and worked there for two years. Those were turbulent times because of the start of the Vietnam War. Working in the Bureau of Far Eastern Affairs, I was consequently involved in scrambling to create a legal defense for the actions of the American government. That was a very difficult and challenging period.

Another job I had in the Legal Advisor's office was to follow the negotiations concerning the Military Bases Agreement. I began to focus on the Philippines because the U.S. had huge military bases there. The American government had actually taken over the Philippines many years earlier, but the agreement between the two governments had not been carefully examined for a long time. In fact, the agreement that existed was not entirely fair to the Philippines.

As a result, I went on a special trip to help the American Embassy in its negotiations with the Philippine government to draw up a new agreement that would more fully recognize the sovereignty of the Philippines. I met U.S. Ambassador William Blair, and we had some good discussions with the Filipinos and the local staff who were working on the agreement. When I was about to leave, I asked, "Mr. Ambassador, have you ever considered having a lawyer here in your embassy to help with all the important legal issues being discussed now?" And he said, "Well, I'll give some thought to that." The next thing I knew, I received an invitation to come to the Philippines as the legal advisor for that embassy, and I jumped at the chance! That was to be my next adventure: to move to the Philippines for an extended period.

I did not go to the Philippines alone, for I had recently gotten married. After I went to Washington, I had met Eliza, who had come there for many of the same reasons I had. She was working in the Peace Corps. After our wedding, we began our international journey by moving to Manila in 1965 for two and a half years of interesting experiences. We traveled all over that region and had a wonderful opportunity to experience diverse cultures. Meanwhile, the embassy successfully concluded work on the Military Bases Agreement. In the end, it was modeled after the agreement the U.S. had with NATO countries, so it recognized the Philippines as a sovereign nation that we should treat like our Western allies.

When that tour ended, I began to seek another opportunity to work abroad for the State Department and applied for a position as a legal officer at the American Embassy in Geneva, Switzerland. That plan eventually worked out, but it had to be delayed; therefore, we returned to Washington early in 1968. Those were really difficult times because we came back to the riots that followed the assassination of Martin Luther King Jr., and protests against the Vietnam War were at their height. Frankly, I was quite happy when we could leave the U.S. for Geneva at the end of that year.

Just before moving abroad, we started our family. We had applied to adopt a baby in Washington and had heard that our application was accepted. Then, a few days before our departure date, the social workers said they needed to conduct a home visit. We thought that would be difficult since we had already packed up all our furniture and shipped it to Geneva; so we had our home visit in the car, and it seemed to work out okay. We received our final approval and took our new daughter to Geneva in a baby basket. Her basket fit perfectly beside us on the plane, and that trip with our little girl was a wonderful way to begin our next adventure.

Life in Geneva was very different from our experience in the Philippines. The Western offices of the United Nations, as well as those of many other international organizations of all types, were based in Geneva. We therefore had the opportunity to see diplomacy at work in a much broader context than before. While I was there, I had a wide variety of assignments. I attended many social council meetings and ended up involved in negotiations with the Soviets concerning the exploration of outer space. Probably one of my biggest jobs was related to the war on drugs, which President Nixon initiated while I was in Geneva. I had to make connections with all the United Nations personnel involved in international drug control policy, and we were party to drawing up several international treaties on drugs. One of the advantages of this project was the chance to meet Vladimir Kusevich, who headed up drug control for the United Nations. Vlado, who was from Croatia, became a good friend. We had a lot of business to do together, and it was a joy getting to know him well.

Just before the end of the Geneva tour, my parents came to visit. At that time we were living in an apartment on the fourth floor in a little residential area above Lake Geneva. I remember so well sitting on the balcony with my dad and telling him that I had been thinking about coming back to Harrisonburg and working in the law firm. Thus, on that balcony in Geneva we created Hoover & Hoover, the law firm we set up in 1971 when I returned from Europe. I was already formulating some dreams about community involvement and teaching, and those early thoughts helped motivate my decision to return.

The 1970s were really a time of growth. I was deeply involved in growing the law firm, growing my family, and growing lambs. In the firm I began to consider bringing in associates and found two young men who eventually became senior partners; in my view, David Penrod and Dale Davenport are two of the best lawyers in the area. Those were really wonderful decisions that I helped make while my dad was still in the firm.

In time, we Hoovers became guilty of some nepotism. My dad took me back into the firm after my years abroad, and then he also hired his nephew. (We even hired my ex-wife after she completed law school.) So when David Penrod brought his son into the firm, I said, "David, you're doing the right thing by following the excellent tradition that my family has established." David later brought another son into the practice, so there are now three Penrods in the firm. Since I retired, no Hoovers remain as active partners—but we started the tradition of making the firm a family operation.

In addition to expanding the law firm, we also expanded our family. We had the joy of having a son born in 1972, so those years provided the dual pleasure of raising young children and young lambs on a twenty-three-acre farm. Where did the lambs come from? Well, one day my cousin drove up with some lambs in the back of his truck and said, "I'm just going to drop these off and see how you like them." I did not really know what to do with those lambs; but they stayed, and I got more and more interested in them. Within a few years, I had a sheep farm. For about twenty-five years, I was raising lambs, and it was a wonderful thing to do with a growing family. I have such special memories of my young children, who often helped me with the sheep and had their school friends come out to watch the sheep being sheared.

At this point in life, I moved into the phase I now refer to as my period of community involvement. Not long after I came back into the law practice, I was asked to become the attorney for Rockingham County. That was a challenging, time-consuming job, but I valued the chance to help develop a Rockingham County comprehensive plan. We developed a large representative group from the community to help us and received excellent input. These were the early days of comprehensive planning for the county; afterward, we were pleased to hire the first county planner to continue what we had initiated.

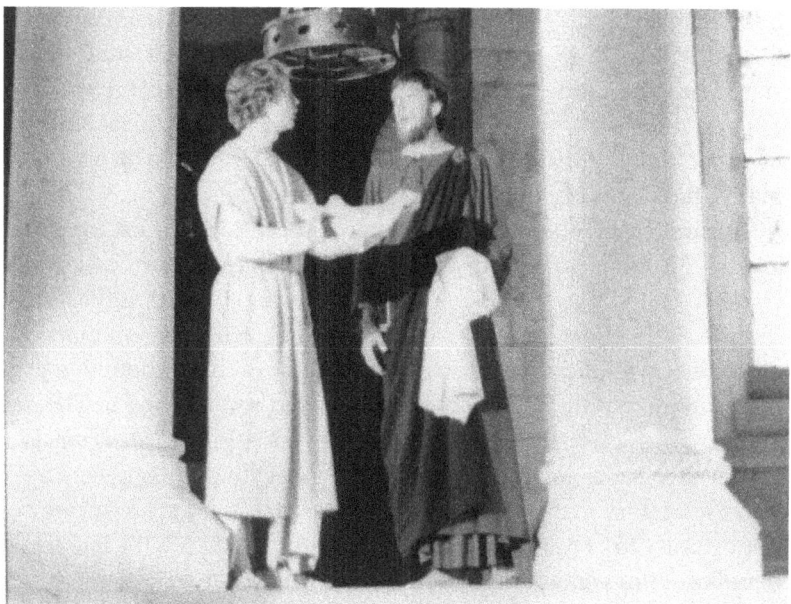

Larry Hoover singing the role of Saint Peter in the production in France of the film Visit to the Sepulcher, *which premiered at the Kennedy Center. With him in the photo is Curtis Nolley.*

Meanwhile, I decided to explore opportunities to use the teaching instinct I had sometimes felt. As a result, I met with the dean at Washington and Lee University School of Law and indicated my interest in teaching as an adjunct professor. I went on to teach a class on International Organizations, based on my experience in Geneva, and also one on Land Use Planning. Those courses were difficult and not very well attended, and they only lasted one semester each. But teaching them was a good experience for me, and I hope that a few of those students benefited. Actually, my law firm later hired a student from the Land Use Planning class, so my teaching did bear fruit.

In addition to legal work and teaching, I quickly became involved in other community activities, such as the Shenandoah Valley Choral Society and the Bach Festival Choir. I also joined the Kiwanis Club and took on some leadership responsibilities with that organization. I served as president of the club for a year; it was the first time I had ever been the presiding officer of a group, and I felt honored to have had that opportunity. During those years, I also began to support the public radio station. I remember one day tuning in to what turned out to be the new WMRA station; I did not even know it existed! At the start, I simply made announcements inviting people to come and find out about the station and join in its support. I ended up becoming a member of the WMRA advisory board, where I learned a lot about the many challenges of public radio broadcasting.

Amid these busy years, I began what I might call my spiritual journey. It was inspired in part by people in Staunton, especially Fletcher and Margaret Collins, who became really dear friends. They founded The Theater Wagon of Virginia, a traveling group that concentrated on medieval musical drama. I knew nothing about that dramatic genre, but I got quite involved and did some acting in Theater Wagon productions. One of those plays was *A Visit to the Sepulchre*, which literary critics say is one of the most frequently performed plays in history. After several performances, I had the life-changing opportunity to be part of a group who went to France in the late 1970s to make a film version in the abbey where *A Visit to the Sepulchre* was first performed in the twelfth century.

It was a marvelous experience to stay in the little French town where the filming took place; we also put on a live performance for the local community before we came home. Upon our return, the film was premiered at the Kennedy Center, which was quite thrilling. In the film, I played the part of Jesus' disciple Peter, and Curtis Nolley filled the role of the disciple John. I had not known Curtis well, but we became close friends through this experience. After all, we lived together in a monastery for three weeks and attended as many as five services a day in the monastery chapel! In the end, I made a commitment to Curtis, who had just been hired as the choir director at the First Church of the Brethren in Harrisonburg. It had been my home church, though I had not attended services for quite a while.

On the way back from France, I declared, "Curtis, I want to be in your choir." When I joined that choir, I also rejoined my home congregation in the Church of the Brethren (COB) and became an active member. I later served as a member of the General Brotherhood Board of the COB and participated in many discussions about issues within the denomination.

The next step in my spiritual journey happened when I became involved with a group called On Earth Peace. This peacebuilding institute was founded by M. R. Ziegler, who was one of the giants of the Church of the Brethren. He was connected with people who wanted to strengthen the traditional peace witness of the church. I made a number of trips to New Windsor, Maryland, where M. R. was teaching young people about peacemaking concepts and leading them in peace witness activities. At one time the Church of the Brethren considered On Earth Peace an official church agency, and it still recognizes its ministry of reconciliation. I am so happy I could be part of this work in its early days.

By this time my first marriage had ended, and in 1980 I decided to marry Pat, a friend whom I had met in my law school days. Actually, Pat had gone to peace meetings in New Windsor with me a couple of times; and when we decided to marry, we asked M. R. Ziegler to officiate. When we talked to M. R., he said he would be delighted. As the date drew near, I began to wonder whether M. R. was authorized to perform marriages in the state of Virginia. I went to the clerk's office and discovered that, sure enough, his authorization had expired! Thankfully, he was able to come to Harrisonburg and renew his authorization before we took that next big step.

Our honeymoon in Croatia was a great way to start a new marriage. My Croatian friend Vladimir Kusevich, with whom I had worked in Geneva, heard that we were getting married and considering a honeymoom trip to Croatia. He called and said, "You've got to stay in my villa!" He had a small place in Splitska, an ancient village on the island of Brac, just off the coast of Croatia. We readily agreed and worked out a plan for transport to the coastal town from which a ferry would take us to the island on which his villa was located.

We arrived in plenty of time and enjoyed a romantic dinner before heading down to the pier to board the last boat leaving that evening. Time passed; we rode and rode, but no island appeared. When I began to ask questions, I learned that hardly anyone spoke English, and I got a bit nervous. I finally found out this ferryboat was headed to a different island and would not return to its departure point until the next morning. We had to sleep on the ferryboat that night; but when we returned, we saw our friend Vlado standing on the pier, smiling and waving as we arrived. He realized that we had taken the wrong ferry and had come to rescue us. What an interesting way to start off our honeymoon!

Another really important event happened on that honeymoon trip. When my friend Don Wells heard that we were going to Europe, he said, "You've got to stop at Caux and visit the Moral Re-Armament International Conference Center. That group is doing wonderful work with peacemaking initiatives." I was not so sure I wanted to interrupt our honeymoon, but Don was very persistent; so we decided that on the way back, we would visit Caux, Switzerland, just outside Geneva. In fact, when we arrived, we were welcomed to a special event. Every summer Moral Re-Armament would have a big gathering at this center in Caux, and the participants would discuss ways to bring about peaceful change all over the world. After our visit, both Pat and I felt like we had come home when we arrived in Caux. The atmosphere was so warm and welcoming and positive that we immediately knew we had done the right thing to stop there.

In Caux, we stayed at a hotel on the hill behind the Conference Center, near Lake Geneva. It was a beautiful setting, and we could sit on our balcony in the evenings and look out over the lake. I hate to admit this, but on that first evening, we lit up cigarettes. A voice came out of the dark night, saying, "There's no smoking at Caux!" We took that admonition seriously, and very soon afterwards we stopped smoking altogether. We continued our connection with the group at Caux and with the people involved in it, and those relationships have been an important part of our experience ever since then. In 2001 Moral Re-Armament changed its name to Initiatives of Change, and it now operates centers in Latin America, Japan, India, and Africa. It is a global network speaking out for peace and moral renewal, and I am pleased to have had a connection with that work.

Don Wells, who sent us to Caux, had come to the Valley with a group called The Fellowship of the Inner Light. It was founded by Paul Solomon as a kind of New Age interfaith spiritual group with psychic overtones. It was attracting a lot of people, and some of its leaders decided to hold a conference in Rockingham County. They needed a special use permit for such an event, so a public hearing was held to consider their application. The room was packed with people who were extremely skeptical about this group and the ideas they were promoting. The opposition was so strong that the board unanimously voted to deny the permit. Don Wells came to talk to me the next day; a friend from law school had given him my name. Don's story sounded very strange, but it interested me because freedom of assembly is a constitutional issue. After our discussion, we filed action in a state court to enjoin the county from denying this group's application because such an action violated a constitutional guarantee of freedom. We felt good about the arguments that we made and expected a positive response, but the judge ruled against us.

What to do? We went back to my office and stayed up all night; finally we decided to enter our plea at the federal court in Harrisonburg the next day. I was unsure whether we could turn to the federal system after losing in the state system, so I contacted a law firm in Charlottesville with expertise in that field. They advised us to go ahead. At the hearing, Judge James Turk said there was no valid reason for the county board's denial except on the basis of the so-called "potty issue." The group had to provide adequate public bathrooms for the event. Inner Light promised to bring in porta-potties, and Judge Turk then ruled in our favor.

We were celebrating the decision at lunch when I got a call saying Rockingham County was appealing its case to the Court of Appeals in Richmond, and it would be heard that afternoon. We rushed to Richmond, along with one of the Charlottesville lawyers. He defended our right to be heard in federal court, and then I presented the facts about the case and the county's denial. By a 2:1 decision, the Court of Appeals affirmed Judge Turk's ruling, and The Fellowship of the Inner Light held their conference. That was probably the most dramatic legal experience I will ever have; it was certainly the most exciting!

On another occasion, Don Wells inspired me to explore one more unfamiliar road. I had been to the 1980 Annual Conference of the Church of the Brethren, where I became particularly interested in the peace position of the church. I mentioned to Don one day that I wanted to figure out how to get more involved in peacemaking because it was such a great tradition. Just a few days later, Don said to me, "I've just heard about a process called mediation, and I think we ought to introduce it to the Shenandoah Valley. Can you help?" We decided to organize a conference and bring in people who could explain the mediation process to anyone who was interested. One speaker would be Ron Kraybill, whom I had recently met at Eastern Mennonite College (EMC), and he helped recruit others. I also contacted a group from the American Bar Association that was beginning work on this topic. When we held the conference, over a hundred people came—lawyers, counselors, pastors, and others who wanted to learn more about mediation.

After the conference ended, Don said he thought I should teach a class in mediation at Mary Baldwin College. I replied, "Don, I've never even mediated a case. How can I possibly teach a class like that?" When he kept on insisting, I finally said, "If I can find one or two people who are crazy enough to help co-teach, I'll do it so others around here can learn how to do this work." Two counselors, Joe Lynch and Dick Whetstone, agreed to help me; the three of us taught a class of over twenty students. This became the core group, along with a group from EMC, who decided that Harrisonburg needed a mediation center.

Since Ron Kraybill had helped us at the earlier conference, I asked him to come down from Pennsylvania to lead training sessions in 1980-81. We had thirty-some people sign up for the first session that Ron conducted. During that session, there was so much conversation about starting a center that I went ahead and prepared the papers needed to form a corporation. During the luncheon that concluded the training, I got people to sign the articles of incorporation.

Larry Hoover singing with his cousins in the May family in a performance to support the Gemeinshaft Home.

From that point on, the Community Mediation Center (now the Fairfield Center) was up and running. It was the first mediation center in the state of Virginia. Kathryn Fairfield then developed and led a team that traveled around the state to train other groups, so we helped spread the mediation process throughout Virginia.

In addition to the Mediation Center and the training teams, another love of my life has been the foundation and operation of the Gemeinschaft Home, which is the residential location of a re-entry program for ex-offenders. Titus Bender, Barry Hart, and I had a big part to play in getting that program started. A special memory for me is the acquisition of the property where Gemeinschaft is located. Barry was originally a part-owner of that house. He and his friends had bought the house on Mt. Clinton Pike and were living in it, but it was such a big house that they also used it to provide sanctuary for refugees who had no place to stay. Thus, it already had a history as a place for people who needed a safe residence while they were recovering from whatever circumstances had made them homeless.

When Barry and his friends decided to sell the property, we began to think that it would be a nice place to house this re-entry program for those making the transition from prison to community life. About this time Chuck Colson came to Harrisonburg to be the speaker at the annual Prayer Breakfast. Colson had just gotten out of jail himself and was very interested in prison ministry. He spoke about what happens when people get out of jail. He discussed the problem of recidivism and the need for former offenders to become involved in a community where they can try to complete their recovery.

After the Prayer Breakfast, which was held at the Belle Meade Restaurant, Chuck Colson said, "Those who want to talk more about this issue, come down and join me in the basement meeting room." Barry, Titus, and I had attended the breakfast, so we all went downstairs and told Chuck our story. We explained our idea about starting a re-entry program in this house that was for sale, and Chuck warmly approved what we were doing. He said, "You guys, follow your instinct; do whatever it takes!" Then he turned to the rest of the group and asked, "How many people in this audience would like to be a part of this plan?" A dozen or so people were down in that basement, and several hands went up.

We talked to each of them afterwards, including Elmer Kramer; he operated Highway Motors just outside Harrisonburg and was active in the Catholic church. Elmer said, "This is a really good idea. Whatever you need, just let me know, and I'll be glad to help." Elmer, who became the first treasurer of Gemeinschaft, had a huge mailing list of community friends from whom he solicited funds to start the program.

After that meeting, we began to talk to others who had been encouraged by Elmer's stepping forward. One of them was Lewis Strite, who was very interested in establishing this new program. When it came time for the sale of Barry's house, Lewis and I and several others were there. It was not an absolute auction because a minimum price of $55,000 had been set for the purchase. We kept talking about buying the house for Gemeinschaft, and Lewis said, "We really need to give this matter some thought and pray over it." So we all joined hands and prayed about whether to take a leap of faith and buy this house. Then Lewis said, "If it brings no more than the asking price, I'll pay the ten percent cash required to buy it."

As the auction went forward, the bids never reached $55,000; the top bid was something like $51,0000. At that point Barry and his friends had to decide whether to accept the lower amount. Since they really needed the $55,000, they were considering whether to end the auction and try again at a later date. Our group quickly got together and decided to pay the full amount right then even though we might have bought it later for a little lower price. Once we made that decision, the sale could go through. Meanwhile, Barry struggled over what to do; he felt he had a huge conflict of interest because he was both a seller and a purchaser. However, his lawyer advised him that it was really all right to handle the sale this way.

In the end, we bought the house for $55,000. Lewis rushed out to the front lawn and stopped the auction before it shut down. He himself paid the ten percent in cash, and after that, with the help of the marvelous fund-raising arm of Elmer Kramer, we completed the purchase. We had to borrow money, of course, but we were able to take out a mortgage on the house. The rest is history, and today Gemeinschaft continues to operate in that building.

In addition to my involvement in all these community projects, I became really interested in educating lawyers about mediation and conflict resolution; so I went to Washington and Lee University, where I had some connections, to see if I could teach a course in mediation there. One of my friends on the faculty said, "I think you should come here and offer a class in negotiation." Negotiation, of course, is the core process of mediation, and I agreed to do that. I believe it was 1985 when I started teaching at the School of Law. That first course began a long teaching career for me; I have since taught courses in negotiation and mediation at Washington and Lee University, the University of Virginia, and Bridgewater College.

Students have found the classes in mediation and negotiation quite appealing. At Washington and Lee University School of Law, the influx of students quickly reached a point at which I could not handle the workload. For a while, I was teaching three sections each semester, which was just too much, so I enlisted a friend to take over teaching half the load. We ended up teaching two sections apiece each semester. We estimate that more than two-thirds of the law students are now graduating with credit for at least one course in negotiation and mediation. That is really satisfying for me because I felt I just had to get the legal community more involved in this method of resolving conflict.

While teaching, I continued my community involvement. The other major organization that I helped found was the Community Foundation of Harrisonburg and Rockingham County. Three or four of us had heard that such foundations were springing up around the country, so we decided to give it a try. Our goal was to start a nonprofit organization that would develop philanthropic funds through donations and bequests and then award grants to help tax-exempt groups improve the quality of life in this community.

We worked hard to recruit a large number of participants and get their input, and they helped us establish this foundation. Our Community Foundation has helped foster and strengthen many wonderful organizations, such as Big Brother Big Sister, the Free Clinic, the Massanutten Regional Library, and the local Arts Council, just to name a few. There is a picture on my desk of the four founders. Since I am the only one of the four who was sitting down and had gray hair, I thought they ought to call me the founding grandfather! But we got that group started, and it is now a very active and successful organization that has made a difference in our area.

One other activity that reflects my heritage and strong connection to the community is banking. My grandfather was named the first chair of the board of directors of the Farmers & Merchants Bank over a hundred years ago, and he served on that board for many years. My father was the legal representative for the Farmers & Merchants Bank and also served on the board. When he had to leave the board at age seventy, the bank invited me to serve, and I chaired the board for a few years. By holding that position, I carried on a special tradition and learned interesting information about the banking industry. I am now an emeritus member of the board of directors and am proud of the fact that three generations of the Hoover family actively served on that bank's board for eighty of its 102 years of existence.

As the years passed, mediation centers began appearing around the state, and the legal community was becoming more interested in this approach to conflict resolution. In the mid-1980s the Virginia State Bar and the Virginia Bar Association set up an Alternative Dispute Resolution (ADR) Joint Committee, and I became the second chairperson of that committee.

The three-year period during which I chaired the committee was a very eventful time for mediation. Harry Carrico, the Chief Justice of the Virginia Supreme Court, had appointed a commission to study the future of the judicial system in Virginia; that group was holding public hearings throughout Virginia. Several of us from the ADR Joint Committee appeared at many of these hearings to speak about the importance of integrating alternative dispute resolution into the legal system.

Our efforts played a prominent role in the report of that commission, which recommended setting up a statewide system to be overseen through the office of the Supreme Court; it would authorize judges to refer cases for mediation and other forms of conflict resolution. Since they needed a statute to present to the Virginia General Assembly, our Joint Committee took on the job of drafting and proposing one. The process took a couple of years, but once the statute was approved and enacted, it really made a difference. Mediation is now widely used by Virginia lawyers to resolve cases, and the change is quite amazing.

Statistics from the McCammon Group, which I helped found in 1995, reveal the impact of alternative dispute resolution on the legal system. The McCammon Group, based in Richmond, Virginia, is made up of retired judges and noted attorneys who undergo extensive ADR training and then handle cases ranging from small personal injury claims to complicated commercial cases. In 2007 more cases were settled by the McCammon Group through mediation than were settled by judges and juries in all the circuit courts in Virginia. Mediation is now routinely seen as a method of case settlement that is more efficient and effective than going to court. People get together and discuss their differences and then rely on such techniques as arbitration or negotiation to get the case resolved.

Another interesting fact is that R. Edwin Burnette Jr., the first chair of the ADR Joint Committee, later became president of the Virginia State Bar (VSB). I read his announcement in the VSB report that he was going to appoint a committee to review and revise the Virginia Rules of Professional Conduct for lawyers. I knew Ed well because he had been my predecessor as chair of the ADR Joint Committee. Of course, I also knew how strongly he supported alternative dispute resolution. I called him up and said, "Ed, when you choose those committee members, be sure to include someone who will see that ADR is properly included in the thinking."

He replied, "That's a fine idea! Do you want to be on the committee? As he probably expected, I said, "Sure." It took us three or four years to get the job done because we did a really thorough review. At first we considered making just some small changes, but we eventually revised the whole format. Embedded in the current rules are seven or eight references to alternative dispute resolutions that serve to remind lawyers of these highly effective processes. I was delighted that this version of the Rules of Professional Conduct went into effect in 2000 because it is now clear that lawyers have an ethical responsibility to advise their clients about the possibility and the applicability of an alternative dispute resolution method such as mediation.

Although I have been deeply involved in my community for several decades, I have also tried to maintain some of my connections overseas. In 1993 I took a three-month leave of absence from the law firm and spent a so-called sabbatical in India. I had been to India three or four times before, and I wanted to refresh relationships I had established through the organization that is now called Initiatives of Change. This group has an International Conference Center on the

Asia Plateau in India, and it is quite similar to the one in Switzerland. I had been there on an earlier visit and really wanted to spend more time attending events at that center.

Before going to the conference center, I spent three weeks at a health camp in Tamil Nadu, southern India, recommended by a good friend. There we participated in yoga classes and health classes, using the mantra "Who Am I?" The pronoun *I* was, of course, the spiritual self, and we were challenged to use self-inquiry to get in touch with the inner self, (written with a capital *S*). After three weeks in the health camp, we spent another week in a Gandhian ashram with a friend I had made on an earlier trip to India. He gave us a real introduction to a Gandhian ashram and also to the nearby community that provided a wonderful exposure to the local culture.

The only commitment I had made before this sabbatical was to lead a mediation training class at the Initiatives of Change Conference Center in Panchgani, a beautiful location on the Asia Plateau. Unfortunately, after the health camp I had developed a very, very sore foot because of a bug bite that had become infected. I could put no weight on that foot. There I was, confined to bed at the conference center one day before mediation training was supposed to begin. I knew that people had come from all over India just to enroll in this class. How could I possibly fulfill my commitment? It was a five-hour trip by car back to Bombay for medical attention, and I was at a loss.

However, in walked a man who had come for the mediation training, and he asked about my injury. He said, "I'm a surgeon, and maybe I can help you." After he inspected my foot, he said, "See if you can get to the infirmary they have here at the center. I'll take care of your foot so you can start the class tomorrow." Then he added, "I came all the way across the country just for this training, so I'm going to make sure it happens." When I got to the infirmary, he cut out the infected area, bandaged my foot, and sent me back to my room. Much to my surprise, the pain had eased enough for me to walk. Now my only concern was how to survive day-long training sessions; but I learned how to lift my leg and rest my foot on a stool whenever I needed to, so the mediation training went on as scheduled. It was indeed a remarkable experience that I will never forget.

About this time I became involved in the Caux Scholars program, which is also sponsored by Initiatives of Change. This program was being held every summer in Geneva, Switzerland, to teach conflict analysis and resolution as well as peacebuilding initiatives to people from all over the world. It included scholarship assistance to help attendees who otherwise could not afford to come. However, the funding had run out, and the program had not been held for a few years.

The leaders wanted to know if I would help revive it, so for three years I went to Caux in the summers and worked with the Scholars Program. Barry Hart from EMU was on my faculty, and we had some wonderful experiences there. When I felt I needed to leave and return to teaching at the law school, Barry was named academic director. After fifteen years in that position, he retired, and now Carl Stauffer, from EMU's Center for Justice and Peacebuilding, is the academic director. Thus, there has long been a special connection between EMU and the Caux Scholars Program, and I am glad that tradition continues.

The other part of my spiritual journey that has been important in my later years is the Enneagram. It is a personality profile that really concentrates on self-awareness. Helen Palmer, who was my teacher and one of the people who has made that process more understandable to students, says that our personality preoccupations are teachers that help us develop our consciousness. The Enneagram has been so meaningful to me that I took the intensive training needed to become certified as an Enneagram Teacher in the Narrative Tradition, and it has become a standard part of my negotiation and mediation classes. I ask all my students to type themselves and then discuss how the type they have identified in themselves affects the way they deal with conflict in terms of their own behavior. It has been a real blessing for me to be involved in the use of the Enneagram; understanding my own preoccupations has been a vital part of my own spiritual journey.

In 2006 I retired from the law firm, but I soon assumed other responsibilities. I go back to the office only occasionally but continue to be a member of the Board. Working with the Blue Ridge Community College Educational Foundation has helped me get to know wonderful people whom I would not have met otherwise. I have also enjoyed serving on the Board of Directors for Shenandoah Valley Public Television (WVPT) and the Board of Trustees at the American Shakespeare Center; in addition, I have served on the Board of Reference at the EMU Center for Justice and Peacebuilding. For quite a while I continued my teaching career as an adjunct professor at Washington and Lee University

I must express special thanks to Pat, my partner and wife, for encouraging and supporting all my interests and efforts over the years. Her three children and seven grandchildren, along with my own two children and grandchild, have added so much purpose and meaning to my life.

My final observation is that the self-awareness I have gained, especially through working on Enneagrams, has helped me better understand the life journey that I have described. Of the nine Enneagram types, I have turned out to be a mediator. Is that a surprise to anyone? In other words, I am the type who can see and understand many points of view, although it is not always easy for me to identify my own perspective. I realize that many of the activities in which I have been involved were often not self-generated but were instead my response to suggestions or opportunities generated by others. However, I have now come to trust my own instincts or inner knowing more easily, whenever such opportunities arise. I believe that this personality trait will continue to shape and define my journey.

December 2010
Revised August 2015

Allon H. Lefever

Faithful Business Executive

Allon speaks from experience about Wall Street and about integrating his Christian faith with his business career (his calling). He originated a list of "Core Values" for building trustworthy relationships and innovative leaders in the many businesses he has developed and monitored. Allon has also participated on boards of service organizations such as MEDA (Mennonite Economic Development Association) and the Fuller Center for Housing. He enjoys sharing an amazing family history of "sixteen generations of faithfulness."

Photo by Frances Coburn, photographer with Museum of the Bible

ALLON H. LEFEVER

My Life Journey: Business as a Calling

When I shared my story at the January 14, 2013, ACRS Breakfast, I had just returned from four incredible days in Hammond, Louisiana, where I had attended the Fuller Center for Housing board meeting. (This is the organization that Millard Fuller founded after leaving Habitat for Humanity.) At the worship service that concluded our session, we "broke the spirit of limitations," by shouting, dancing, singing praises, and praying!

It was indeed a privilege to visit Laplace, Louisiana, a town of 24,000 about sixty miles west of New Orleans, located on the delta near the Mississippi River, where Hurricane Isaac had hit the previous September. A unique combination of factors had converged to create an eight-to-ten foot flood surge, causing 7,000 homes to take on water and leaving 2,000 houses still unlivable—a tragedy for this town's primarily blue-collar residents, many of whom worked in nearby oil and chemical refineries.

In response to the need created by such disasters, Fuller established the program Save a House, Build a Home. In many cases, a bank donates a foreclosed or abandoned house to the Fuller Center, which arranges its renovation with some donated labor and materials. It then sells it at no interest or rents it as a nice two-to-three-bedroom home for about $275 per month to a needy family. Much of the labor is provided by teams of volunteers from around the country. For example, one of the Laplace teams was made up of six Amish men from Indiana, who amazed everyone with their hard work.

During our stay, the board members visited houses where Fuller had sent work teams. I met and talked with Mr. Stanton, who had lived with his wife in their home for twenty-one years. When the four feet of water receded, they started the cleanup, removing damaged items and particleboard kitchen cabinets that had disintegrated. They cut away and discarded many square feet of saturated drywall. Unfortunately, the Stantons did all this work before the arrival of the Federal Emergency Management Agency (FEMA) inspector, who declared, "You don't qualify for a $5,000 Disaster Recovery Loan because there is not enough proof of substantial damage."

The good news, the inspector said, was that they could apply for a FEMA grant. Mr. Stanton did apply, and he had just received the response after four months' wait. The letter announced that he had indeed qualified for a FEMA grant—of $57.67! His reaction? "Ain't nobody doin' nothing good in Waaaashington!" Needless to say, he appreciated the Fuller Center work teams!

The wonderful, inspiring people of flood-ravaged Laplace showed their appreciation to the Fuller Center by piling food in front of us: Cajun oysters, crawfish, blackened alligator meat, and "King Cake." This cake has a plastic baby Jesus hidden in it, and whoever gets the slice containing the figurine must bake the next King Cake. I enjoyed two of those cakes during my time there and was greatly relieved that I never found the baby Jesus!

My recent experience in Louisiana is just one of many special memories that come to mind when I review my forty-five-year career. It is difficult to find a single focus in my life's mix of agriculture, industry, technology, academics, church, community, and family. Therefore, I have decided to organize the story of my journey around three main themes: the influence and importance of family, the challenge of integrating faith and career, and the fulfilling role of church and community involvement. In each of these areas, I will note the supreme importance of values.

For History Buffs

My family story includes sixteen generations of faithfulness.[1] It begins in 1510 with the birth of my twelfth great-grandfather, the Frenchman Meagen Lefever, in the beautiful province of Alsace with its charming city of Strasburg, founded by the Romans near the beginning of the Christian era. At the age of thirty-three, Meagen Lefever was granted a coat of arms by the Royal Duke of Antoine. Lutheranism was spreading in the region, and the Lefevers became Protestants around this time. With their official coat of arms, the family felt safe from political or religious persecution. However, only nine years later that area was overrun by princes from the court of the German emperor, Charles V. The Lefever family fled over 100 miles to the valley of the River Yonne in the shelter of the Vosges Mountains south of Paris, where they made their home for the next thirteen years.

The Roman Catholics in the area began to call these French Protestants "Huguenots." As my eleventh great-grandfather, John Lefever, grew up, persecution increased. On Sunday, August 24, 1572, the Catholics launched the Massacre of St. Bartholomew, killing several thousand Huguenots in Paris, including many at a wedding party. In religious wars over the next thirty years, an estimated 70,000 people perished. The Pope sent congratulations, falsely assuming the Huguenots had been eliminated. But in 1598, Henry IV, a friend of the Huguenots, issued the Edict of Nantes, which ended the wars for a while and enabled my tenth and ninth great-grandfathers to enjoy some peaceful years.

The peace did not last. On October 18, 1685, Louis XIV revoked the Edict of Nantes, making Protestant marriages and emigration illegal and also compelling the Huguenots to be baptized and instructed by Catholic priests. My eighth great-grandfather, Abraham Lefever, and his family got caught in this turmoil; he, his wife, and six of their children were murdered by Catholics one evening. Only Isaac, my sixteen-year-old seventh great-grandfather escaped, possibly by hiding in a barn. He had somehow managed to take his father's Bible with him; the rumor was that his mother had hidden it in a loaf of bread. This Bible, printed in Geneva in 1608, is nine-and-a-quarter by six inches and four inches thick. It is now on display in the library of the Lancaster County Historical Society in Pennsylvania.

Another Huguenot family, silk merchants by the name of Ferree, lived nearby along the Rhine River. This family took in Isaac Lefever, and he eventually married their daughter Catherine. Soon thereafter, my sixth great-grandfather, named after his martyred grandfather, was born. (He would become my so-called first "American grandfather.") Then the father of Isaac's adoptive family, Daniel Ferree, passed away, leaving Madame Ferree a widow.

Within two years of baby Abraham's birth, Queen Anne of England issued a proclamation inviting Huguenots to come to England and from there "settle to the island of Pennsylvania." Thus it was that Madame Ferree's family, including Isaac, Catherine, and little Abraham Lefever, were granted consent to emigrate to England on March 10, 1708. Upon their arrival, Madame Ferree met personally with William Penn, who immediately introduced her to Queen Anne, from whom Madame Ferree obtained "a patent of naturalization and permission to colonize America." This document was dated August 27, 1708; six weeks later, the ship *Globe* left for America with twenty-five names on its register. This ship, which set sail on October 15, 1708, finally arrived in New York on December 31, 1708.

Almost four years later, on September 10, 1712, William Penn's commissioners deeded 2,000 acres of Lancaster County, Pennsylvania, land to the Ferrees and Lefevers for the grand sum of 150 pounds—or 9.8 cents per acre for rich Lancaster County soil. (As of this writing that land is worth around $30,000 per acre!) The families arrived at their destination late on a summer afternoon; from a hilltop overlooking the Pequea River, the land looked so good to them that they called it "Paradise," the name of a small town that now stands in the heart of Lancaster County.

Native Americans emerged from the woods along the Pequea Creek, and one of them spoke enough broken English to communicate: "Indian no harm white man; white man good to Indian; go to our chief; go to Beaver."[2] They did so, and with the humanity that distinguished those Native Americans, Chief Beaver gave his wigwam to the Ferrees and Lefevers to use that evening. The very next day Beaver took them to meet Tawana, the chief of the Conestoga Indians who then occupied that area. (This same Chief Tawana had signed a famous treaty with William Penn thirty years earlier in 1682.) Thus, these ancestors of mine became the first white settlers in Paradise, Pennsylvania; today a plaque commemorates the first white child born in the Pequea Valley, a son of Isaac and Catherine Lefever. (He was a younger brother of my sixth great-grandfather, Abraham.)

Four years later Madame Ferree died and was laid to rest in a plot now known as Carpenter's Cemetery. My seventh great-grandfather,

Isaac, is also buried there, with his tiny gravestone about fifty percent submerged after centuries of settling into the fertile Lancaster County soil.

Over these twelve generations, my great-grandfathers have been the last sons in their families four times, and two of those were the twelfth child born to their parents. Let us just say that miracles do happen. Despite the laws of mathematical probability, I am here today!

My Personal Story

I was born on September 14, 1946, the first child in a wonderful Christian family. My father and mother had just returned from WWII Civilian Public Service (CPS); both had served in mental hospitals. Just before my birth, my father had added extensive greenhouse capacity to a third-generation vegetable and flower business, where he worked in partnership with his father; they had ten or more employees. From a young age, I had a close working relationship with both my grandfather and my father in that business. My father paid me by the carnation box (three cents for fifty-four bands to a box), and he took me along in the big delivery truck as we delivered cuttings to other growers.

My father developed a requested brand for our carnations, even though most of them were sold wholesale in Philadelphia. My mother enjoyed supporting Dad and the business, helping bunch and pack the flowers and preparing chocolate and cookies for break time. She did not, however, like to be out front with the customers or make business decisions.

When I was five, my father helped found Philhaven Hospital, a non-profit behavioral healthcare facility, and the other founders asked him to become the first administrator. I vividly recall his struggle over leaving the flower business he loved, but he felt called to serve in that startup capacity. He said that Rob Gardner's song "I'll go where you want me to go, dear Lord" kept ringing in his ears. His younger brother took over the greenhouses, and we moved to Lebanon County, Pennsylvania. In a few years, however, we moved back to resume greenhouse operations, and my father took over my grandfather's share as well.

Grandpa was a successful businessman, but he always gave priority to his full-time ministry at Mellinger's Mennonite Church, which he pastored for many years. He was a tall, gentle, caring man who was quite curious about the world around him. At home he followed the strict "no radio or TV" rules of Lancaster Conference in those days, but on the job he "tuned in" because he enjoyed knowing about politics and economics. He even listened to our musical choices: Elvis, the Everly Brothers, and eventually the Beatles!

When I was only twelve or so, my father put me in charge of the neighborhood boys he hired to care for the acres of plants we raised every year. My father, like his own father, was a well-organized manager of the business and its employees, so I learned a lot about management just by watching and following their examples.

My father and grandfather were also active in many community organizations, of which my father was often the treasurer. I frequently overheard conversations as he worked with startup Christian organizations, assisting them in finding ways to meet payroll and solve other problems. He was especially active in the Middle Atlantic Growers Association, and a highlight for me was traveling with him to Association meetings, often held at Dupont's Longwood Gardens in Delaware.

I attended Christian schools except when my father served at Philhaven Hospital, but by high school graduation I was eager to hear non-Mennonite views about God and religion. I began questioning and rebelling against some of the Mennonite rules of the day, such as strict dress codes and restrictions on movies.

Then came the Vietnam War; I drew a low number, making me subject to the military draft. Upon passing the physical, I claimed conscientious objector status and was asked to help found a new voluntary service (VS) unit in Albany, New York, where I worked as a counselor in a home for emotionally disturbed children.

After my high school sweetheart, Doris Blank, and I were married, she joined me in Albany as the unit hostess. While the boys I oversaw were in school, I was able to take college courses in psychology and economics at an adjacent division of Russell Sage College. In Albany, I was in a setting where I had to explain what conscientious objection meant, who Mennonites were, what I believed, and why I opposed war. I gained a new appreciation for the peace stand of our church, a view that gained some acceptance since many people opposed the Vietnam War. Others disagreed, of course, but it was a maturing and grounding time for me.

My plan was to join my father in the flower business after completing my required time in VS; I hoped to add more capacity to the business as he had done thirty years earlier. However, times were changing. Refrigerated aircraft began flying in fresh flowers to our primary Philadelphia market, and prices for heating oil were escalating. I was worried that the business was declining, but I was reluctant to discuss my concerns with my father since we had already developed expansion plans. But when I finally spoke up, to my absolute surprise and relief, he agreed with me. He had those same concerns but had remained silent rather than destroy my dreams. In hindsight, my decision not to rejoin the business was a huge fork in the road, but it was the right decision because the flower industry in Lancaster declined rapidly in the following decades.

Since I was not going into business with Dad, I decided to acquire more education. For a while, I cut carnations early in the morning and attended Millersville State University later in the day, graduating magna cum laude with a BA in social studies. I was then accepted into the PhD program in economics at Pennsylvania State University (PSU), which also awarded me a graduate assistantship. However, I soon faced another decision. Graduates of that program were taking jobs that just did not appeal to me, such as doing research with the Federal Reserve or teaching in a remote college in Nebraska. Also, by now we had two little boys, and finances were tight.

After I passed my PSU PhD candidacy exam, Doris and I went out for dinner to celebrate. As we sat by a window and watched the gently falling snow, we discussed this fork in the road. Should I continue pursuing the doctorate or complete an MA and then seek a job? We decided I should leave the PhD program, finish the master's degree, and most likely enter the banking field. I actually felt a deep sense of peace as I began quietly looking at options during that last semester of study. By spring, with my MA in economics in hand, I received an offer from Fulton Bank, the largest in Lancaster, to work in mergers and acquisitions. Instead, I decided to take an intriguing planning and corporate training job at a food processing company, Victor F. Weaver, Inc., in New Holland, Pennsylvania. This job had challenging and interesting potential; the company was clear about its values—and I could always go into banking later!

THE INTEGRATION OF FAITH AND CAREER

Within a few months of my employment at Weaver in 1973, the Russians began buying corn, and corn prices soon exploded. The company needed someone to write a hedging policy and set up a program to enable control of our feed costs. I got the nod and thus the chance to report to the founder's son, who was about to transition into the position of CEO. Suddenly, at a young age I was the rookie member of a senior management team who was in the right spot at the right time, with just enough knowledge and preparation to handle the opportunities that came my way. Yes, I was lucky, but I also believe the saying that "Luck is what happens when preparation meets opportunity."

Within a couple of years I was vice president of operations with a lot of responsibility. What does it mean to be in charge of a team of managers and nearly 2,000 persons in an operation you are expected to lead at the age of thirty-three? I began to realize that leadership was above all about setting the parameters and establishing the guidelines for the culture of the organization; it was about being a role model, even a mentor. My role was increasingly more about getting things done through the leadership and motivation of others than about doing all the many tasks myself. This is an important lesson one must learn as one's span of responsibility grows.

Along with that realization arose new questions about my deeper goals in life. I certainly believed in engagement; in fact, I saw business as a significant way to become engaged in the lives of people and in the community. I truly loved business—its innovation, its organization, its accountability; I now also began to view and understand business as a calling.

Yet certain questions continued to bother me. First, why did so many individuals, including church members, express negative views about people in business? Some church publications even criticized Victor Weaver for taking advantage of minority members when in fact he did much to help them. (For example, he provided ESL training, GED classes, driver's license preparation, and bilingual human resource personnel.) Ironically, companies such as Armstrong Cork, a local Fortune 500 company, came to observe and learn how Weaver retained and developed minority members because Armstrong could not retain enough such employees to meet Affirmative Action goals.

Second, how could I make a meaningful contribution to the thousands with whom I came in contact, including employees, vendors, and worthy community organizations?

Finally, how could I use my own experience to help alter the misunderstandings and misconceptions held by some in the church about the nature of business?

By now our sons Rod and Jeff and our daughter Deb were growing up fast and participating in many events, some of which I needed to attend. Though I did fairly well, I often said "yes" to so many community and work-related activities that maintaining a balance between work and family became a challenge. One evening, probably after I missed a family event, my wife Doris confronted me. Her speech went something like this: "If you can schedule everything else in that little Daytimer book of yours, then you can certainly schedule the family for at least one night a week. So which night do you want?"

I picked Friday since it seemed the least likely to have a work-related conflict. We let the kids take turns deciding what do on family night, so we had many adventures, which ranged from bowling to attending Phillies games to visiting the Green Dragon, a local flea market with cotton candy that one of the boys loved. This was a wonderful thing Doris did for our family and me. She forced me to prioritize: to do what deep inside I actually wanted to do instead of letting other things use up the time required.

When I was refining my leadership skills, I was blessed to have a boss and an organizational culture that encouraged the development of employees and affirmed the dignity of all persons. However, I often wondered how to incorporate into business certain beliefs that were near to the heart, such as my faith. To be honest, I was quite "professionally oriented" or "results oriented"; however, I was not always comfortable with the relational aspects of the workplace. Nonetheless, I had a burning desire to be a positive leader. How could I provide the right kind of leadership in my work environment, in the policies I created, and the way I managed people? How could I be a witness to my beliefs and still recognize and respect diversity of belief, even non-belief, without becoming intrusive or violating equal opportunity laws?

I began to search for authors who had written about integrating faith and occupation. In doing so, I discovered the Mennonite Economic Development Association (MEDA), an outstanding organization that not only emphasizes finding "business solutions to poverty," a goal that resonates with me, but also publishes the *Marketplace* magazine, which includes stories about how business persons are applying their faith in the marketplace. In addition, MEDA holds an annual convention that provides excellent training, speakers, and chances to share ideas with others. My involvement with MEDA has been tremendlously meaningful. It includes nine years of service on the board and participation in many MEDA projects. As a result, I now have wonderful friends all over the U.S. and Canada who are dedicated to applying their faith to their business.

In the workplace I increasingly saw the critical importance of culture, values, and respect for the dignity of all persons. While acquiring three businesses in the South to supplement Weaver's production capacity, I found new ways to integrate faith and work. Many opportunities came in the way I treated persons joining our company; some took the form of policy, and others occurred during vendor relationships. For example, at one of our acquisitions we held a Christmas party for our employees in rural North Carolina. As I was setting up a Power Point presentation, the restaurant owner came over to say, "You know I'm doing you a helluva favor!"

I calmly asked, "What do you mean?"

He replied, "I don't normally allow Negroes in my restaurant. The whites don't like it, and it could kill my business!"

I then had the chance to tell him that I understood his perceived risk but that our philosophy was to treat all persons with equal respect.

Later that evening I heard one of the most moving prayers in my experience. This prayer of blessing on our food and on our company, coupled with an expression of thankfulness for a "good job," was delivered by an African-American man who worked for us as an egg gatherer. He was poor and uneducated but also a pastor to his people, a good man whose prayer was so vivid and powerful that it has stayed with me to this day. I only wish the restaurant owner could have heard it!

My boss, Dale Weaver, who always encouraged community involvement, inspired me to serve on the boards of various organizations, such as the Lancaster Chamber of Commerce, the United Way, Goshen College, MEDA, and quite a few others. I began to realize the many opportunities business provides for believers to share in the secular world, as we rub shoulders with those who see the world through a different lens. It is a way to move beyond the comfortable environment of the church; thus, I value the secular networking possibilities that exist for Christians in business. I suppose present-day Pharisees might accuse us of dining with sinners, but what a wonderful chance to extend our witness.

After sixteen good years, the day came when Weaver, Inc., was sold to Holly Farms. I then faced one of the most difficult days of my life because I had to inform sixteen salaried employees whom I had hired over the years, people loyal to me, that their jobs no longer existed because Holly Farms already had those functions at headquarters. Even though I spent hours planning the most dignified explanation possible, it was an emotionally wrenching experience.

In addition, Doris and I again faced a fork in the road because we had to decide what was best for our family. Should I accept a senior executive position with Holly Farms, even though we would have to move to company headquarters in North Carolina? Or should I pursue an intriguing option with High Industries, Inc., which would keep us in a familiar place? After much prayer and discussion, we chose High Industries, where I would be responsible for developing new companies for the High family. Over the next eleven years I had the exciting opportunity to research venture possibilities, select a business idea or develop a plan, and then help start or acquire a new business. We started or acquired ten companies, and I discovered what fun it was being entrepreneurial and building new work teams!

In my first year I was able to work with the Highs in articulating the High Industries Core Values, which I built upon as we started each new company. Those values helped define our culture, and they helped attract persons who desired to join a company with our stated ethics because they saw it as a place where they wanted to work. I had many opportunities to express my personal beliefs and found myself increasingly able to share them with others. My goal was not to convert others to my religious position but to clarify my personal beliefs and the way they would impact the way I conducted business and treated others.

When the opportunity arose to take public one of the High companies, I entered a high-flying world. Now I was interacting with investment bankers in New York City and attorneys for the Securities and Exchange Commission in Washington, D.C., so I had a new forum in which to present the way we tried to operate our companies and implement our values. Not everyone was interested, but some wanted to know more. There were people who admired our emphasis on Core Values and found our respect for the dignity of all people refreshing.

Meanwhile Rod, my older son, graduated from Goshen College with a business degree and went on to the Tuck School of Business at Dartmouth to earn a master's degree in business administration (MBA). It was 1991, and professors were telling the MBA students about a new communication device called the Internet, which was going to change the way the world communicated! Rod graduated and got an excellent job in banking, but he was ready to be entrepreneurial. As a result, in 1993 my son and I and a friend (Carlton Miller, president of one of the High companies) formed an Internet Service Provider (ISP) as soon as it was possible to offer Internet services to the general public. We focused on such values as promising only what we could deliver and respecting the dignity of all people. We emphasized these values as we hired workers who were fascinated by the Internet and excited about joining our firm. The company grew rapidly, with many of the hires being young, first-time associates.

Two stories will illustrate the importance of our Core Values in the rapidly growing Internet business. For example, no one anticipated the extent to which pornography would become prevalent in the Internet industry. But about six months after we started business, a young employee asked, "Are you aware that the site of one of our customers contains a lot of pornographic images? You claim to care about the dignity of all persons, but the content on that site isn't very dignified, especially for women!" We checked, and he was absolutely correct.

When we told the site owner to eliminate the pornography within three days, he replied, "I have this domain on all my letterheads, and I will sue you if you cut us off. Just remember that I have several businesses with you!" Three days passed, and nothing changed. Fortunately, our ISP business agreement specifically mentioned the intent of our ISP "to transmit wholesome content"; on the basis of that statement, we shut down his service.

Over the next five years, our business expanded from two to 1,500 employees, and many of them heard about our shutting down that site to preserve a culture of dignity for all. However, if we had not defined our Core Values in the legal agreement, the outcome might have been different.

Five years later we decided to take our Internet company public by combining a number of ISPs into a large national ISP. We found several companies ready to merge with us and join our business plan. We held a Founders Conference at the Watergate Hotel in Washington, D.C., to share the vision and the plan. As we were fine-tuning the Power Point presentation for our meeting with the New York investment bankers, we reviewed the slide showing our Five Core Values. The lead banker, who was standing in the back of the room, suddenly declared, "The presentation is already too long, so take that rubbish out!" After a brief discussion, Carlton Miller, my son, and I decided to keep the Core Values slide in its place. After all, it was our presentation, and that statement was an important part of who we were.

The next morning, as I presented to and discussed our Core Values with seventeen owner groups, the lead banker looked indignant. But three company presidents came up afterward to ask more questions about our core values, saying, "That's the kind of company we want to be part of!" This experience reinforced in me the courage to speak openly about our deepest values, especially the need to treat everyone with dignity.

I resigned from High Industries in 1998 to join my son Rod in the rapidly growing Internet business. We were able to take the company public by doing an initial public offering on March 25, 1999, opening on Nasdaq at 11:00 a.m., raising $215,000,000, and rallying seventy percent from our opening price on our day of issue. We were interviewed on CNBC that evening as the biggest gaining stock on Wall Street that day. It was quite an exhilarating event!

Within a year and a half, the second largest ISP, Earthlink, wanted to stay ahead of Microsoft Net and also gain on the gorilla of the industry, AOL. As a result, we were bought by Earthlink, Inc., and I became their vice president of mergers and acquisitions. This position provided me the chance to integrate Core Values into a much larger public company. In fact, I was able to work with the company's president and its communications division to help further the development of a Core Values culture within Earthlink.

Then Shirley Showalter, who had heard about our sale to Earthlink, called to see if I would consider coming to Goshen College, where she was president. She asked if I would be willing to direct their Family Business Program and teach in the college business department. I hesitated at first but was fifty-five, the very age at which I had promised myself I would get out of the so-called corporate rat race. Books such as Bob Buford's *Halftime: Moving from Success to Significance* were helpful in the decision process; they provided great ideas for a strategic plan for the remainder of my life. Thus, Doris and I moved to Goshen, and I made the transition from the business to the academic world. Learning about this new world was a wonderful and interesting experience.

But still another change lay ahead. Eastern Mennonite University (EMU) called about its search for a director of the MBA program. This was a somewhat easier fork in the road to take, for by then we knew we wanted to move back east. So we moved to Harrisonburg, Virginia, and for five years I directed EMU's MBA program until the call of business tugged too hard once again. With my numerous board services and volunteer activities, the teaching schedule seemed a little too rigid. However, I still occasionally lecture in entrepreneurship and venture creation classes at nearby James Madison University, and I do consulting work with young entrepreneurs and startups. You can be sure I always teach my students to write business plans with core values right up front, along with their vision and mission statements. Also, in my consulting, I help companies articulate and put their core values in writing and think about how to use those values to shape their culture and policies.

As I review my life's journey, it is clear that for me business has definitely been a calling. I see business as "a forming of communities to make a crucial contribution to society." My belief is that creating good jobs and providing wholesome products and/or services are ways to foster personal dignity and are therefore fundamental for a civilized society to function well. Managed properly, the business entity helps make this a better world. In fact, I consider business to be "passionate creativity, hopefully for the betterment of humanity."

While I understand the need for handouts in situations such as emergencies and natural disasters and while I admire the work of groups such as the Mennonite Central Committee, I also see the role of business enterprise as essential to a society that functions well. It is one of the best ways to help people break out of the poverty cycle. The community engagement fostered by business, the creativity of business, the opportunities furnished by business, the jobs provided by business, and the dignity available to persons who have meaningful work—all these factors are crucial elements of the foundation for a sustainable society.

Today, at age sixty-nine, I have moved into serving on numerous boards of directors, consulting, and overseeing a couple of small businesses. I divide my time by thirds! About a third of my time is spent serving on eight corporate boards and three non-profit volunteer boards. Another third of my time goes toward overseeing a couple of small businesses, including the Hampton Inn and Suites in Woodstock, Virginia, along I-81. The remaining third is devoted to consulting, traveling, and spending more time with my family, especially so I can fully enjoy our ten grandchildren.

FULFILLMENT THROUGH CHURCH AND COMMUNITY INVOLVEMENT

I came from a Christian home; my grandfather was the pastor of my home church; my father founded and served in a number of church organizations. Thus, I had in my family great role models who taught me that service is truly important. The concept of serving God by serving others is part of my heritage.

As a young teenager, I accepted Christ as my savior at Mellinger's Mennonite Church in a revival meeting led by none other than Myron Augsburger. This decision definitely established a direction for my life, although I later found the new rock-and-roll world appealing and struggled with a lukewarm faith. I did not fully claim the way of Jesus until after my teenage years. However, I matured a lot during my VS assignment, and my wife Doris encouraged my spiritual growth.

When I was still a young man, my entrepreneurial juices began to flow; at age eighteen I helped start both a Christian softball league and a bowling league. As I completed my education and settled into my career, I had other opportunities to get involved in community and church causes. Being willing to say "yes" and become involved was always easy for me, as I enjoy starting new things. When I was taking college classes, I felt some inward indication that a career such as teaching might be my calling. But when I entered the business world and saw so many ways to help people and do good works, I increasingly felt that this was where God wanted me to be. With the help of positive mentors, groups like MEDA, and friends who were integrating faith and business, I became more confident about sharing openly with others and thereby expressing my faith in the business world. I found special satisfaction in contributing to the direction setting and management oversight of organizations.

Allon Lefever, serving as Chair of the MEDA Board, presents Gil Crawford, CEO of Microvest, a painting from MEDA as a note of congratulations to Gil and his team for having just achieved $50,000,000 in microloans loans to the poorest of the economically active. MEDA had formed MicroVest in 2003 to provide microloans to the poor around the world.

As time passed, I became certain this was the way I could best work toward the common good. I now believe business is a special calling for some people, and I consider two principles to be essential in building a "sacred culture," if I may call it that. In my experience these principles have been effective in forming a positive culture, and they have provided an interesting approach to communication with persons in our secular society, including people who are not interested in religion and maybe cannot understand our church jargon. But they can grasp the importance of values and servant leadership.

Basic to my life's journey is the first principle: Integration of my faith into my business career must begin with my inner character. I must ask myself some important questions related to this principle. Who am I inwardly as a person? Have I defined my personal core values? Have I written them down anywhere? How can my personal values be carried out in the workplace? Do I live what I proclaim? (There is nothing worse than claiming respect for core values and then disregarding them in daily life. If I am not going to live by them, then I should not advocate them.) How can I show God's love to those with whom I come in contact? How can I show respect for all while helping persons achieve meaningful work and dignity?

The financially successful person must ask additional questions: What do I do with the resources I have been given? Do I buy an expensive vacation home? Do I buy a big yacht? Do I golf all the time? Or do I find ways to help the poor, to minister to those who need material or emotional assistance? In short, do I seek ways to become meaningfully involved in the lives of others?

The second principle to which I subscribe is the establishment of written core values that guide the way an organization wishes to operate. In both the corporate and the non-profit world, I like to see owners of the business, or the senior management of the organization, involve their employees in an interactive discussion of what the corporate core values should be. This conversation builds ownership in the process for employees and provides feedback to owners on such matters as content and the existence of sensitive areas. If one of your values is collaboration and respect for the voices of all participants, following this process will teach that value.

At High Industries, senior management developed a set of corporate core values and then sent a report to our 2,200 employees, asking for their input and suggestions. We received over 150 responses. A number felt our list of fifteen statements was "too long—I can't remember them all!" In addition, there were other helpful suggestions. After taking this feedback into consideration, we ended up with two broad categories: *building trustworthy relationships* and *being innovative leaders*. We also developed content sub-points that supported those two categories, including statements like "finding creative ways to make this a better world." Some companies choose to be forthright in acknowledging God as central to their purpose and values; others are more subdued or subtle in what they put in writing.

I have also had the privilege of serving on twenty-six non-profit boards, including community chamber boards, community development and technology boards, Christian schools (elementary through university), retirement communities, and hospitals. These organizations are usually committed to a particular cause or mission, and their values and culture are driven by the nature of the organization. For example, hospitals focus on quality of care and patient safety, while educational institutions emphasize developing the whole person. But each of these organizations has a unique culture, and each one needs to nurture its associates carefully to assure desired behavior. And if a group needs to work at changing the corporate culture, that process definitely requires a lot of interactive communication.

I will share an example from recent experience. In my Hampton Inn business, we begin with a clear statement about our "culture of caring." In every employee interview, we explain that our goal is to have a "caring culture." We spend time defining that concept, discussing its practice, and training employees to follow four specific principles: (1) We care for one another as our co-workers. (2) We care for our guests. (3) We care for our local community. (4) We care for the world at large, our global community.

At the Hampton Inn, customer service and customer safety are non-negotiable; therefore, I stress the rule "Always cover the front desk." We once hired a night auditor who had never before worked an overnight shift. When the breakfast hostess arrived at five a.m. one morning, the young man was nowhere to be seen; she called the general manager (GM), who rushed in to help. Finally, at 7:30 a.m., out came our young night auditor; he had fallen asleep in a vacant room!

The GM fired him on the spot because she felt his behavior was an unpardonable safety violation. When she called me to report the incident, she said, "I had to fire the auditor because you say that we should 'never, never leave the front desk unattended.'"

Another of my rules is not to second-guess the GM, so what was my response? Fortunately, I had asked the young man a few days earlier how he was adjusting to the night shift, and he admitted that sleepiness was an issue. Not wanting to override the GM, I discussed with her what it meant to be a caring culture in this unusual setting. Should we call in the employee, discuss the situation, and consider giving him another chance? We mutually decided to have that meeting, at which the young man shared his struggle to stay awake and begged to keep his job. After listening to his story, the GM and I agreed to give him that second chance. Three years later, he is a valued employee who has earned a promotion.

Without emphasis on a "caring culture" as one of our core values, my guess is the GM would not have been willing to reconsider her initial decision. Had we not taken the time to consider exactly what we meant by "caring for one another as our co-workers," that young man would have been a casualty on week two of his new job! Both my GM and I learned from that experience how the culture could help set the tone for dealing with the unexpected.

Every chance to serve brings new learning and usually new satisfaction. Here are some opportunities that have been especially meaningful for me: I served on the MEDA board of directors for nine years and chaired it for two. I also serve on the Sorona board, which helps provide capital to entrepreneurs around the world, supporting the creation of jobs and fostering hope, dignity, and community leadership.

I recently chaired the board of directors of LCC International University, an internationally recognized liberal arts institution in Lithuania. It provides a broad-based education within a Christian academic environment. The transformation of the students as they develop new worldviews is amazing. These individuals can truly help develop a more civil society in their countries by emphasizing ethics in business and other organizations.

I have also enjoyed being on Habitat for Humanity local boards and recently served on the national board for the Fuller Center for Housing.

Service on the boards of Virginia Mennonite Retirement Community and Rockingham Memorial Hospital has been rewarding. I have especially appreciated the chance to evaluate numerous health systems and then become part of the innovative Sentara Health System.

Allon Lefever discusses some thesis options with Monika Bidvaite, an LCC student from Russia whom he and his wife, Doris, helped sponsor.

Being a part of the Rotary Club has been another meaningful involvement on the community level.

I very much enjoy reaching out to the secular world through the networking that business relationships provide. As a small subculture, Mennonites really do have some pillars of strength that can have a positive impact in the larger world. We may not realize how many people admire these attributes and find them appealing. Of special significance are our peace position, our emphasis on service to others, our emphasis on and practice of community, and our integrity and ethics, especially when they are accompanied by an attempt to put them into practice. These values are greatly needed in a world that often seems devoid of peace, service, community, and integrity. I feel comfortable and confident in sharing them as my priorities.

I currently serve on the board of Museum of the Bible, where there is great respect for our beliefs. This ecumenical group is dedicated to providing the world's greatest Bible museum, only three blocks from the White House in Washington, D. C.!

Participation in the community of believers is also an crucial part of my commitment to follow Christ. Becoming involved in the work of the church continues to be fulfilling for me. I am thankful that in my lifetime I have seen better bridges built between business and the church. Each community has gained respect for the other's gifts, and by working together, we learn from each other. That has been particularly satisfying for me to see and experience.

As a Christian, I have one more question to consider: What is our responsibility if we are given much? In Luke 12:48, Jesus says, "For unto whomsoever much is given, of him shall be much required" (KJV). While I still enjoy the challenge of business, I am now less interested in the process of accumulation than I am in giving away more than I make. I do not have a boat on the Chesapeake, but I do have a family foundation that our family formed after Rod and I received Earthlink shares upon the sale of our company.

Today my wife and I, along with our three children and their spouses, are on the board of directors of an organization we call the Ripple Foundation. Our children picked this name because we believe that even a small ripple can make a real difference! We know it will never be the size of a Ford or Gates foundation, but our objectives are to provide seed money for struggling startups, as well as contribute to other worthy causes.

Each of the eight directors of our foundation can donate up to $1,000 per year to any cause of his or her choice, so long as it is a 501-C-3 charitable organization. This year, both of our sons, at the height of their business careers, have made more significant contributions than Doris and I have been able to do. Interestingly, my daughter has been the most creative in helping fund a number of small charitable endeavors. As a family, once or twice a year we process requests that have come in and make mutually agreed-upon decisions about donations. In an unexpected way, working together as the Ripple Foundation has become a bonding experience for our family.

Given my life experience, I think I have finally figured out how to manage a successful journey through life. I recommend a simple four-step formula: (1) begin with solid values; (2) approach everything life sends your way with a positive, can-do attitude; (3) marry a good spouse; (4) raise children smarter than you are! On a more serious note, if you count Doris and me as travelers on our family's journey, the Lefevers now have a rich heritage of fifteen faithful generations, with our children representing Generation Sixteen!

In terms of our legacy, Doris and I are pleased to see our children following in the footsteps of previous generations. Our son Rod and his wife Lauri, who live in Lancaster, Pennsylvania, are active in their church and in Christian education. Rod, a highly ethical businessman, is currently moderator of Forest Hills Mennonite Church. Our second son, Jeff, and his wife Michelle are part of a community church in Minneapolis, Minnesota, and Jeff serves on the development team of the Christian school their children attend. Our daughter Deb and her husband Ross attend a combined Mennonite/Church of the Brethren fellowship in Ann Arbor, Michigan. Like her father, Deb seems to jump from one thing to the next, but she stays busy as a self-employed entrepreneur. All three of our children have good, solid marriages. Yes, as parents, we have so much for which to be grateful, and we pray that God will continue to guide us, our children, and our wonderful ten grandchildren—Generation Seventeen!

January 14, 2013
Revised November 2015

Notes

1. The information in this family history section is drawn from *The Pennsylvania LeFevres*, George Newton LeFevre and Franklin D. LeFevre, compilers (Strasburg, Pa.: The LeFevre Cemetery and Historical Association, 1952, 1970).

2. Ibid., 6.

Peggy B. Shenk

A Woman for All Seasons

If you are expecting "inside stories" about the EMC/EMU presidents whom Peggy served as secretary, administrative assistant, and assistant to the president, you will find truthful and respectful ones here. If you wish to read stories about a Mennonite childhood in the home of an pastor/evangelist, those are here. If you are looking for stories from a pastor's wife in a segregated community, those, too, are here. And if you are interested in stories from the heart of a loving parent, they certainly are here in this moving memoir.

Photo by Paul Beiler, August 14, 2016

PEGGY B. SHENK

From the Home of an Evangelist to a Desk in EMU's Presidential Suite

Somehow it did not seem right to me for a person without a college degree to be working closely with the president of a college (later a college and seminary and eventually a university). Yet this high school graduate found herself serving a sequence of three Eastern Mennonite University presidents in roles of increasing responsibility: secretary, then administrative assistant, and finally assistant to the president. To fulfill the presidents' faith in me, I added to what experience was teaching me by taking advantage of seminars, lectures, and special classes at EMU and other institutions.

When I retired after twenty-nine years of service, I was both pleased and humbled that President Joe Lapp persuaded the university trustees and the Mennonite Board of Education to do what they had never done before: They granted me the first (and they said probably the last) honorary Bachelor of Arts degree. Further, the trustees gave me a ticket for a tour of Europe led by Lynn and Janet Stutzman. My husband Michael bought his own ticket, and together we enjoyed an unforgettable journey that provided many insights into European culture as well as friendships with our fellow travelers.

My story, however, is not mainly about my roles in the president's office at EMU, although I will offer a few vignettes from those years. Rather, it is about the people and the responsibilities that shaped my life and faith.

Important People in My Early Years

Dr. Robert Hughes

In 1932 Franklin D. Roosevelt won the Democratic nomination for President, Charles and Anne Lindbergh's baby was kidnapped, Amelia Earhart became the first woman to fly solo from Newfoundland across the Atlantic, and the Washington Redskins' football franchise was established. All these events received worldwide recognition. However, my husband says the most important event that occurred on May 21, 1932, was the birth of a fifth daughter to Milton and Ruth Haldeman Brackbill. I was born in a large bedroom on the second floor of a sixteen-room, 200-year-old stone farmhouse in Malvern, Pennsylvania. Dr. Robert Hughes was there, as he was many times in my early life.

My parents named me Margaret Louise after two of my mother's good friends: *Louise* (Lehnhof), a German neighbor whom we called Aunt Louise, and *Margaret,* also a neighbor whom we called Aunt Peggy. That is how I became *Peggy* to all except my grandparents and a few others who did not believe in using nicknames.

Before I was two years old, I became deathly ill with erysipelas, a condition caused by a mosquito bite. The infection from the bite moved from one arm across my chest to the other arm. For several weeks my life hung in the balance. My father, who had felt a call to the ministry at the time of my sickness, asked God for my healing and promised that he would answer that call. (He was chosen by lot the same year and became co-pastor at the Frazer Mennonite Church in Frazer, Pennsylvania.) Also, Dr. Hughes was there, driving the two miles from his home office in Paoli almost daily to check on me.

When I was eight, I contracted a horrible case of whooping cough. I can remember seeing my parents sitting by my bed, watching so I did not strangle while whooping! Once more Dr. Hughes took care of me, and he had to tell me I couldn't go to Bible school that year. He even gave me a red rose from his rose garden. Years later, when he congratulated me at my wedding, he said that I was the one who had given him all his gray hair!

Grandma and Grandpa Haldeman

My maternal grandparents, Fannie Auker Shirk and Cornelius Ralph Haldeman, shared our Malvern farm home. This multigenerational living arrangement was common back in the days when William Penn deeded the land on which Grandpa Haldeman's farmhouse stood to a Mr. Malin. In the early 1900s my grandparents bought the farm and moved there from Berryville, Virginia. In addition to the large stone farmhouse, springhouse, and barn, the property included several acres of land for truck farming, a tenant house, and a large building that housed a cider press. Although we lived in Paoli, we always moved to "the farm" at Malvern each summer. When my grandparents were no longer able to operate the farm alone, they offered to sell it to one of their three daughters and her family. My parents bought it and arranged the house to accommodate two families. Two rooms in the middle of the downstairs and a big bedroom reached by the back stairs became my grandparents' rooms.

Since my parents were very busy, I spent a lot of time with my grandparents. Grandpa and Grandma kept a stool at their table for "Margaret" if I decided I liked their meal better than what Mama was serving. During those years, Grandma and I had many good times together. At least once and maybe twice after I learned to read, Grandma and I read through the Bible, each of us reading every other verse; as we finished each chapter, we marked it off on the American Bible Society Bible reading grid. We also memorized parts of or whole Bible verses for every letter in the alphabet. I still remember many of them:

A. "**A**ll things were made by him and without him was not anything made that was made."
C. "**C**hildren obey your parents."
J. "**J**esus wept."
P. "**P**ray without ceasing."
X. "**E**xodus," Grandma would always say.
Z. "**Z**acchaeus come down."

Grandpa and Grandma often seemed as busy as my parents. Grandpa Haldeman worked part time in my uncle's farm markets but came home every evening. I remember how he and Grandma worked together many evenings canning fruit and vegetables. Grandma often came to our kitchen to prepare vegetables for our supper. Also, she had flowerbeds that she and I tended faithfully. Bulbs needed to be dug up in the fall, divided, and replanted in the spring. I have such good memories of those times with Grandma Haldeman.

What a joy it was years later when, as a young married woman, I brought my firstborn son Mike from Florida to Pennsylvania for Grandma Haldeman to see and to hold! She died, though, before our second child, Janie, was born. My parents, as well as my sister who lived nearby, cared for both Grandma and Grandpa in their own home in their final days.

When Grandpa and Grandma Haldeman had bought the farm in Chester County, there was no Mennonite church closer than Spring City. Thus, whenever the weather permitted, they hitched up the horse and buggy on Sunday mornings and drove the thirteen miles to that church. Later they and a group of Mennonites in the Chester County area met in an eight-sided, one-room schoolhouse on Diamond Rock Hill, closer home. Some years after that my grandparents and parents became charter members of the Frazer Mennonite Church, built along the Lincoln Highway. A *missional* church long before that designation came into use, it was on the edge of Lancaster Conference not only in terms of geography, but also in the way it did church.

Life with My Pastor/Evangelist Father, Milton Brackbill

Those listening to my father's sermons could not have known that his early life was difficult. His mother (Hettie Good Brackbill) died when his younger sister Elsie was eight and he was eleven. (Just a few years before this writing, Aunt Elsie Brackbill Harvey died at the age of 102. She was EMU's oldest living alumna.) Because Daddy's father (Benjamin Franklin Brackbill) felt he could not take care of these two younger children, he sent them to live with his parents in Lancaster County, Pennsylvania. He considered his two older sons (Charles and Harry) capable of living at home and fending for themselves.

My father remembers that living with his grandparents was an unhappy time for him because his grandfather was very strict. Once when he found my father looking at himself in a mirror, he informed my father that looking into a mirror was a sure sign of pride; therefore, he was going to hell faster than a horse could trot!

Actually, the Brackbills and the Haldemans must have met earlier. Before my grandmother Brackbill's death, she and my grandfather Brackbill lived in Philadelphia with their three small boys (Charles, Harry, and Milton). For Grandpa Haldeman to find work when his and Grandma's three little girls (Grace, Myrtle, and Ruth) were small, they moved to various locations, one of which was Philadelphia. Eventually, it was discovered that these two families probably attended the Philadelphia Mission at the same time. Two of the Haldeman girls later married two of the Brackbill boys; my parents, Milton and Ruth Brackbill, were one of those couples.

MAKING A LIVING
WHEN A PREACHER RECEIVED NO SALARY

Daddy seldom received any money other than an infrequent reimbursement for travel expenses when he conducted revival and evangelistic meetings. As far as I know, the Frazer congregation never gave him any wages except just before his retirement. In those days ministers were expected to serve the church without pay while supporting their families.

Once when Daddy was invited to Tampa, Florida, for revival meetings, he took Mama, my sister Betty, and me with him on a trip that turned out differently than we had expected. We drove there in our 1937 Dodge and stayed with church families. On our way home after the meetings, we had barely enough money for meager groceries and gas. The minister at Tampa had said that since Daddy had brought his family along and the Ybor City members had taken care of us, there would be no honorarium for Daddy's services. When we got hungry, we would stop so Mama could heat tomato soup over a can of Sterno for a meal. I am sure we had oranges and probably cheese and crackers. It was a long trip, though, and Daddy kept a small stick by the gearshift in the front. When Betty and I became too spiteful to each other, he would wave it around, singing at the top of his voice, "Makes me love everybody." We never felt the stick, but we got the message!

In my parents' early years, Daddy worked on a butter-and-egg delivery route and later helped his brother Harry at the farm market on the home place and at the markets in Wayne, Villa Nova, and Ardmore. Mama was busy baking bread, rolls, doughnuts, and shoofly pies to help make a living and pay the tuition for my sisters, who were attending Eastern Mennonite School (EMS) in Harrisonburg, Virginia. (This was before Lancaster Mennonite High School was established.)

A New Source of Funds

When I was six years old, my oldest sister was planning to be married. My parents remodeled the springhouse at our home in Malvern into a two-room cottage with the soon-to-be-married couple in mind. Before the wedding, however, they learned about a job with living quarters where she would be a housemaid and he would be the chauffeur. Since my sister and her husband did not need the springhouse for a home, it became the first of five buildings that my parents built or renovated to start the Brackbill Motel, advertised as having "a Christian atmosphere." Our overnight guests could also purchase a full-course dinner for a dollar.

In the early '40s the Brackbill Motel was the first one east of Philadelphia on Route 30's Main Line, a prime location. An unofficial historic region of suburban Philadelphia, this area contained affluent towns built along the old Main Line of the Pennsylvania Railroad, which ran parallel to U.S. Route 30, the historic Lincoln Highway. In the nineteenth century the Main Line also became home to sprawling country estates established by Philadelphia's wealthiest families, many of whom had another house in the city and many of whom hired trustworthy Mennonite girls as their servants.

We rented out rooms in our large house as well as in the motel. It was not unusual for Daddy to wake one of us and say, "There is a family downstairs that has been looking for a motel. It is late, and their children are tired and sleepy. Would you please put clean sheets on your bed, straighten up your room, and go to a third-floor room to sleep?" We always responded to him but not always cheerfully!

Although Daddy saw to it that our home was filled with music, reading material, laughter, and good conversation, it was also filled with work; Mama and Daddy worked right along with us. We washed all the sheets, pillowcases, and towels from the motel every day except Sunday. On Monday we would have to wash twice the usual number. Since we did not have a dryer, we hung everything on the clotheslines and then ironed the pillowcases. To feed all our guests and our family, we froze bushels of corn, prepared cases of cans of tomatoes and string beans to be processed at the cannery, and made washtubs of chow-chow. When things got tense because we were tired and did not feel like working another hour or two or three, Daddy would bring out his reel-to-reel tape player and put on good singing groups and gospel music to brighten our moods.

When Daddy was away for meetings, Mama needed to work extra hard at baking and selling her goods and operating our tourist home and cabins. My sisters and I had to work hard, too. There was time, however, for swimming in the pond in our meadow. I do not think my wool bathing suit dried out all summer, because it was usually wet when I would put it on for another swim.

AN EVANGELIST/TEACHER WHO FACED QUESTIONS

Daddy was a true evangelist both in his home church and community and also in the wider Mennonite brotherhood. He was invited to hold revivals and evangelistic meetings throughout the Mennonite denomination from the east to the west coasts and from Florida to Canada. When I was around six years old, the members of the Frazer church joined our family at the Paoli railroad station to see Daddy off for six weeks of meetings and Bible schools in Oregon and Idaho Mennonite churches. To us it seemed as if he were going to the far ends of the earth.

Daddy was a self-taught person. An avid reader, he would stay up until one or two o'clock in the morning, waiting for tourists at the motel. He did not sleep as he waited but read, prayed, studied the Bible, and prepared his sermon notes. He filled his Scofield Bible with notes in the margins, and he often preached just from those notes. He was a fine Bible scholar and teacher and a very effective preacher/evangelist.

However, Daddy's interpretations and applications of various Scriptures were somewhat ahead of his time, and they were not always considered in line with traditional Mennonite beliefs. These views contributed to his being terminated as an instructor in the Six-Week Winter Bible Term at Eastern Mennonite School after serving in that position for about ten years. A staunch premillennialist, he was in agreement with the predominant teaching on prophecy in the Virginia and Lancaster Mennonite conferences. However, some in Virginia felt that he had been too much influenced by the Calvinistic teaching of the evangelical churches along the Main Line, the Bible conferences of Keswick and Sandy Cove, and the popular preachers in Philadelphia.

The EMS allegations also related to his interpretation of certain aspects of the nonconformity adhered to by the Lancaster and Virginia conferences. For instance, he did not consider all of the ordinances of the (Old) Mennonite Church, such as the prayer head covering and other aspects of "plain dress," to be essential to salvation. He did not oppose the Mennonite ordinances in his teaching, but in private conversation with colleagues, he openly expressed his views.

A teenager at the time, I had learned how to type. Thus, I was the person who typed Daddy's responses to the allegations directed at him by the EMS administrators. Men of the church and teachers at the school I was attending were saying that my daddy should not return as a Bible instructor. He responded in kind, peaceful ways without acknowledging that his beliefs were incorrect. As a daughter who felt her father could do no wrong, I thought he should be telling them that they were wrong and defending himself!

VISITORS FROM NEAR AND FAR

My parents' involvement in their business and the church brought the larger world into our home. Mennonite girls working in homes along the Main Line frequently spent their days off in our home (because their parents' homes were too far away for a day's trip) and their Sundays at the Frazer Mennonite Church, where my father was the minister. At Sunday dinners, they and other guests usually filled our dining room table, which easily held twenty-two persons. We also learned early to accept people from other denominations and cultures. Students from Moody Bible Institute visited our home and church, and colportage people made their rounds selling Bibles and other Christian books. A Christian man from India came annually to our home on his spiritual pilgrimages.

When each of us five girls married, Daddy accepted our husbands as his "sons," and many conversations went on around our table when we were home together. Four of the sons-in-law became ministers and had a lot to talk about with Daddy. One of the ongoing conversations in the '40s and '50s was about the great revival in East Africa among our missionaries there.

MY PUBLIC STEPS OF FAITH

I would often go along with Mama and Daddy for revival meetings when he was preaching at a church close enough for him to come home each night. From babyhood up, I heard Daddy's revival and evangelistic sermons. Since a number of people who attended our church were not Christians, Daddy, as I remember, gave the invitation to accept Jesus almost every Sunday morning. Thus, it was not surprising that at the age of seven I felt that I should stand when he gave an invitation to accept Jesus Christ as Savior on a Sunday morning at our church.

I was perfectly willing and even eager to put my hair up and wear a covering, a cape dress, and black stockings as was the custom for women and girls in our church when they were baptized. My father, though, was not eager for me to join the church at such an early age with all that church membership entailed. He did assure me of being saved, which was what I wanted. Baptized when I was around eleven, I enjoyed participating in our church youth group, Gospel Echoes, which met every week. We became quite accomplished as a choir, and we distributed a little paper, *The Way*, in West Chester every month.

I wore a head covering with my pigtails during the fifth, sixth, and seventh grades at our public school. There were no other Mennonites in our school, but no one made fun of me. Fitting in was not a problem for me since our family always had friends who were not Mennonites, and we knew many people in our community who belonged to non-Mennonite churches. Further, a number of persons who were welcomed into our church had last names unfamiliar to our Mennonite heritage: Henry, Burgess, Mosteller, Hinkles, Malin, Emory, Cooper, Goddard, and Lamp. These families made a significant contribution to the church and community.

One community event that increased our friendship with families other than Mennonites was the Frazer Summer Bible school, which Uncle Harry Brackbill had begun. He invited the other churches in our community to join in this effort to hold a two-week-long Bible school for boys and girls to attend in the mornings. Members from those churches helped teach or contributed in other ways. For example, the Episcopal Farm School for Boys loaned its bus, which my father drove to gather up the children. I attended Bible school for many years and then became an assistant teacher and finally a teacher in my later teens.

That Bible school grew so large that children were bused to the East Whiteland Consolidated Public School and the Presbyterian church for classes. The man who owned the buses in that area loaned them to transport children to and from Bible school, and the state police directed traffic at several locations. At the height of the Frazer Summer Bible school era, over 600 children attended.

After Michael and I married and moved to Sarasota, Florida, I could not imagine missing out on the Frazer summer Bible school. With Michael's blessing, I took Mikie, who was seven months old, and a teenage girl from our church and went by train to Paoli to help teach. I did that only one year because I was later needed at the Newtown Gospel Chapel, where we served in the African-American community in Sarasota. I seemed to be the only one who could handle an energetic class of boys who were difficult to control and teach at the same time. Somehow I did it!

EMS AND MICHAEL

There were no Mennonite high schools except Eastern Mennonite School (EMS) in Harrisonburg when my sisters and I were ready for high school. Elementary schools in Virginia did not include eighth grade then; however, my sisters, who had gone to eighth grade in Pennsylvania and then to EMS as freshmen, told me that the eighth grade in Pennsylvania was practically the same as the freshman year at EMS. Since I was eager to finish school quickly, I begged my parents to see whether I could skip the eighth grade in Pennsylvania. Thus, Daddy took me to Virginia a day or so before school started so I could meet with Elsie Martin, principal of Park School (in Park View) and attempt to test out of eighth grade. I remember little about those hours except that I wrote answers on the blackboard in response to her questions, which probably involved spelling, math, English, and social studies. At the end of the day I received a certificate for eighth grade and could enroll at EMS as a high school freshman at thirteen years old.

I was not alone at EMS but found my first year there difficult. I roomed in the dormitory with two other girls from our church, and one of my older sisters started college at EMS at the same time. Even so, I was extremely homesick and spent a lot of time in my sister's room. However, she was having boy friend troubles and was about as sad as I was. We went home only twice: at Christmas time and at the end of the school year.

The next three years were better because I lived with another sister, Grace, her husband Charles Hostetter, and their family. Altogether, we were six people with two rooms up, two rooms down, and one very tiny bathroom. Once or twice Daddy also lived with us while he taught in the six-week Bible term. It was during this time in high school that I made an adult commitment to Christ during one of the revival meetings.

In my second year at EMS I met Michael Shenk. He was fifteen and I was fourteen. The summer after our sophomore year we did not see each other at all, but we did write often. I discovered in Michael a kind, gentle spirit; in comparing him to Daddy, I felt he had the same excellent, endearing traits. We graduated from high school in 1949 and became engaged in February 1951. We have been married over sixty years, and he is still the love of my life.

OUR CALL TO FLORIDA

After our marriage, we lived in Denbigh (Newport News), Virginia, and bought Michael's grandfather's house at what was called The Crossroads. We were invited to teach Sunday school at the Huntington Avenue Mennonite Church in downtown Newport News. In addition, we helped in the early African-American mission efforts in that city. I think both of us felt something of a calling to help in mission churches.

At one church service we heard our bishop, Truman Brunk Sr., tell about the beginning of an African-American mission in Sarasota, Florida, called Newtown Gospel Chapel. It did not surprise either of us when Brother Truman asked if we would consider a call to the mission effort begun by Rhoda Ann Stoltzfus, a young woman in Sarasota. She had gone out on her own on Sunday afternoons and gathered children together on someone's porch to tell them Bible stories. The group had become so large that Myron Augsburger, then pastor of the Tuttle Avenue Mennonite Church, said his church would help find a building and volunteers to start a Sunday school.

Now this group was asking for a pastor. Myron and Bishop Truman Brunk both felt that Michael would be just the person for that position. We also felt a call from the Lord to go as they requested. Michael, however, was an only son, and his father had a large peach orchard. It would have been easy for his father to ask Michael to stay with him in the orchard business. However, Papa did not hesitate for a moment. He was not only willing to let Michael go, but he also encouraged us to follow the Lord's calling.

We thought we had carefully planned our move to Florida. Going with us in our 1949 Ford Coupe as we left Denbigh, Virginia, in September 1953 was helpful Helen Mabel, Michael's twin sister, and an older woman who needed transportation to Sarasota. Two of Michael's friends drove his father's pickup truck, loaded with all our possessions and our collie dog, Alpha. Checking on her at one stop, Michael decided she would be more comfortable if she were not tied. He thus saved her life.

Arriving a day and a half later at the house we were renting, we waited and waited for the truck. Finally, we started north to look for it. Just outside the city limits, there it was, moving strangely sideways. In a rainstorm the driver had run off the side of the road and over-corrected so sharply that the truck had turned fully over, landing right side up on its wheels, facing north instead of south. Friendly truckers had stopped to help gather up items and tie a tarp around the truck to hold everything together. But there was no dog. Thanks to the vigilance of the county sheriff, she finally turned up safe and sound, but at a home 130 miles away near Ocala. When we got there to pick her up, her tail would not stop wagging!

A welcome event the evening we arrived in Sarasota was the appearance of a man who was helping in the Newtown work. When Michael met him at the door, the man asked if Michael's father was at home because he wanted to meet his new pastor! He was quite surprised that this young fellow standing in front of him was going to be his pastor. He was gracious, though, and we became good friends and coworkers. From this point on, we enjoyed our ministry at Newtown chapel and made many good friends, whom we would invite into our home. However, to some it seemed quite different for African-Americans to come into our white neighborhood because the nation was grappling with integration in the early '50s, and Sarasota was still fully segregated.

THE CHALLENGES OF ANOTHER CONGREGATION

When the Augsburgers left Florida for Myron to continue his studies and serve as part-time pastor at Eastern Mennonite College (EMC, formerly EMS), the Tuttle Avenue congregation invited Michael to take Myron's place as pastor. Our time at Tuttle Avenue had its challenges, especially for me. Michael could be objective about church matters, but I tended to take every issue personally. Also, Michael, who had a busy schedule pastoring while working part time, was gone almost every evening. After we enclosed our carport to turn it into an office, many of the people who came to see Michael often came into our house as well. Our children seemed perfectly happy because we lived on a street with many playmates, and our backyard was usually full of children. However, this was a difficult time in my life because we never seemed to have any time alone as a family.

I thought about the big farmhouse in Malvern, Pennsylvania, where my parents still lived and always warmly welcomed us. After suggestions from our family doctor, Michael and I decided that I should go north to their home for a few weeks. I took Donnie with me, and Michael kept Janie and Mikie. Soon, though, Michael brought Janie to Pennsylvania because she was so homesick for her mother. Relaxing in the comfort and love of my parents' home and surroundings, I felt ready within a few weeks to return to Florida. While I was gone, Michael had made helpful changes. He had moved his office from the house to the church and established office hours that allowed him more time with his family.

In the 1960s the Mennonite congregations in Florida were struggling with the issue of charismatic renewal. Those who embraced the charismatic emphasis felt that a true Christian needed the experience of being filled with the Holy Spirit and speaking in tongues. One often heard stories of miraculous healings. I remember going into our bedroom and kneeling down by our bed, asking the Lord to give me this experience if it was his will. I did not have any of those unusual experiences, but I did experience a peace about my own Christian life and yielded myself more fully to the Lord.

However, the members of our church had various viewpoints, and Michael wanted to pastor all of these people. Some outspoken persons criticized him because they wanted him to support only their position. I realize now that this criticism was harder on me than on Michael because he felt that in time most people would cooperate.

Our Return to Virginia

In 1969, when the Tuttle Avenue Church in Sarasota gave us a sabbatical year, we moved to Harrisonburg for Michael to complete his college training. To my surprise, Myron Augsburger, now the president of Eastern Mennonite College and Seminary (EMC&S), asked if I would serve as his secretary while we were in the area. After prayer and with Michael's total support, I accepted Myron's invitation. I enjoyed working for him during the 1969-70 academic year.

In 1971, events moved quickly. We had returned to Virginia late that summer after deciding to leave Sarasota. Michael was going to teach part time at Eastern Mennonite High School (EMHS) and become the part-time pastor of Trissels Mennonite Church near Broadway. Myron, who had asked a faculty member to fill in as his secretary during the 1970-71 session, told me that the job would now be mine if we planned to stay in Harrisonburg permanently.

Although I was much more ready to make this decision than Michael, we mutually decided to make this area our home. I had been a stay-at-home-mom during our seventeen years in Florida. However, since our youngest son Don was in the sixth grade and Mike and Janie were in their teens, our family was now ready for me to take a job. Also, Michael was soon asked to get his guidance certification and work full time at EMHS as the guidance counselor.

Our church life also underwent change. When Michael became a full-time teacher at the high school, he resigned from Trissels. It was not long, though, until he was asked to become the interim pastor at Valley View, a small church in the Criders area. Our son Don and I stayed on at the Trissels church because we thought Michael would not be at Valley View very long, and Don was then the organist at Trissels. When it appeared that Michael would continue to serve at Valley View, I began going with him; after several months Don followed. (It has been an answer to our prayers to have our children involved in the church and community in significant ways.) At Valley View I was especially happy to be considered just another member, and I liked its family spirit. We served at that church for thirty-six years until Michael's retirement in 2011, when our son Mike succeeded his father as pastor.

NOTES FROM MY DESK IN THE PRESIDENT'S SUITE

Myron Augsburger's tenure

My previous office experience included typing for my preacher-father, serving as Michael's secretary, and working as the church secretary during our Tuttle Avenue years. My years in the EMC president's office during Myron Augsburger's tenure also required office skills but provided many learning opportunities as well. Myron was involved not only in the many aspects of college administration but also in Inter-Church Evangelism, an organization in which he had been active before his presidency. This ministry opened the door for him to introduce Mennonite thought and theology to people in many other denominations. Indeed, after hearing Myron speak in the United States and in Europe, students from other denominations entered EMC and the seminary.

Myron, as a theologian and Anabaptist scholar, also authored books with an Anabaptist theme, thereby supporting his intention to preserve the Anabaptist-Mennonite tradition at EMC. I typed several of his books on an electric typewriter, using little slips of correction paper when needed. (The last book I typed was on a Selectric with a roll of correction tape.) Using only his handwritten scripts, I typed the chapters, and he edited them. I typed them the second time for his second editing, and finally I typed the finished copy. That method was a far cry from the technique of cut-and-paste now prevalent in the computer age.

Other concerns also seem a bit outdated in this modern era. For example, when I began working at EMC, the president's office was responsible for preparing faculty and staff contracts. Salary scales had not yet been adopted. One faculty member refused to sign her contract, which called for a salary of $666.00. Her reaction was not because of the small amount but because of the ominous use of those numerals in Revelation.

The arrangement of the administrative offices on the main floor of the old central building presented an unusual situation. In the presidential office suite, the office of the president's assistant, then Linden Wenger, was behind my office. In fact, to enter either the president's or Linden's office, a visitor needed to go through my office. Following the student uprising at Penn State University, Virginia state police visited college presidents to recommend procedures in case of emergency. Linden informed me that if students stormed President Augsburger's office, he could simply climb out his back office window!

Good humor typically pervaded the atmosphere of our offices. On one occasion when President Augsburger was off campus, he phoned to ask me to give Linden a note stating that a box was waiting for him. Linden was to call a particular number to find out where he should pick up the box. Linden soon came into my office with a red face and a hearty laugh to tell me that the phone number was that of Lindsey's Funeral Home! We had forgotten that it was the first day of April.

On one of Myron's sabbaticals in Basel, Switzerland, he prepared an Anabaptist calendar with a historic Anabaptist event on each of the 365 days. He mailed these handwritten items to me, and I typed them in draft form for his editing. After my retirement I found several of these calendars and gave one to a Puerto Rican member of Valley View Church who had wholeheartedly embraced the Anabaptist way of peace. Myron would often say to me, "With your experience, you should really be granted a degree in Anabaptist history."

Actually, I learned about much more than theology and Anabaptist history in the president's office. For instance, from Myron I heard all about swans. They mate for life and must not be placed in a pond or lake with snapping turtles. He also told me that he had sold swans to the park in Hagerstown, Maryland. One day park officials called in a panic while Myron was out of the office and said that for no discernible reason, one of the swans had died. When I got in touch with Myron, he said to ask them if they had snapping turtles. They did. They then remembered that the swan had met its death when it was grazing at the bottom of the pond.

Before Myron left office, Michael and I joined him and Esther to help with a Middle East tour, which included Egypt, Israel, and four days on a Greek cruise ship. In Egypt we saw the mummy of King Tut in the Cairo Museum, rode the train from Cairo to Luxor, the Valley of the Kings, and enjoyed a sailboat ride on the Nile at sunset. The Aegean cruise included stops at Mykonos, Ephesus, Patmos, Rhodes, Crete, the beautiful island of Santorini, and Athens. This trip, along with Myron's commentary, made famous places come alive for me.

I was grateful to Myron Augsburger for the opportunity to serve as his secretary. However, when new presidents were chosen for Eastern Mennonite, I offered my resignation each time because I did not want the incoming president to feel that I automatically came with the office. Moreover, I realized that each president would have an entirely different approach to carrying out the duties of his office and wondered if I had enough flexibility to make the changes required.

Richard Detwiler's tenure

Richard Detwiler contacted me soon after he was chosen president of the college and the seminary in 1980 and asked me to continue in the office as his administrative assistant. I was accustomed to Myron's rapid-fire way of outlining whatever he was telling me. Soon after Richard became president, he asked me over the phone to do certain tasks while he was gone. There was a long pause, and I finally asked, "Are we finished?" He assured me we were not finished and went on conversing in his leisurely fashion, which I soon learned to appreciate.

Richard Detweiler's Spirit-led churchmanship was much needed in those years. At that time the church's higher education programs were under severe scrutiny by a group in the denomination. They felt that the college was selling the church short on some Mennonite distinctives as well as certain doctrines. They were concerned about topics such as the dress code or lack thereof and faculty whom they felt were not fully committed to the Mennonite church. Some of the doctrines under scrutiny were the inspiration of the Bible, miracles, the resurrection of Christ, and the virgin birth. A pastor at heart, Richard related well to students and even to critics of the institution. He told me he thought he could always find a way to get along with everyone he knew. However, at one point in his presidency, he asked me to enroll him in a seminar at another institution; it was entitled "How to Get Along with Difficult People."

Richard and his wife Mary Jane were true examples of servant-leaders. Shortly after Richard assumed the presidency, Mary Jane became ill with transverse mylitus. The disease progressed, making it difficult for her to walk, and she spent time at the University of Virginia Hospital. An independent woman who always wanted to serve rather than be served, Mary Jane persevered and even made meals for guests. Richard not only felt responsible for the health of the institution but also felt he should fulfill his responsibility as Mary Jane's helper. At one point in her illness, she stated that to her, Richard was just like Jesus.

At the end of his presidency Richard commented, "It was not all a bed of roses: The administration building burned, Eastern Mennonite High School withdrew from Eastern Mennonite College and Seminary governance, and all the trustees resigned!" (Actually, after EMHS left the umbrella of EMC&S, the trustees had had to resign to be reappointed to the new organization.) Although this statement was a humorous one, the administration building fire was quite traumatic for Richard. When I first saw him after the fire, I suggested that we supply coffee and refreshments for the firefighters. He was carrying his briefcase and other papers, but he said, "Oh, we must!" He immediately shoved his briefcase into my arms as he hurried into the cafeteria to get drinks for the firefighters. I was truly left holding the bag!

In 1986 after five years in the presidency, Richard felt he had helped foster healing in the relationship between the denomination and the institution. In consultation with others, he agreed that it was time to find someone who could continue what he had begun and also help to achieve a more stable fiscal situation.

On the day Richard was to leave the office, one last paper needed his signature. I put a little yellow sticky note by the place he was to sign and wrote on it, "Once more before we part." He signed the document and then wrote on the sticky note, "But we shall still be joined in heart and hope to meet again." We also had a "Sorry" card I had given him after one of my mistakes; we had often passed it back and forth during his five years in office. When I spoke at his roast at the faculty meeting in Laurelville before he left office, I gave the "Sorry" card back to him one last time. I was truly sorry he was leaving.

Joseph L. Lapp's tenure

Joseph L. Lapp was chosen to succeed Richard as president of EMC&S. Joe and I were well acquainted since he was chair of the board of trustees, and in 1977 I had been appointed Secretary to the Board and Corporate Secretary of the Institution. Soon thereafter, Joe approached me about continuing in the office with the title Assistant to the President. I accepted and served in this capacity until I retired in 1999. My workload now involved more administrative details, and I enjoyed working with the president's cabinet, trustees, faculty, staff, and students. This workload would be quite demanding for both Joe and me. In one of our first one-on-one meetings, Joe asked me what time the president's office opened. When I told him 8:00 a.m. or before, he regarded me with an expression of disbelief. He was used to lawyer's hours!

Joe was the first EMU president who was a lawyer, not an ordained minister. I think at times he felt this distinction more than he needed to. The one responsibility that was totally new for President Lapp was the number of speeches, sermons, and convocation addresses he needed to prepare. However, he tackled the presidential job with gusto, and his hearty laugh would ring out in the office suite.

Interestingly, his ponytail days inspired many written and oral opinions. I even had a file folder marked "Ponytail." It contained a record of all the phone calls and other conversations I fielded regarding the inappropriateness of Joe's ponytail. I finally told one woman who went on and on about how undignified it was for the EMU president to wear a ponytail that it was just a phase he was going through.

Joe was quite considerate of the former presidents and would regularly visit them. He also practiced inclusiveness and appointed and worked well with women as colleagues. He told members of the president's cabinet early on that he did not want "yes" people but that they should be prepared to support their opinions. Joe openly appreciated their efforts. *The Wall Street Journal* kept him up to date on the silver market, and on special occasions he gave the cabinet members silver dollars.

As president, Joe also traveled extensively for the university for speaking engagements and development work, and I always knew when he had experienced airport layovers. He would take out of his wallet receipts for Mrs. Field's Cookies and coffee and sometimes a paperback book if he had experienced a long wait.

Through the years with President Lapp, I was a member of the President's Cabinet, the Lectureship Committee, and the Strategic

Peggy Shenk receives an honorary Bachelor of Science degree from President Joseph L. Lapp on her retirement in June 1999. The president requested this degree from the EMU trustees and Mennonite Board of Education as a one and only honorary degree given by EMU.

Planning Committee. I served as recording secretary for these groups as well as the President's Partnership Council and EMU trustees. When people asked if my job were stressful, I could truthfully reply that when you enjoy your job, the stress is not debilitating. Actually, I liked my job. In fact, when I began thinking of retirement, I wondered if I still had a life outside the office. I found that I did. One of my biggest joys is that Michael and I have more time together since he has finally retired not only from pastoring but also from his landscaping business.

OUR CHILDREN

When I think about the days our children were teenagers and going through some rough times, I am reminded of the verse in Proverbs 22:6, as it reads in Eugene Peterson's *The Message*: "Point your kids in the right direction, and when they are old they will not be lost."[1] Our children all attended Sarasota Christian School, which Michael had helped to establish. Mike finished his first year of high school at the public Sarasota High School and then went to EMHS. Janie was in middle school when we moved to Harrisonburg in 1971, and Don was in elementary school. They then went on to graduate from EMHS.

Our older son Mike married Ramona Kline, who is the director of the Minnieland Private Day School in Harrisonburg. They have three children and two grandchildren. Mike worked for over twenty years at Williamson-Hughes Pharmacy. He and Ramona and their family attended Valley View and helped tremendously with the singing and Sunday school work. Later Mike joined Michael as associate pastor at Valley View. He was voted in as pastor upon Michael's retirement and also became an overseer in the Northern District of Virginia Conference. He is very much like his dad, and we are happy to have him as our pastor.

Our daughter Janie is a self-employed home health caregiver who is much appreciated by the many older persons to whom she has ministered. When I received letters from my colleagues on my retirement, Ira Miller, former dean of the college, wrote that the best gift I had given them was our daughter Janie, who took care of him and his wife for a number of years.

Janie married Jerry Myers, and they have one married daughter. In Janie's late teens she told us one evening that her boy friend was coming to meet us. Our family was all at home that evening, and we waited and waited. Finally, this 1969 Camero came slowly rumbling into our drive. Our daughter-in-law Ramona looked out the window and said, "Mama, I think he's black." I said, "That's fine." However, Jerry still had an ordeal to face.

Uncle Charlie Hostetter was visiting, and I can still the two of them sitting on the couch while Uncle Charlie quizzed him about family, work, and the Christian life. Jerry responded, "Yes, sir," to every question; he passed the test and soon became a much beloved member of our family. I later asked Janie why she didn't tell us he was an African-American before that first visit. She replied, "You always said you did not care what color our friends were, just so the one we chose to marry was a good person."

Our younger son Don graduated from EMU and taught theater there for two years when Barbra Graber was on leave. He spent a year traveling with MCC Players, who performed in churches throughout the U.S. and Canada. He then decided to move to California to see what he could do in the dramatic arts. Fortunately, he had strong secretarial skills and could make a living while auditioning and acting.

During our first visit with Don in California in 1977, he told us that he was tired of trying to be someone other than the person he truly was: He was gay. Don needed to be away that evening, so Michael and I walked many blocks in Pasadena while discussing our feelings. We concluded that although we needed time to sort through our reactions, we loved Don unconditionally and would support him in his convictions. Our children have always been assured of our love and acceptance even though we might not always agree with them.

Michael and I wanted to share our knowledge of Don's orientation with our siblings but were not sure how some of them would react. When we did, they were wonderful and nonjudgmental. All of them loved Don, and that did not change.

My father called one evening and said he was thinking about Don. Out of the blue, he asked me if Don was homosexual. I can remember exactly where I was standing in the house—in front of a mirror. I looked at myself and thought, " I cannot lie to Daddy" and said, "Yes, he is." Daddy said, "I thought so. I will need to do some more reading and studying about that." There was only love, and Daddy and Don continued to have a warm relationship.

Don attended The Church of Truth in Pasadena for a few years and was their music director. Later he joined the choir of the San Marino United Church of Christ, whose motto is "God Is Still Speaking." He became the choir director and soon began working in the church office as the administrator. Then the church asked him to consider becoming their pastor. They had known him for more than ten years and were assured of his Christian commitment and his abilities. Before that, the church had encouraged him to begin a drama program. He did, and they had had several successful years of dramatic performances, which the church hoped would be a ministry in the community. We were present when he received a unanimous vote to become their pastor. We were also present when he received an excellent evaluation after his first year as pastor and another unanimous vote to continue as pastor.

When Michael became an overseer and a member of the Faith and Life Commission of the Virginia Conference, he felt he should share Don's sexual preference since homosexuality was such a controversial topic. He concluded by saying, "I have strong faith in Don's Christian commitment and feel I could go to heaven on Don's coattails." I myself have no need to debate the various interpretations of biblical teachings about sexuality. I only know what I see and experience in Don's life and those of others whom I have met. We are grateful for all our family members, and although we are far from perfect, we love and respect each other.

In addition to our own three children, there are many others whom we consider to be surrogate family members. We have two apartments in our home, and for the last thirty-five years we have rented them to nieces and nephews as well as a whole series of international students and their families. The latter have been from India, Ethiopia, Kenya, Germany, Brazil, Palestine, Thailand, and Russia.

At the time of this writing, a Kenyan family lived with us in the upper and lower apartments while we lived on the main floor of the house. Their family members included Mary, Leonard, Zoe, Joy, and Noel Parakuo. Mary worked in custodial services at EMU and took one class per term at EMU. Leonard was a CNA at Harrison House (a home for profoundly handicapped persons) and also milked a hundred or more cows each evening on a farm west of Harrisonburg. Zoe was in her first year of college at EMU and doing well, Joy was at Thomas Harrison Middle School, and Noel was at Waterman Elementary. We were CuCu and Babu (Grandma and Grandpa) to them all.

Because of our relationship with this family we had the privilege of hosting their relatives from Kenya. We often talked of going to Kenya because we wanted to know more about their home, communities, and church. One day Mary came to me and said she and Leonard were going home to Kenya in a few months and they wanted us to go with them.

Peggy and her husband Michael Shenk receive a cow as a gift of friendship and respect from their dear friend Jonah Meja on their visit to Kenya in 2011.

We spent twelve days visiting in Kenya. It is hard for me to describe the wonderful feeling of family as we went from place to place. With the help of skilled interpreters, Michael preached in Leonard's and Mary's home churches. Mary said that they were the best sermons she had ever heard him preach. We also visited a number of schools, some of which were in very poor areas.

Looking Back

I am thankful to have been born into a home where love was easily expressed in word and deed. As long as they lived, my parents maintained a strong influence in our lives and in our children's lives. We all knew they prayed for us daily; and when they died, one of my sisters began praying for each of us every day.

I am particularly grateful for a loving and supportive husband and thankful that he is in partial remission from his chronic lymphocytic/leukemia (CLL). I thank the Lord also for our children and their spouses, who are dedicated to the church and to helping others. I am grateful for loving grandchildren and our two great-grandchildren. In retirement, I look back at what we have experienced and thank the Lord for his faithfulness and for our family and friends in the church and community.

February 2013
Revised June 2015

NOTE

1. Eugene H. Peterson, *The Message: The New Testament, Psalms and Proverbs* (Colorado Springs: NavPress, 2007, paperback; 1995, leather-bound).

Shirley Hershey Showalter

Once a College President, Still a Teacher

As we come to the last chapter in this book of memoirs, we turn to the author of her own book-length memoir, Blush. *Shirley used scrapbooks and a variety of other resources, as well as memories, to tell detailed and truthful stories of her growing up—the people and events in her life and her inner responses. Here she turns to us, drawing convincingly on her experiences, to show us how and why we should begin writing our stories.*

Photo by Joyous Snyder

SHIRLEY HERSHEY SHOWALTER

Why Writing Memoir Is Hard... And Why You Should Do It Anyway

Editorial note: Like the other chapters in this volume, this essay was the basis of a presentation made at an ACRS breakfast meeting. Unlike the other memoirs, however, it offers not so much the story of the author's life as it does her reflections on the process of memoir writing. This process resulted in the publication of many personal essays and Shirley's delightful book-length memoir, Blush. *One of her goals is to encourage other writers to reflect on and write about the ways the history and culture of Anabaptism have shaped their lives. Her website www.shirleyshowalter.com includes a place to sign up for weekly writing prompts called Magical Memoir Moments.*

> I owe the Lord a morning song
> Of gratitude and praise,
> For the kind mercies he has shown
> In lengthening out my days.[1]

The filmmaker Samuel Goldwyn once said, "I don't think anyone should write his autobiography until after he's dead."[2] I'm beginning to think, after six years of writing numerous personal essays and one book-length memoir, that Goldwyn was right. In fact, on some days, I think this whole process might be shaving a year or two off my life. Of course, this essay was written smack dab in the middle of the process, and we all know why the phrase "murky middle" exists.

The middle place, however, offers some opportunities that no other vantage point can boast: the ability to stand between the beginning and the end, between the good and the bad. This piece stakes a claim to the middle position and asks what is good and what is bad about writing a memoir. My argument will sound a lot like the great platitude of the sports world: "No pain, no gain."

Behind that generic truth hides a deeper one. After exploring both the pain and the gain, I will explain why I think all of us should write or record or at least verbally share stories about our lives.

Pain: Why Memoir Writing is Hard

All writing is hard work. Watch a child trying to write a paragraph while twisting her hair into a knot or another biting his lower lip. Remember the pain of your first research paper? Well, practice may produce better outcomes over time, but the pain only gets worse!

William Styron once said, "Let's face it, writing is hell."[3] But perhaps the most famous description of all is this one: "Writing a novel is like traveling from Vladivostok to Paris on your knees." No one seems to know with certainty the author of those words, but all writers know the feeling, and any author who claims to enjoy writing all the time is not to be trusted!

The posture of being on one's knees makes an overt connection to prayer, which is a good analogy, I think. One thing prayer and writing have in common, at least in my experience, is that they attract distraction. As soon as I determine to do either one of them and settle myself down in my chair, my thoughts run wild:

- Those plants look like they need water.
- My nose itches.
- What shall I make for lunch?
- Maybe there is a new picture of the grandchildren in my inbox.
- I think I hear a ping on my computer. Facebook status update!

Writing, like meditation, requires persistence in silence. Those first minutes of "monkey mind" thoughts about other things give way only when you sink down lower below consciousness. Some days you can get there soon; other days the chatter and little interruptions never end, and you reach the end of a day with nothing to show for it.

Writing about oneself is doubly hard. Many people get stopped before they start. Where do I begin? What will people think if I tell the truth about my life?

Here is a paradox for you: It takes ego to write a memoir, but ego unleashed is an ugly thing. Some memoirs go down the path of revenge, self-pity, or whininess. No wonder the words *memoir* and *narcissist* often appear in the same sentence.

Yet a memoir without conflict loses the main ingredient of story. Some writers, especially those taught to value peace at any price, brush over conflict and paint with only the bright, sunny colors, leaving out the shadows.

Mennonites have always emphasized the importance of humility and modesty, especially for women. So a Mennonite woman memoirist pushes the boundaries for some readers, not least of whom might be herself. Not surprisingly, when I wrote my first draft, I could hear voices whispering, "Who does she think she is?"

The truth about my life is that I loved attention when I was a child; as a first-born, I got a lot of it, especially at home. I had a mother who loved to dress me up and encouraged me to enter contests as a teenager and who named me after a movie star, Shirley Temple. A mother who sadly left her jewelry, make-up, fashionable dresses, stylish coats, and chic hats behind when she joined the church at age eighteen. A mother who loved my exuberance and aspiration yet disapproved of pride when she thought she saw it in me. She herself struggled to find a place for her gifts in the church and was happy when she saw me develop as a Bible quizzer and Sunday night speaker in the Mennonite Youth Fellowship, yet she was not at all sure that I should go to college. My father was even less sure.

I had to learn the hard way, in school and in church, that I was not the center of the universe. When that happened, I blushed. I also blushed when I tried to pretend to sophistication I did not have or when others made fun of Mennonites in general or of me in particular. Hence the title Herald Press and I chose for my memoir was *Blush: A Mennonite Girl Meets a Glittering World*.

When you begin to reflect on the themes of your own life, you inevitably find embarrassing, painful situations. You will be tempted to turn away. Don't. Your story probably lies somewhere close to those pain points. For example, when I wrote about Mennonite courtship, I remembered one young man I had not thought about in years, a high school senior I dated once or twice who was diagnosed with an aggressive cancer soon after our last date. I did not consider him my

Shirley Hershey Showalter autographs a copy of her memoir Blush: A Mennonite Girl Meets a Glittering World, *September 19, 2013, at Lititz Mennonite Church, Lititz, Pennsylvania. Each member of the audience was given a little bag of "Grandma Herr's Sugar Cakes" made with the recipe printed in the back of the book.*

boyfriend, but when I heard the news about him, I was sad. I never went to visit him, fearing he would think I was "serious" about him, not trusting myself around either death or romance.

At the time, avoidance seemed a wise choice. Now I regret that I did not have the strength to be present for a dying friend. Perhaps my regret about what I did not do at age seventeen contributed in some small way to later hospital visits and later acknowledgments of failure.

The biggest fear many memoirists have stems from the fact that it is impossible to tell your own story without also telling the story of the other characters attached to your life. You leave yourself open to their criticism and correction if you include them. If you let all those characters read your book, you may get confused. If you give them veto power over what you say, you may end up losing your own voice.

Ironically, you can also offend people by leaving them out of your story. So it is best to write for yourself as your first audience and then to an "ideal reader" who needs to hear your story. Strive always to be truthful, but recognize that your truth may not always match the memory of others in your life. Choose those whose opinion matters most to you and share your story with them. Listen to their critique, but change your work only if you were wrong about factual details, time sequence, or other external forces. Your feelings and thoughts are your own, and you need to find your own internal truth.

How you tell your story can be one of the biggest challenges of all, especially if you choose to write a lengthy memoir or autobiography. The longer the form, the harder the task will be. I got started by writing short pieces called "personal essays" in the 1980s and 1990s. In fact, I began to think of memoir as my favorite genre only after the *Kalamazoo Gazette* newspaper offered a literary awards contest in 2007. The category that most appealed to me they called *memoir*.

Remember the little girl whose mother encouraged her to enter contests? Well, she still exists inside the adult Shirley. I decided to test whether I had any memoir to write about. I spent a weekend at Gilchrist, a nearby retreat center, and invited God to guide my memory and my hand. I came back from that weekend with three stories. The experience of writing them was holy. "The Fresh Air Girl" won first place in the newspaper contest. Eventually it became a chapter in my longer memoir.

When I proposed a book-length memoir to Herald Press in 2011, I knew my greatest challenge would be structure. I felt very comfortable with the essay form of ten to twenty pages. But how could I create a long memoir with enough suspense and action to sustain the reader's interest all the way to the end?

I had attended a few workshops on writing memoir, and I remembered this piece of advice: "Throw your character into a pot of boiling water and then turn on the heat." The trouble was, however, that my "boiling water" was pretty tame stuff by the standards of most memoirs. I would have to find a way to dramatize and make sacred everyday life on the farm and church. And I would have to find a structure that held all this material together. I was relieved and a little amused when I discovered author Paulette Alden's great description of my own problem:

> But it wasn't a straight-forward or easy process to turn that short piece into a book. A book is so *long*! I had to find a structure, I had

Shirley Hershey Showalter was called to the presidency of Goshen (Ind.) College in 1996. Here she strolls and converses with students in September of that year when the campus was covered in maple leaf color. She promised students when she took office that she would continue teaching as her schedule permitted. Over the eight years of her presidency, she taught a course on The Literature of Spiritual Reflection and Social Action three times.

to figure out what to put in and what to leave out, and what order all the material should be in. I had to get in backstory, which would give meaning to the present action story.[4]

I was relieved to discover that some writers did not follow the narrative arc (with a carefully designed introduction, development, conflict, and resolution) in memoir writing. Like me, they enjoyed the short essay and hoped to weave thematic threads through a series of chapters that could stand alone as essays. The model that I found particularly helpful was Mildred Armstrong Kalish's *Little Heathens: Hard Times and High Spirits on an Iowa Farm in the Great Depression*.[5]

What I eventually came up with was a structure similar to Kalish's, in which title, introduction, conclusion, and thematic allusions throughout the book do the work of the narrative arc. I know that some readers, especially those that love a rippin' fast read, will find my book slow, maybe even boring. But I counted on finding readers who appreciate the small-scale dramas of long-ago farm life and long-ago Lancaster Conference. Most Mennonites know how huge those small dramas can seem to those who lived them.

Finally, writing memoir is hard because it is often done at a computer. I have spent too many hours in front of screens ever since I first bought my own personal computer in the early 1980s. My jaw, neck, and shoulders take a beating as I sit for hours at a time, straining for the right word. I walk an hour each day, do strength training, yoga, and massage; but I still feel aches and pains in my body, especially when a deadline looms.

GAIN: WHY MEMOIR WRITING IS IMPORTANT

Even when writing memoir causes suffering, as it undoubtedly does, we should still do it. The stories of our lives matter to God, to our family, and to our community. The Bible itself, a book full of stories, is proof of this fact. True, very little of it is written in the first person, but some of it is. Jesus, for example, in John 12:32 (KJV) says, "And I, if I be lifted up from the earth, will draw all men unto me." Our Bible quiz team in the 1960s spent a lot of time talking about the meaning of that sentence. Now I see it as a one-sentence memoir!

Sometimes I am consciously aware of writing as a spiritual experience. One of my favorite proverbs is this one: "A word fitly spoken is like apples of gold in pitchers of silver."[6] I can testify to the joy of wrestling mightily for the right word or sentence, and then suddenly, like grace, receiving words as gifts. Sometimes the tears flow also, an outward sign of the inward connection between joy and sorrow, pain and gain.

The sentences I love most in other authors' work flow like music and poetry. One example is this sentence from *My Antonia*, by Willa Cather: "That is happiness: to be dissolved into something complete and great."[7] From among the many other lovely ones she wrote, Cather chose those words to be inscribed on her tombstone. A few years ago I placed flowers and a stone on her grave in Jaffrey, New Hampshire, gazing at those words etched in stone and recognizing that Willa Cather was still alive! She was alive in my heart. Her words had cheated death.

That spiritual connection between writing and the eternal value of the fitly spoken word applies to our own lives and also to those we love. In my case, I felt the desire to write a memoir in part to honor my eighty-six-year-old mother while I could still talk with her about the details of my story. I dedicated the book to her. We spent hours together going through memorabilia—photos, clippings, report cards, calendars, and souvenirs. Each one of them brought new memories. My father died in 1980, so I couldn't talk with him. I know some day I will not be able to talk with Mother, either. But writing the memoir brought us closer and taught both of us things we did not know about each other.

One of the pieces of memorabilia I found was a valentine that Mother wrote to me in 1969 several months before I got married. The note said,

> You are the dolly I never had,
> You are the figure I lost long ago,
> You are the stories I never wrote,
> You are the plays I was never in.

I realized by writing a memoir how much of her own life, her hopes and dreams, my mother poured into me. A quotation from Carl Jung came back to me in a new wave of understanding: "The greatest tragedy of the family is the unlived lives of the parents."[8]

I had another force pulling on me as I wrote. Just as my mother has connected me to the past and to the ten generations of my Mennonite family in America, in the same way my young grandson connects me to the future. I drafted the text of my memoir while living temporarily in Brooklyn, New York, and while working as "granny nanny" for baby Owen. How would Owen know what it was like to milk cows and sled down the hill and pick bluebells along the creek bank unless I told him my stories? And how will he know what I believe and how my faith was transferred from generation to generation unless I sing him my songs?

For me, writing a memoir, despite all the pain in the process, has been a great adventure. I am always happy when I am learning. In this case, I had to learn much not only about writing but also about history, technology, and social media. I enjoy the process after the writing and editing even more than the early retreat weekend in 2007 when three stories from my childhood came so easily to my hand.

Now, as I blog at www.shirleyshowalter.com and get to know readers interested in memoir and in my Mennonite story, I am already entering conversations that I look forward to on book tour. My logo on the website includes these words: "Discover the power of writing your story." The circle will not be complete until you find your own way to tell your story. By all means, start with the short form: a journal, a scrapbook, a story. Or just pull up a chair and tell your story to a friend. Children make a great audience and will help you simplify, which is part of the process of figuring out what a story is *about*.

Memoir writing has drawn me back to the very beginning of my life. I think of my childhood as a magical time. Time mattered little, partly because it matters little to all children and partly because time changed things so slowly in my Mennonite farming community. But space—that was different. I was a tiny creature set in a vast landscape, able to explore freely and safely. Every day brought a new adventure.

When indoors, I had a favorite way to play. I would line up chairs facing the front of the room and place my little brother, my dolls, and our stuffed animals on the chairs. Then I would sing, preach, and teach. Whatever I had gathered in my last adventure would pour forth out of me. Learning was exciting, but it was not complete until I shared what I learned with others.

This memory brings me to my final point about the value of memoir. It should help us understand more fully who we are and where we are headed. Most human beings, especially most Americans, do not take time to reflect deeply, but when we do, the rewards are great.

I chose a personal mission statement in 2004, before I realized I would write a memoir. I chose it while a friend was dying, and I think of her whenever I say these words: "My mission is to prepare for the hour of my death one good day at a time and to help others do the same."

Chaplains and doctors tell us that the tasks of the dying are fourfold.[9] They need to find a way to convey these ideas to those they love:

> I forgive you.
> Please forgive me.
> Thank you.
> I love you.

I tried to say all these things in my memoir. I will need to say them many more times before I die. I thank God for "lengthening out my days" long enough to allow me to study my life, not because it is more important than other lives but because it is not.

Maybe Samuel Goldwyn was right after all. We should write our autobiographies after we die. Only after we die to our need for importance, the very force that drives many of us in our youth, can we find the deeper stories of our lives—the stories that connect us to all other parts of God's brilliant, eternal, yet ever new creation.

September 10, 2012
Revised August 2015

Notes

1. Amos Herr, "I Owe the Lord a Morning Song," Lancaster County Bishop, 1890 (published in nine hymnals).

2. Samuel Goldwyn, http://quoteinvestigator.com/2012/03/14/goldwyn-autobiography/ (accessed Aug. 21, 2015).

3. William Styron, http://www.theparisreview.org/interviews/5114/the-art-of-fiction-no-5-william-styron (accessed Aug. 21, 2015).

4. Paulette Alden, "Writing a Book-length Memoir," http://paulettealden.com/articles/writing-a-book-length-memoir/ (accessed March 1, 2015).

5. Mildred Armstrong Kalish, *Little Heathens: Hard Times and High Spirits on an Iowa Farm in the Great Depression* (New York: Random House, 2008).

6. Proverbs 25:11 (KJV).
7. Willa Cather, *My Antonia*. (New York: Houghton Mifflin, 1918, 1954), 18.
8. Carl Jung, https://www.goodreads.com/quotes/22674-the-greatest-tragedy-of-the-family-is-the-unlived-lives (accessed August 21, 2015).
9. Ira Byock, M.D. *The Four Things that Matter Most: A Book About Living* (New York: Atria Books, 2004).

THE APPENDIX

The Anabaptist Center for Religion and Society: Forging a Future

The Anabaptist Center for Religion and Society (ACRS) with each new volume in *The Geography of Our Faith* series has in its Appendix provided reflection and an update on its activities. Volume 4, the last of the series, coincides with several key points in the development of ACRS and Eastern Mennonite University (EMU). As Ray Gingerich has noted in his Series Editor's preface, Volume IV has the distinction of being launched during the centennial celebration of the founding of Eastern Mennonite University. The series itself has documented some of the changes as well as constants in the life of the university. In Volume 1, and to some extent in later volumes, many of the contributors had direct connections with the founders and early teachers, administrators, and students of what has come to be known as Eastern Mennonite University. The series can thus be read as a companion story to the official history prepared by Dr. Donald B. Kraybill for the centennial celebration (*Eastern Mennonite University: A Century of Countercultural Education*, Penn State University Press, 2017).

    The memoirs in these volumes have also provided real life examples of persons who have lived out the values of commitment to the Mennonite church, community, and service. ACRS has provided a context in which persons from a variety of life streams have been able to come together to reflect on contributions and issues of importance to the church and society, as well as challenges for the future. It seems fitting, then, that as Eastern Mennonite University celebrates 100 years of institutional life, ACRS' *Geography of Our Faith* Series recognizes the contributions of some thirty-five persons—fifteen in Volume 4—who have given life to the Anabaptist values at the core of EMU's history.

ACRS Activities

Breakfast Series Presentations

The ACRS Breakfast Series presentations of personal stories from which the four volumes have come have gathered an eclectic group of Anabaptist retirees who continue to meet for a monthly presentation planned by ACRS. In recent years the speakers have focused on times and events that were important milestones in new directions for our North American churches. Beginning with the Civil Rights movement for integration in our communities, media productions on mental health, restorative justice programs such as the Victim Offender Reconciliation Program (VORP), and school discipline—there are persons in this community who have been active participants in the growing commitment to following Jesus in living out peace and justice. Thus, the ACRS breakfasts continue to explore the wider global vision and interactive programs of our brothers and sisters.

The Annual General Meeting

In addition to the breakfast presentations, in the past ACRS also provided forums and other types of opportunities to engage in a more systematic and conceptually oriented analysis of topics of current interest in the church and society. However, the Provost's Office at EMU eventually developed the University Colloquium Series, which provided a broader-based space to fill the niche that ACRS had earlier identified in the life of the university. ACRS then moved to feature a longer presentation and time for discussion at its Annual General Meeting in May as an intermediate venue between the University Colloquium Series and the ACRS Breakfast Series. For example, the ACRS 2016 Annual Meeting featured David Myers, an Anabaptist working in the faith-based section of Homeland Security in Washington, D.C. He shared the struggles and successes of working from an Anabaptist orientation in the federal government environment. Since the Myers presentation was well received, future ACRS Annual Meetings will offer more such windows into critical avenues of service.

Occasional special issues forums

ACRS continues to search for ways to provide opportunities on an *ad hoc* basis for small groups of persons to gather to discuss pressing current issues in society and the church. An example of this would be the Mennonite World Conference (MWC)/ACRS-sponsored farewell gathering for César García, General Secretary of MWC, and his spouse, Sandra Baez, from Colombia, who were completing a study-leave at Eastern Mennonite University. César shared some of the challenges and opportunities he faces in his responsibilities with Mennonite World Conference, especially in light of the current forces in the world that increasingly threaten to divide societies and the church.

Orie O. Miller's biography

Since the content of Volume 3 was compiled, ACRS undertook the joint publication with the Mennonite Central Committee of *My Calling to Fulfill: The Orie O. Miller Story* by John Sharp of Hesston College (Harrisonburg, Virginia: Herald Press, 2015). ACRS is pleased to offer this major contribution to the literature on leadership in the Mennonite Church during its most vigorous institutionalization era. The first volume in *The Geography of Our Faith* series linked us to the early days of EMU by giving those of us whose lives span the time between the infancy and maturity of the university the opportunity to build a bridge between those two eras with our stories. Similarly, the Orie O. Miller biography also links those eras in Mennonite and Brethren in Christ institutional development.

The Leadership Conference

The Orie O. Miller biography served as the basis for an ACRS-inspired conference on leadership, "Leading into the Common Good: An Anabaptist Perspective," April 7-9, 2016. Conference participants came from a variety of Mennonite educational and denominational institutions and agencies. The registrants ranged across a wide age span, underscoring the challenge of generational transitions in leadership style heard in the presentations and conversations. Also highlighted were many changes in the past seventy-five years in the way institutional loyalty and identity are expressed by current Anabaptist communities.

Dr. Jim Smucker, then EMU graduate dean, provided overall leadership for the conference which was officially sponsored by ACRS, EMU's School of Graduate and Professional Studies, Mennonite Central Committee (MCC), Mennonite Economic Development Associates (MEDA), Mennonite Health Services, and MennoMedia. Co-sponsors included Anabaptist Mennonite Biblical Seminary, Bethel College,

Bluffton University, Canadian Mennonite University, Conrad Grebel University College, Goshen College, and Hesston College.

Mennonites filmed through a different lens

ACRS has provided the context and structure to help Buller Films develop the initial phase for the production of a film on the Mennonites in the United States from the perspective of persons who are not Mennonite but who have knowledge of how Mennonites have engaged the world. This major film project, just in its initial developmental stage, holds great promise to provide an example of how small religious groups can have an impact on the larger society with which they are often at odds. It will also allow Mennonites and other Anabaptist groups to look at themselves through a different lens. The project is being designed to meet the funding requirements and quality of production standards so that it could be suitable for public television as has been the case with some of Buller Films' past productions.

OPPORTUNITIES AND CHALLENGES FOR THE FUTURE

Engaging differences and divisions

ACRS has been very supportive of the Center for Interfaith Engagement (CIE) since the latter appeared as part of EMU. We have supported many of the CIE activities as a co-sponsor or as participants in its programs, which focus particularly on interfaith interaction. Within ACRS there has been a history of wanting to create spaces in which the different faith traditions could engage each other. ACRS has also been committed to providing spaces for different Christian streams in the Shenandoah Valley to engage each other on topics of mutual interest, but on which there is disagreement.

We will continue to organize more encounters so that spaces are created in which disagreements might be converted into opportunities to develop stronger relationships within a theologically diverse community. These efforts complement activities already in place like the Mennonite Central Committee and Church of the Brethren relief sales, which bring persons together from different Anabaptist groups to work on a common project. Other activities like the post-disaster reconstruction sponsored be Mennonite Disaster Service also play an important role in providing opportunities for different communities to interact. ACRS believes that it can offer a space for theological discussions in the Shenandoah Valley among groups within the Anabaptist tradition and across different streams of Christianity, as well as among other religious traditions from around the world. The growing xenophobic tendency in the United States in the past fifteen years makes ACRS' commitment to strengthening social bonds across religious, ethnic, and social differences a high priority.

Stories as models for service

In his closing paragraph of the Appendix to volume 2 of *The Geography or Our Faith* Series, Ray C. Gingerich, a founding member and former director of ACRS, draws on an agrarian metaphor to describe the influence hoped for through ACRS' chosen activities:

> Through story telling, forums, colloquiums, research and publishing, cross-cultural exchanges and new ventures in interreligious relationships, the seeds of a passing generation are being harvested. Our hopes are that these seeds will be treasured, not as museum artifacts, but as verdant elements of an inheritance that, when cross-fertilized with the creativity and commitment of the current generation and planted into the fertile soil of its culture, will spring forth into a new communal breed of twenty-first century Anabaptists—instruments of peace and well-being in the trajectory set by our ancestors. ["The Continuing Story of the Anabaptist Center for Religion and Society," in *Continuing the Journey: The Geography of Our Faith*, ed. Nancy V. Lee (Telford, Pa.: Cascadia Publishing House, 2009), 366.]

—*Vernon Jantzi, Director, ACRS*

THE EDITORS

Nancy M. Farrar retired in 2006 after thirty years' service in the James Madison University Writing Center, where she specialized in writing across the curriculum. Previously she had taught literature and composition at Longwood College, Mars Hill College (N.C.), and JMU. During her professional career, she also edited a wide variety of manuscripts, ranging from doctoral dissertations to a plumbing manual. She especially enjoyed helping edit essays in this fourth volume of ACRS Memoirs, *Making a Difference in the Journey: The Geography of Our Faith*, because her older son is active in a local Mennonite church and her younger son is currently associate pastor of a Church of the Brethren congregation in Harrisonburg.

A reader of mysteries since middle school years, **Audrey A. Metz** wrote one in elementary school that featured a cat as the clever sleuth. Fortunately, she says, it was never published. She graduated from Christopher Dock High School, with one year at Eastern Mennonite College. Her favorite subject in elementary school through college was English. She loved "Comp" assignments, was a reporter for the school newspaper, and was encouraged by her English teachers to keep writing.

She has been published by Mennonite Publishing House and a women's magazine, *Lady's Circle*. While living in Sarasota, Florida, she wrote, compiled, and edited a newsletter for her church, the Bahia Vista Mennonite congregation. She enjoys writing but identifies with writer Dorothy Parker who said, "I enjoy having written."

Kathy D. Fisher grew up happily in southern Ohio in a Conservative Conference Mennonite home. After graduating from EMC (now

EMU), she went to Egypt under the Mennonite Central Committee and then returned to the U.S. to get an MEd from Temple University. From there, she spent years teaching English as a Second/Foreign Language in Riyadh, Saudi Arabia; The United Arab Emirates; Columbus, Ohio; and more recently at James Madison University and Eastern Mennonite University in Harrisonburg, Virginia.

She was married to Albert N. Keim from 2000 to 2008, when he passed away. As a member at Park View Mennonite Church and the EMU community, she is blessed to be home from her wanderings.

Nancy V. (Burkholder) Lee, co-editor of ACRS Memoirs 1 with her husband Robert Lee, editor of ACRS Memoirs 2, and managing editor of ACRS Memoirs 4, has taught English courses at Rockway Mennonite Collegiate in Canada, Goshen College, and universities in the U.S., Japan, and China. She served in the latter two countries with her husband under Mennonite Mission Network and Mennonite Partners in China. Among her publications are these: *Getting Acquainted with the New Testament*; *Developing English Writing Skills*; and "In Japan, 1954-66: Among Many Discoveries, a Far-Reaching One" in *According to the Grace Given to Her: The Ministry of Emma Sommers Richards* (Elkhart, Ind.: Institute of Mennonite Studies, AMBS, 2013).

www.ingramcontent.com/pod-product-compliance
Lightning Source LLC
Chambersburg PA
CBHW071657170426
43195CB00039B/2221